A Paddler's Guide to Everglades National Park, Second Edition

University Press of Florida

Florida A&M University, Tallahassee
Florida Atlantic University, Boca Raton
Florida Gulf Coast University, Ft. Myers
Florida International University, Miami
Florida State University, Tallahassee
New College of Florida, Sarasota
University of Central Florida, Orlando
University of Florida, Gainesville
University of North Florida, Jacksonville
University of South Florida, Tampa
University of West Florida, Pensacola

Other Books by Johnny Molloy
50 Hikes in the North Georgia Mountains
50 Hikes in the Ozarks
50 Hikes in South Carolina
60 Hikes within 60 Miles: San Antonio & Austin (with Tom Taylor)
60 Hikes within 60 Miles: Nashville
A Canoeing & Kayaking Guide to the Streams of Florida (with Elizabeth Carter)
A Canoeing & Kayaking Guide to the Streams of Kentucky (with Bob Sehlinger)
Backcountry Fishing: A Guide for Hikers, Paddlers, and Backpackers
Beach and Coastal Camping in Florida
Beach and Coastal Camping in the Southeast
The Best in Tent Camping: The Carolinas
The Best in Tent Camping: Colorado (with Kim Lipker)
The Best in Tent Camping: Florida
The Best in Tent Camping: Georgia
The Best in Tent Camping: Kentucky
The Best in Tent Camping: Southern Appalachian and Smoky Mountains
The Best in Tent Camping: Tennessee
The Best in Tent Camping: West Virginia
The Best in Tent Camping: Wisconsin (with Kevin Revolinski)
Day & Overnight Hikes along Kentucky's Sheltowee Trace
Day & Overnight Hikes, Great Smoky Mountains National Park
Day & Overnight Hikes, Shenandoah National Park
Day & Overnight Hikes, West Virginia's Monongahela National Forest
From the Swamp to the Keys: A Paddle through Florida History
Hiking the Florida Trail: 1,100 Miles, 78 Days and Two Pairs of Boots, and One Heck of
   an Adventure
Hiking Mississippi
Mount Rogers National Recreation Area Guidebook
The Hiking Trails of Florida's National Forests, Parks, and Preserves (with Sandra Friend)
Land Between The Lakes Outdoor Recreation Handbook
Long Trails of the Southeast
Paddling Tennessee
Paddling Georgia
Trial By Trail: Backpacking in the Smoky Mountains

A Paddler's Guide to Everglades National Park

Second Edition

Johnny Molloy

University Press of Florida

Gainesville · Tallahassee · Tampa · Boca Raton

Pensacola · Orlando · Miami · Jacksonville · Ft. Myers · Sarasota

Library of Congress Cataloging-in-Publication Data
Molloy, Johnny, 1961-
A paddler's guide to Everglades National Park/Johnny Molloy.—2nd ed.
p. cm.
ISBN 978-0-8130-3360-0 (alk. paper)
1. Canoes and canoeing—Florida—Everglades National Park—Guidebooks.
2. Everglades National Park (Fla.)—Guidebooks. I. Title.
GV776.F62E937 2009
917.59'3904—dc22
2009006567

The University Press of Florida is the scholarly publishing agency for the State
University System of Florida, comprising Florida A&M University, Florida Atlantic
University, Florida Gulf Coast University, Florida International University, Florida
State University, New College of Florida, University of Central Florida, University
of Florida, University of North Florida, University of South Florida, and University
of West Florida.

University Press of Florida
15 Northwest 15th Street
Gainesville, FL 32611-2079
http://www.upf.com

For my brother Pat

This book is a guide to the paddling region of Everglades National Park and waters north of the park. Every effort has been made to make this book as accurate as possible. Neither the descriptions nor the maps in the book can be assumed to be exact or to guarantee your arrival at any given point. Use your good judgment in this and any wilderness endeavor.

Contents

Preface

Welcome to the second edition of *A Paddler's Guide to Everglades National Park*. To paddle the Everglades was a dream of mine for nearly a decade before my first trip in the early '90s. Everybody has heard of the Everglades, but I heard of *paddling* the Everglades while canoeing the Boundary Waters Canoe Area Wilderness of Minnesota. About that time, an old college buddy from the University of Tennessee, Tom Lauria, had taken a new job and moved to Miami. It only seemed natural that we would combine a reunion with a trip to the Everglades, as by this time I had become completely immersed in the outdoor life.

We drove to Flamingo, rented a canoe, then struck out for the Glades, completely blind as to what to expect. I still remember the first night at South Joe chickee—watching the sky turn red, not believing we were camping in the Everglades! The fishing was good, but the water was far more open than we expected. The following year, we took off from Everglades City and hit the Gulf. The scenery was incredible and so were the waves, nearly swamping us after a cold front blew through. Every year thereafter some new adventure took place. The first trip around Cape Sable just blew my mind. It made me realize how precious this natural preserved coastline is in our era.

Later, the trips became longer and longer, and I spent long periods in Everglades National Park. By this time I had started writing outdoor guidebooks. I could see a comprehensive guidebook covering all the commonly paddled waterways of the Everglades was needed. Also needed was more information on the campsites, gear, and just what it is like out in the Glades. I ran into so many paddlers who were surprised, as I was, too, on my first adventure, by the Everglades backcountry—from the vastness of the water to the maze-like mangrove. I decided to write a guidebook about the paddling area of the Everglades.

After hooking up with the University Press of Florida, I set off for the Glades to write the first edition of the book, meeting with park personnel, getting their helpful input, then striking out on trip after trip one winter, paddling over 500 miles while researching. I would rise from my tent in the morning, load my craft (I used both a canoe and a sea kayak), then set out on a new route. While paddling, I would record information on a microcassette recorder, making notes on maps, eventually landing at a backcountry campsite. After unloading at a campsite, I would have a bite, set up camp, then hook up my laptop computer to a power inverter, which was then hooked up to a portable power pack. I would then type up literal on-site reports while the information was fresh in my mind.

While paddling, I stored the computer inside a dry bag inside another dry bag, then crossed my fingers. The miracles of modern technology made writing the book easier, but it never stopped a headwind or turned the tides in my favor or made the mosquitoes go away. But overall, writing this book was a wonderful experience and a dream come true.

Since penning the first edition of this book, I have returned to the Glades year after year after year: at this writing, I have spent more than 270 nights in the backcountry. For this second edition, I spent another entire winter in the park, paddling over 600 miles. This time, I decided to include the Ten Thousand Islands National Wildlife Refuge, Fakahatchee Strand State Preserve, Collier-Seminole State Park, and the Rookery Bay National Estuarine Preserve, which are adjacent to the north end of the park, extending from Tiger Key north to Cape Romano. This is a popular area and paddlers frequently use the Everglades' Gulf Coast Ranger Station as a jumping-off point, so it was a natural inclusion.

Also, since the first edition, the Everglades paddling area has undergone many changes, not only from natural forces but also because of park decisions to close or open paddling destinations. Beyond detailing these changes, I added some new routes in the park and repaddled the old ones, taking new pictures, making notes with a digital recorder, tracking mileage with a Delorme Earthmate PN20 GPS—and making lots of new friends in the backcountry! I hope you enjoy this new edition as much as I enjoyed researching and updating it to make your Everglades experience as rewarding as possible.

Leave No Trace Principles

- Plan ahead and prepare thoroughly
- Travel and camp on durable surfaces
- Dispose of waste properly
- Leave what you find where you find it
- Minimize campfire impacts
- Respect wildlife
- Be considerate of other visitors

Introduction

The national park system of our country is an American legacy. This system preserves and protects special and unique natural features scattered about the land. If these parks had not been established, many scenic and environmentally important treasures would have been lost. Everglades National Park is no exception. A century ago, South Florida was perceived as a swampy no-man's-land, where a few settlers and the last of the Seminoles survived among inaccessible vastnesses. Then, Henry Flagler completed his railroad to Key West, and the appeal of this warm country became apparent. The rush for land and water to accommodate the homesteaders was on! From the time of the Seminole Wars, people dreamed of draining the Glades. The Everglades was paradise in the rough—if they could be drained and canalized. The realization that this ecosystem should be preserved competed with the realization that much money could be made by "taming" the Everglades. A struggle ensued, and by 1947 Everglades National Park was established. Even though the park is the most sizable one east of the Mississippi and contains the largest roadless area in the lower forty-eight, the entire Everglades ecosystem has not been not preserved. Far from it. Vast tracts to the north have been drained, Lake Okeechobee has been diked, and the natural flow patterns of the River of Grass have been changed for good. What is left of the Glades continues on.

But all is not doom and gloom—there is much to see and even more to realize and appreciate. Imagine South Florida today, with its

Pelicans skim over open water. Photo by Constance Mier.

population bursting at the seams and vying for all the resources available, without an Everglades National Park: condos in the Pinelands, strip malls on the old Ingraham Highway, high-rises looking over Florida Bay from Cape Sable, bridges connecting the Ten Thousand Islands. It might very well have been like that.

The Everglades have been permanently altered, but they aren't dead. On the contrary, they retain many of their original characteristics. The Everglades are a vast spread of seemingly endless sawgrass, mangrove, sea and sky. You can see birds, fish, gloomy tidal creeks, dolphins rising for air on wide rivers, the world's best sunsets from Cape Sable, and unspoiled islands in the Gulf of Mexico, where deserted beaches are yours to walk. All you have to do is get in your craft and paddle.

That is the purpose of this guidebook—to help you most effectively paddle the Everglades. With this book, you will have a realistic idea of what paddling the Everglades is like, how to get on the water, what to take with you, and where to go and stay in the Everglades backcountry. There are over fifty routes described in this guidebook, covering not only the Wilderness Waterway and the Gulf of Mexico, but all the commonly and many not so commonly paddled routes in the entire park as well as waters to north of the park up to Cape Romano.

Each route description begins with an instructive, easy-to-read information box that gives you a brief overview of your route. The beginning, end, distance in statute miles, and estimated paddle time get you oriented. Potential tidal influence, potential wind influence, navigational challenge, highlights, and hazards help you size up the route. Campsites on the way and connections with other routes help you plan your overall trip through the backcountry. A narrative overview and running commentary on the route follow, giving general directions and alerting you to any significant natural or historical sites and other route connections along the way.

A special section about campsites is included. Here, you'll find details about each individual campsite in the paddling backcountry: where it is, what it's like, and how much use it receives. Everglades backcountry paddlers can then cross-reference this information with the route information to develop a comprehensive, realistic itinerary for a watery adventure lasting from one night to two weeks.

For reference once you're out there, backcountry pastimes such as fishing and birding are also detailed. Using all the data in this book can add up to a successful trip. So reserve some of your precious time, study this guidebook, plan a trip, and then go do it!

What It's Like—Paddling the Everglades

It's seeing an osprey carrying a grunting Jack Crevalle in its talons.

It's paddling 9 miles into a head wind until your arms ache.

It's seeing porpoises jump out of the water in unison as the sun sets on the Gulf of Mexico.

It's looking out and seeing nothing but no-see-ums on your tent window.

It's being swamped at Northwest Cape trying to debark in northwest winds.

The author drags a sea kayak up the beach on Cape Sable. Photo by Mark Carroll.

It's being pulled into Lake Ingraham by a strong tide rushing through the Mid Cape Canal.

It's recognizing the constellations reflecting off a glassy bay as fish splash in the distance.

It's huddling behind your tent on Mormon Key, trying to make coffee with fumbling fingers as a north wind pierces you to the bone.

It's camping on Fakahatchee Island, considering the settlers who are buried at the cemetery there.

It's hooking a tarpon on a light rod with 4-pound test line.

It's spending the night lost somewhere near the Roberts River.

It's watching the sea oats sway on Panther Key.

It's watching motorboats parade by from Darwins Place.

It's dragging your kayak up the beach on Cape Sable.

It's a never-ending paddle on a hot still day in Florida Bay, where the mirages in the distance cause paddlers to believe their strokes toward an unseen goal are futile.

It's being cooked a fresh fish dinner by some fellow campers at Camp Lonesome.

It's frantically loading your canoe as the mosquitoes drive you to finish your morning coffee in the boat in Broad River.

It's walking deserted Highland Beach, and seeing deer.

It's hearing gentle night breezes tap your canoe against the chickee as you drift off to sleep.

It's thinking about all the passersby who once got freshwater from the Cape Romano's wells.

It's paddling your sea kayak over topaz waters to North Nest Key.

It's drying out your gear on the dock at Plate Creek chickee.

It's seeing an alligator sunning himself at your campsite on Alligator Creek.

It's inhaling the pungent waters of The Nightmare as the winds howl through the canopy of branches overhead.

It's watching minnows dart about the crystal-clear water of Rocky Creek.

It's leaning against a cooler as an all-day rain falls at the Rodgers River chickee.

It's contemplating in the middle of the night whether the spirits of Mr. Watson's long-ago-murdered laborers really do haunt the Watson Place campsite.

It's looking out on white capping waves from behind a sheltered island on Whitewater Bay with miles ahead of you.

It's reeling in a red from the Lane Bay chickee.

It's seeing a manatee in the warm waters of Dusenberry Creek.

It's running aground on a mud bar while shortcutting Broad River Bay.

It's walking the sandy flats of Rabbit Key at low tide on a moonlit night and wondering if you can walk all the way to Fort Myers.

It's trying to guide your canoe to the safety of the Chatham River as stained 4-foot waves batter your canoe into Gun Rock Point.

It's watching the red fireball of the sun drop into the Gulf of Mexico from Cape Sable.

It's the sense of fear that sets in when you realize that your navigational skills have led you astray while the sky darkens into night.

It's mentally calculating how many strokes of the paddle it will take to cover the remaining mileage of your day's journey.

It's realizing the ground on which you are camping was built up hundreds of years ago by the daily piling of discarded shells by Calusa Indians.

It's noticing sharks in the waters of Whitewater Bay as you fish, and realizing your canoe lies awfully close to the water's surface.

It's having seawater slowly fill your boat while crossing a choppy Second Bay.

It's paddling toward the rainbow's end after weathering an afternoon thunderstorm.

It's being awakened by a bull gator's bellow near your chickee and wondering whether he's looking for a mate or a meal.

It's playfully surfing the waves in your sea kayak while being blown by a friendly wind to Pavilion Key.

It's being pestered by raccoons at Pavilion Key who leave their sandy footprints all over your boat.

It's exploring the interior of Mormon Key, looking for signs of previous inhabitants.

It's lying in a wet sleeping bag at Oyster Key after a midnight storm caught you with your tent fly down.

It's seeing Chokoloskee Island after paddling in a storm through Rabbit Key Pass.

It's watching the sky darken at Canepatch, while you ram down dinner after paddling for ten hours, then racing to the tent as swamp angels buzz all around you.

Natural History

The Everglades. Just about everyone has heard of the Everglades. But what are the Everglades? Ask twenty people and you get twenty different answers. Yet most conceptions of the Everglades center around two mental images. First image: Everglades as jungle. Tall trees tower over gloomy swamps with snakes hanging from tangled vines. Alligators lurk beneath coffee-colored waters, while strange birds deliver stranger calls that echo across the ooze. Second image: a limitless plain of verdant grass growing out of water. The sun beats over the harsh bleakness, punctuated only by violent thunderstorms. An occasional bird flaps its wings across an endless horizon.

Neither image is entirely incorrect. The jungle scenario comes close to describing the nearby Big Cypress Swamp, while the river-of-grass scenario somewhat describes one of the Everglades' several ecosystems. The vastness of the 1,500,000-acre Everglades National Park, the largest roadless area in the lower forty-eight, encompasses several environments that together form a fragile, complex ecosystem like no other on the face of the planet.

To describe the Everglades we must first go back in time. Over the past two million years the peninsula of Florida has been alternately exposed and inundated as cycles of glaciation came and went. Sediments were deposited from the Appalachian Mountains to the north, forming the surface of the Everglades. After the final glaciation some 6,000 years ago, the sea rose to its present levels and the shoreline of the state took its present shape. A warmer, wetter, more tropical climate ensued. Some temperate vegetation stayed in South Florida, while other more tropical vegetation migrated north from the Caribbean. Then the Everglades, a mere infant as far as ecological systems go, began to evolve and dominate the South Florida landscape. To conceive just how dominant the Everglades were, consider that the Everglades National Park encompasses only one-fifth of the historic Everglades.

Water has always been a defining element of the Everglades. Its flow has been drastically changed by man over the last century. Before canals, agriculture, and Miami, this aquatic maze originated in lakes just south of present-day Orlando. Creeks flowed south from these lakes, merging to form the Kissimmee River and other creeks, which in turn flowed southward into massive Lake Okeechobee, more than 700 square miles in size. Water spilled over the south shore of this inland sea into a 50-mile-wide river only inches deep. The river was hidden by an expanse of sawgrass extending southward as far as the eye can see. Beneath the sawgrass the water flowed, glimmering in the sun, heading southwesterly in a shallow trough with a slope averaging less than 2 inches per mile. This "sheet flow" was punctuated with dense islands of trees and other vegetation. These islands, called hammocks, stood slightly higher and drier than the sawgrass. Eerie-looking dwarf cypress trees formed other tree islands.

The water of the Everglades has always come and gone with the seasons. And down here there are two seasons, wet and dry. The wet season starts around the end of April, when warm, moist air flows north from the Gulf of Mexico and the Caribbean, then dumps water in sporadic yet certain storms all over the Florida peninsula.

This wet season climaxes as the days slowly get shorter and disturbances head west from Africa, building over the warm Atlantic waters, sometimes forming hurricanes, sometimes not, but dumping water all the same, often several inches in just a few hours. The waters of the northern lakes, near today's Orlando, along with local rains, filled the Glades. Then, sometime in November, the first cold fronts pushed all the way down from the north, leaving brilliant blue skies broken by occasional storms. The flow of the Everglades slowly diminished until the wet season returned again.

Depending upon the season, fire has played an important role in shaping the Everglades. When thunderstorms reign over the region, bolts of lightning strike, starting fires that spread through the sawgrass. In spring, while the soil is still dry, fires can burn down to the peat layer, slowing development of marsh and swamp habitat and allowing water to flow through the sawgrass. In the wet summer, when water levels are high, usually only dead growth burns, creating a fantastic sight as flames stretch across the landscape.

Today, as in the past, the water flows ever south and west, merging into wide tidal rivers bordered by mangrove, inevitably mixing with the salty water from the Gulf of Mexico and Florida Bay. It is here that the world's greatest mangrove forest thrives. But as robust as these trees grow, they are flattened with frightening regularity by hurricanes, which shape the Glades as surely as does the flow of water from Lake Okeechobee. Surrounded by the mangrove forest and nearly inaccessible to humans are the coastal marshes, where sawgrass forms a plain. More accessible are the coastal prairies of Cape Sable. Salt-tolerant ground cover such as sea purslane grows atop limestone marl. Abutting the ocean on the continent's edge is pristine beach, rare in Florida today.

Beyond the sawgrass and mangrove of the mainland, in the shallow waters of the Gulf of Mexico are outlying islands, known as "keys." These mangrove islands, with occasional beachfronts, extend northward from Key West into Florida Bay and reach their greatest numbers near Everglades City in the storied Ten Thousand Islands. Rich tropical marine vegetation grows in Florida Bay, creating an important link in the web of life for the aquatic and avian animals of this salty side of the Everglades.

And there are other environments in the Everglades. The Pinelands thrive on a limestone extension of the Atlantic Coastal Ridge. This land, though dry by Everglades standards, is often inundated for two or three months per year. Slash pine, cabbage palm, and palmetto dominate this fire-dependent community. Saline flats, brackish bays, and cypress heads—other elements of this complex natural world—subtly blend and merge and meshe to form a fascinating landscape worthy of a lifetime's study.

The historic Everglades are no more; the natural flow of water has been permanently disrupted; the Kissimmee River has been straightened; the south shore of Lake Okeechobee has been dammed; the

Caloosahatchee River has been channelized; the sawgrass has been drained, plowed over, and pushed under for sugarcane; canals have been dug all over the eastern Glades; Main Park Road acts as a dam; Florida Bay suffers aquatic blooms from excess fertilizer; almost all wildlife has been reduced in numbers. The Everglades will never be what they once were, but with care and management as a national park their recovery can continue.

Impacts of Modern Civilization on the Everglades

The historic flow of water from central Florida has been the key component in shaping the Everglades. But since the mid-1800s, plans have been in the works to drain, channelize, and otherwise "improve" the Everglades. Between 1882 and 1916, several canals were constructed that diverted the historic flow through the sawgrass to the east and west coasts of the state. Then, Lake Okeechobee was diked. More canals were added; others were enlarged to tame the Everglades. Yet problems like flooding, fires, and residents' disrupted water supplies led to more extensive water control, managed by the Central and Southern Florida Project for Flood Control and Other Purposes. This CS and F Project, authorized by Congress in 1948, was mostly in place by the mid-1960s.

The project eased flooding, made a more reliable water supply, and opened up a huge expanse of land south of Lake Okeechobee, formerly sawgrass, for agriculture. In the end, only 25 percent of the freshwater Everglades was left intact. Project engineers have attempted to mimic freshwater flows of the past with little success. Freshwater concentrations have become compartmentalized between levees and canals, instead of flowing naturally through the ecosystem. Phosphorous from agricultural lands to the north have overly enriched some areas, while the decrease in freshwater has led to increased salinity and attendant changes in Whitewater Bay and Florida Bay.

Wildlife, especially the area's once-vast rookeries, has suffered accordingly, save for alligators, which thrive in manufactured canals. Even so, their habitation patterns in the historic Everglades created trails and underwater "alligator holes" that were havens for fish and birds during the dry season. In the changed Everglades, there are far fewer alligator holes and so less of the wildlife that is dependent on them. This is just one example of the alteration of the complex Everglades that park officials, agricultural interests, environmentalists, and the Army Corps of Engineers are playing tug-of-war over. This conflicted interaction of people, land, and water goes on to this moment, colored by the uncertain outcome of the Everglades Restoration Act.

Human History of the Everglades

The Everglades as we know them first took shape around 5,000 years ago. Human habitation soon followed. The Indians that occupied South Florida quickly came to use what the region gave them. They often lived in open, raised platforms with palmetto-thatched roofs, called "chickees." Located on beaches, along rivers, or over sheltered waters, these chickees—and a healthy dose of fish oil smeared on their skin—helped cut down on mosquitoes. Smudge pots, smoldering fires of black mangrove, further kept the "swamp angels" at bay.

In other places, the Glades Indians lived on shell mounds that expanded from one generation to the next, accumulations of discarded remains of oysters, turtles, conchs, clams, and other creatures that were the mainstay of their diet. From the land they harvested heart of palm, coco plums, sea grapes, and game: white-tailed deer, turkey, marsh rabbit, and birds, such as ibis. More important still were the fish abundant in the fresh- and saltwater around them. The waters from Lake Okeechobee, to the mangrove-lined rivers, to the Keys were their waterways, which they traversed in canoes made from hollowed-out cypress logs.

Life in the Everglades was good, and several groups of Indians enjoyed its abundance. The Calusa roamed the northwestern Glades, from the Caloosahatchee River down to the Ten Thousand Islands. The Miamis centered around Lake Okeechobee. The Tequesta ranged along the Atlantic Coastal Ridge down to the Keys. The populations of all of these groups eventually declined and individuals were assimilated once the Spaniards made the opening gambit in their attempt to conquer the people of the Glades.

The Calusa of the Everglades proved to be a fierce lot in the post-Columbian era, as Spaniards combed South Florida in search of gold and slaves to work the cane fields in Cuba and Hispaniola. The Indians and Spanish were wary of one another. An early colonization attempt in 1521 by Ponce De Leon, who named Florida, ended violently with spears and arrows and Ponce De Leon's death. Slavers went after more docile Indians for plantation labor. Many Glades Indians stayed free, lurking to retrieve booty from galleons sunk by hurricanes, as the Spaniards rode the Gulf Stream back to Europe.

Florida passed into the hands of the newly formed United States by purchase in 1818. In the typical pattern, a signed treaty and further white settlement were followed by another treaty and more settlement. The Seminoles, as Florida's remaining Indians were known, were forced farther into swampy South Florida. Federal troops were deployed to get rid of them; they sporadically attacked white settlers guerrilla style. Back and forth went the slaughter during the Seminole Wars. Some Indians were sent to Arkansas, but a few remained unconquered in the Everglades to form the nucleus of the only current residents of the River of Grass, the Miccosukee and the Seminoles, on sites stretched out along the Tamiami Trail and a few other scraps of South Florida land.

Then came the grand plan to drain the Everglades, proposed in the state legislature for the first time the very year Florida became a state, 1845. Reports were hurriedly written, and the Swamp Lands Act was passed by the United States Congress in 1850. The Civil War delayed further action until the great freezes of 1894–95 blasted the orange groves and drove more settlers south to get below the "frost line." Miami sprang up overnight. The Everglades were ripe for the taking. Plumes and alligator skins were, too.

By 1905, the dredges were at work for real. "Land" in the Everglades was selling and reselling, as greedy speculators sold to greedier speculators. The only faster sales were those of plumes from the rookeries, where the birds seemed as inexhaustible as the land. No one bothered to study the environmental impact of canalization or even whether it would "work." Some land was put into cultivation, but settlers on other tracts were discouraged by hurricanes and continued flooding; land values dropped. The Audubon Society came in and began trying to protect the rookeries, which suddenly seemed doomed. Saltwater intruded from the sea. Fires flamed over parched sawgrass. Yet one project, the Tamiami Trail, the road connecting the east and west coasts of lower Florida, was built as men envisioned it. It took 12 years and a lot of lives, but the road was completed in 1928.

Also in 1928, another view of the Everglades was taking shape. A man named Earnest F. Coe saw the beauty and uniqueness of the Everglades in its natural state. He the varied landscapes as a vast national park, then set about a one-man crusade to share his vision. Others joined Coe, and on June 20, 1947, the Everglades National Park came to be.

Of course, controversies and challenges continued to boil, especially concerning the lifeblood of the Everglades, water. There will be more challenges still to come as long as this national park and millions of citizens exist side by side in South Florida. Yet with increased public awareness that the Everglades' health is an indicator of South Florida's future, perhaps the River of Grass will endure.

Hurricanes

In 2004, hurricanes Wilma and Katrina battered the Everglades and much of Florida. As destructive as they can be, though, hurricanes and their effects are a normal shaper of Florida's ecosystems. The state's huge human populations might as well accept this fact, for as long as there is a Florida, hurricanes will sometimes crash into it. Paddlers will notice storm damage all along the Gulf Coast, especially west-facing parts of the mainland and throughout the Everglades' keys. From Cape Romano to Florida Bay, the impacts of past hurricanes will show for years to come: Kingston Key chickee was completely blown away, and most of the mangroves along the Gulf Coast were killed. Their skeletons stand as monuments to the power of wind and water. Shark River Island was denuded of vegetation. Highland Beach, among others, was similarly stripped and more beachfront exposed. Graveyard Creek campsite was whittled down in size, but Cape Sable was opened up. Carl Ross Key was smashed and closed as a campsite. The north edge of Florida Bay was overthrown by mud and its marl prairies scoured. Recovery will be slow. But we might consider that what we call "disasters" happen only where works of human invention have been introduced. The Everglades wouldn't be the Everglades without the shaping force of

Skeletal, hurricane-stripped mangrove at the tip of Shark River Island. Photo by Constance Mier.

hurricanes. Over time, the mangrove coastline will return to a verdant green. Even now, young mangroves are sprouting up among the bleached trunks. Shorelines will build again, sands gathering where they have always gathered. Then another hurricane will come—part of the ongoing cycle of reshaping and rebuilding.

Understanding the Climate

For the Everglades visitor, the paddling season coincides with one of the two seasons that dominate South Florida—the rainy season and the dry season. The rainy season lasts from May through October. During this time, days often start clear, then clouds build and local thunderstorms drop heavy rains; then the skies clear and the cycle starts again. The result is nearly 7 inches or more rain per month, culminating in the hurricane season. Daytime highs reach 90 degrees, dropping to the low 70s at night.

The dry season, mid-November through mid-April, is the time when canoeists and kayakers enjoy the waters of the Everglades. It seems odd that the best time for paddlers is the dry season. But this is the time when days are usually clear, average highs range from the mid-70s to the low 80s, and lows drop to around 60 degrees. On average, there are less than seven days per month of measurable rainfall.

These statistics for Everglades City, Florida, from the National Oceanic and Atmospheric Administration will help you know what weather to expect.

	Nov.	Dec.	Jan.	Feb.	March	April
Average temp.	71	66	65	65	69	73
Average high	81	77	76	76	80	84
Average low	61	55	54	55	59	63
Record high	90	88	88	89	91	95
Record low	33	29	27	30	33	43
Average monthly precip.	1.26"	1.19"	1.56"	1.93"	1.95"	2.06"

Of course, these are all averages. Cold fronts can and do punch down from the north, bringing strong winds and nighttime lows into the 30s. Big thunderstorms storms can hit hard. Dreary rains can last for days. But overall, Everglades paddlers can expect good paddling weather from November through April, though hurricane season can spill into November and April can get really hot. Check ahead on the weather during the shoulder months. And carry a transistor or weather radio with you at all times during your Everglades trip to get the latest weather information.

Navigating Your Way around the Everglades

Many first-time Everglades visitors are surprised to find that the park's actual appearance doesn't match their preconceptions. Its landscapes are difficult to pigeonhole—there are eight different ecosystems within the preserve boundaries. But for the Everglades paddler, there are two primary environments: the coastal mangrove swamp, sometimes called "the inside," and the Gulf of Mexico, also known as "the outside."

The Everglades is the ultimate water park, so it is no surprise that water is the primary element of this and most other environments here. First-time Glades paddlers are amazed at how much wide-open water they travel. For the record, the paddling area of the Everglades is more open water than not. Freshwater from the sawgrass swaths flow south and west, subtly merging with tidal saltwater from the Gulf of Mexico. Here, the brackish water runs to the Gulf, flowing among the world's richest stands of mangrove trees, which seem at first like a continuous green shoreline that all looks the same. There is a ceaseless quality to the mangrove, as it conspires with the flowing water in endless variations of creeks, ponds, bays, inlets, streams, lakes, rivers, undulating shorelines, and keys that can and will confuse novice and experienced paddlers alike.

Now add a horizon unbroken by elevated features to use as guideposts—no mountain peaks or river valleys by which to establish your position. This low profile does make for fantastic weather watching, as clouds move by in every shape and form, but it leaves navigators to find their position by discerning subtle changes in contours of a "more alike than not" shoreline. Canopied creeks corkscrew in seeming circles, and your only view is the 20 feet ahead of your craft.

Then add distance to the navigator's realm. On the far side of a bay, a group of mangrove islands looks like an unbroken seashore. Coastal configurations lose their curves. Water, cloud, and sky meld into distorted mirages. On windless days, the horizon is lost: boats float in the air, birds fly underwater, and islands move imperceptibly.

Throw tidal variation into the mix. The tide is out, and what should be a group of keys is now connected by exposed land. A 100-foot-wide channel becomes a 20-foot-wide creek. Mud flats and oyster bars block a course that is plainly shown as water on your charts.

Then there are the marked channels: canoe trails where all you have to do is follow the numbered PVC-pipe markers; channels in Florida Bay, where arrows on wooden posts keep boaters in deep waters; channels from Flamingo out to the Gulf through Whitewater Bay. And there is also the Wilderness Waterway, the marked route from Flamingo to Everglades City, which many paddlers erroneously think is "*the* route" through the Glades. (It was actually contrived and marked in the 1950s as a motorboat trail in an effort to drum up park visitation.)

So what is it like navigating your way around the Everglades? It depends upon how you do it. A global positioning system (GPS) downloaded with aerial maps or nautical charts showing your exact position eliminates the trouble and worry of figuring out where you are. Having a GPS on you is a wise paddler's insurance. But only a fool comes out here without a backup navigational plan. Even if you have the world's best GPS, you should bring a nautical chart and compass. You will surely use them in the big-picture approach to route planning that complements the little-picture approach afforded by your GPS. Call me old-fashioned, but I believe that using

Wilderness Waterway markers help guide paddlers in the back-country. Photo by author.

a nautical chart and compass is an integral part of the Everglades experience. You study the landscape for known points that correlate with your estimated current position as you see it on the nautical chart in front of you. You fix your current position as certain, then move on to another position. In doing so, you absorb every nuance of the setting around you. This strategy forces you to scrutinize the Everglades. After all, you have a major stake in knowing where you really are.

Navigating here ends up as something between paddling marked channels and negotiating a maze. You may start out on a marked trail, then branch off to unmarked routes. Or you may use portions of a marked route such as the Wilderness Waterway on your trip. A good thing about navigating the Everglades is that there are enough certain fixed positions such as campsites, chickees, signs, and markers to periodically confirm your position, without so many markers that that backcountry becomes a sign-posted highway in the watery wilderness.

What You Need for Navigating

Your primary tools for navigation are a GPS with map downloading capability, a compass, and a nautical chart or aerial maps. Aerial maps, downloadable from the Internet, are increasing in popularity as a substitute for nautical charts. No matter which tools you use though, you must add to them a creative mind.

Most paddlers use a GPS nowadays—some for the downloadable maps and others simply for the reassurance. The models in play can boggle the mind. I use a Delorme Earthmate PN 40 with map downloading capability. I download the appropriate nautical charts onto the GPS, which uses overlay to show me where I am on the chart. The GPS provides other information as well: you can download the locations of campsites to help you navigate. If you decide to rely on downloaded maps, be careful not to spend the whole day staring down at the GPS. I have seen some of my paddling buddies do this, exploring the virtual Everglades rather than the real Everglades in front of them. Bring extra batteries, and consider housing your GPS in a waterproof storage case. Don't make the foolish mistake of relying *only* on a GPS: saltwater can kill it and batteries can die. Furthermore, local, immediate conditions trump whatever the GPS says. Some people won't believe they are where they are simply because the GPS told them otherwise.

Aerial maps and nautical charts are available in numerous incarnations—many more than in years past—and can be found on the Internet and locally at the Flamingo Marina and the Gulf Coast Ranger Station. The three nautical charts published by the National Oceanographic and Atmospheric Administration (NOAA) are #11430 for the northern Everglades and Cape Romano, #11432 for

GPS navigation systems can be reassuring, but use a backup map and compass too. Photo by author.

the central Everglades, and #11433 for the southern Everglades and Florida Bay. But these charts are made of paper, don't last, and aren't practical for paddlers surrounded by water.

Far preferable are the tear-proof, waterproof charts made by Waterproof Charts of Punta Gorda, Florida. These are based on NOAA charts and cost roughly the same, but they are compiled and numbered somewhat differently. Still, they include all the features you need to navigate the Everglades, such as channels, water depths, campsites, and markers. For Cape Romano to Lostmans River, you need Waterproof Chart #41 (Everglades and Ten Thousand Islands). For Lostmans River to Flamingo, you need Waterproof Chart #39 (Lostmans River to Whitewater Bay). For Florida Bay, you need Waterproof Chart #33E (Florida Bay). These charts are available at most bait and tackle shops near the Everglades. You can also get them over the Web at www.waterproofcharts.com.

No matter what chart you use, not every tiny mangrove island and creek will be on it. But there will be more than enough features shown to get you around. For really precise detail, people are turning to aerial maps as well. Aerial maps of the Everglades paddling area can be found over the Internet on such sites as Google Earth.

When choosing a compass, you can get as fancy as you want, but a simple one with a clear plastic base, moveable compass ring, cardinal points, and numerical degree calibrations will do. To find which direction you should go, point the direction-of-travel arrow on the plastic base toward your destination on your chart or map. Turn the compass housing ring until north on the housing ring lines up with north on the actual compass arrow. Line up the map north with the compass north. You are now oriented. Luckily, north in the Everglades is close enough to true north that you don't have to adjust your compass for magnetic declination.

One of your most important navigational tools is a creative mind. Your view of the Glades with a nautical chart is from the top looking down, from the air looking down on the water—a vertical point of view. Your real-life view is from the water surface across the water, a horizontal outlook. Your mind must be able to turn your vertical view on its side to a horizontal view. You must match the features in front of you with the features on the chart. This becomes easier over time and is a function of experience with maps.

When you're looking at your charts at home, it's a simple matter to make your way through the Ten Thousand Islands, down the North Harney River, and from Hells Bay to Lane Bay and so on. It's another matter in the field, but the slow pace of a paddler can be an advantage, because the setting changes slowly. Conversely, the slow pace makes mistakes less forgivable. In this book, the individual routes described are rated for navigational challenge. If you are inexperienced with map and compass, paddle some of the easier (lower-rated) navigational challenges or marked canoe trails, then work your way up. Experienced navigators can paddle the more challenging routes. A GPS with downloadable maps will raise your confidence, no matter your skill level.

Navigational Considerations

Just as there are no other Everglades on earth, there is no paddling experience like the Everglades. The Marjory Stoneman Douglas Wilderness comprises much of the paddling area of the park. Within the wilderness there are truly wild places, but the water column (that is, anywhere there is water within the wilderness) is excepted. That means, unlike areas usually designated wilderness, motorized craft are allowed in the water column. In other words, you will see motorboats on your trip.

Motorboats can be your navigational ally. Say you are crossing Blackwater Sound, trying to reach The Boggies, a channel leading into Florida Bay from Blackwater Sound. A motorboat is on the same route. The west end of Blackwater Sound looks like one continuous shore. You can watch the motorboat power to the channel, helping you figure out exactly where The Boggies are. Also, don't be afraid to flag down a boater to ask for directions. Of course, this can be as embarrassing as pulling into a filling station in a strange city and asking for directions, especially if you are a man.

Birds can be your navigational ally as well. Say you are paddling west across Snake Bight to Flamingo in Florida Bay. The tide is going out, so the water is getting very shallow, but from where you are, the water stretches all the way across the bight. Then you see birds standing in sections of the watery bay. You know to avoid those areas, as they may become impassable.

Distance and horizon can make things look other than they are. In paddling the keys of Florida Bay, for instance, distant islands you are heading for may not be visible on the horizon. Get your position, set your direction, and trust your compass. Similarly, far-off features such as the creek leading past Darwins Place, indistinguishable in the distance, become clearer as you approach them. Again, set your direction and trust your compass or GPS.

Tides can be a directional indicator as well. If you know the general times of tidal variation in a given area, you can tell which way the Gulf is and vice versa. I once spent the night lost, near the Roberts River. The next morning I knew the tide was outgoing and checked it, then followed a series of creeks out to the Roberts River and regained my position.

Numbered channel markers are very helpful for navigation. The Coast Guard maintains a marked route from Flamingo to the Gulf via Whitewater Bay and the Little Shark River. The numbers on the large red and green metal signposts get higher as you head north for the Gulf. There are also Coast Guard–maintained markers heading into Florida Bay from Flamingo and into the Gulf from Everglades City.

The Wilderness Waterway, maintained by the park service, starts in Flamingo and leads to Everglades City. Paddlers follow the Coast Guard markers to #48, just north of Whitewater Bay, then follow rectangular brown signs. These signs are numbered, getting higher the closer you get to Everglades City. The arrows on the signs *do not always* point you in the right direction, so double-check your chart and don't blindly follow the arrows of the Wilderness Waterway.

Paddling at night is a very viable option in the Everglades, especially on a full-moon night, and is a good way to use the tides or avoid windy days. Don't expect to find your way around Hells Bay in the dark, but a less complex area, such as along the Gulf, can be paddled after the sun goes down. What helps are your two urban markers, Miami and Naples. The lights of Miami are visible no matter your position in the Glades. They can be your eastern beacon.

The lights of Naples are much less bright, but in the northern reaches of the park, they are your northern signal. Lighted buoys mark the park's perimeter in the Gulf.

Obviously, the sun can be used throughout the day to help you figure out your position. Keep up with where you are at all times using the navigational helpers described here. Don't try either to paddle for an hour and then reposition yourself or to check your location only every now and then. The more you stay on top of your position the less likely you are to get lost. Finally, do not—I repeat, do not—enter the backcountry without a nautical chart and compass, even if you have a GPS.

Watching Out for Potential Hazards

Imagine a man-on-the-street interviewer asking passersby this question: "What do you think poses the biggest hazard in the Everglades?" Without a doubt the most popular answer would be "Alligators." In reality, wild alligators shy away from people. Food-habituated gators can pose something of a problem, but for the Everglades paddler there are several other hazards that may adversely impact a trip on a far more regular basis. A negative alligator encounter is very, very rare.

Wind can be the paddler's worst enemy, though a moderate tail wind can be a good thing. So can an insect-clearing breeze. But big blows can be dangerous. South Florida in the winter has fantastic weather more often than not—generally sunny and warm, but also regularly windy. The mornings are usually still, but the winds pick up as the morning moves along. And 10–15 knots is average. Days with wind speeds lower than this occur, but so do plenty of days with higher wind speeds. Small-craft advisories are common. Winds normally blow from the southeast, but when a winter cold front steamrolls from the north, the temperature plummets and steady, strong north winds of 15–20 knots can hold for days. Try to plan your trip around the winds, but when this is unavoidable, take smaller channels and use the lee sides of shores and islands to minimize the wind's effects.

When the winds blow, the waves come right along with them. First-time Everglades trippers are often shocked at the vast amount of open water they traverse. And a good wind can turn a glassy bay into a choppy wave trap. Wind may slow your progress, but waves can capsize your craft—real trouble. Listen to National Weather Service forecasts; they predict wind speed and direction. When big winds are expected, try to paddle early in the morning when the winds and waves are generally lower. Consider paddling in the late afternoon or at night for the same reason. As a rule, I try to start early in the day, not only to avoid the winds but also to give myself ample daylight to handle any difficult unforeseen situations.

In windy conditions, try to modify your route to stay in sheltered waters, or at least take sheltered breaks when you can to avoid ex-hausting yourself. Don't try to fight through waves. Roll over them, riding the crest, then drop to the trough as gently as possible, and pull yourself up and over the next crest. Sea kayaks have the advan-tage in big waves. If you are kayaking, make sure any gear outside the craft is tied on very tightly, and consider using a wrist strap to connect yourself to your paddle.

Canoeists have to be more careful. First, try to avoid getting par-allel to big waves. If you are heading in a direction parallel to the waves, paddle at an angle, crisscrossing the waves rather than pad-dling parallel to them. A wave crashing into the side of your canoe can be a quick capsizer. If water is splashing in, try to bail at inter-vals. Otherwise the water in your canoe will lower your waterline, allowing more water in faster, and eventually you will sink. Beware of waves coming from behind; they can drop a lot of water into your boat when you're not looking.

In times of wind, bring rope to tie the corners of your tent to the posts of chickees. Furthermore, wait until late in the day to erect your tent to avail yourself of more space on the chickee and not subject the tent to sun or wind damage. Follow this advice when

A paddler impatiently waits for the tide to reach Highland Beach. Photo by author.

camped on open beaches, as well. These tips come from hard experience: I have had three tent poles break during Gulf-side camping trips.

Have a rope on both ends of your craft in order to securely tie it to a chickee, and pull your boat far above the high tide line on beaches to make sure the boat will be there when you need it again.

When leaving a beach in your craft, aim your boat straight toward the waves and try to time your departure between wave surges, then paddle out at a slight angle to the waves. Do not allow your boat to get broadside to the waves, or it will fill with water and get pounded back to shore.

Tides can be your enemy or friend, much like the wind. Low tides can leave you stranded in the buggy Nightmare or expansive Florida Bay. But apart from causing discomfort or delay, tides can also do real damage. Be careful around man-made canals—a strong tidal pull can take you where you don't want to go or ram you into a tree lying half-submerged in the water. The biggest problem with tides comes when you are cutting corners in rivers and straits or around peninsulas. You will be paddling in one direction, and the tide, flowing perpendicular to your direction, will catch the nose of your craft and turn you over before you know what happened. Watch for direction flow in the water ahead of you—ripples and currents—and adjust your speed and direction accordingly. In rivers and creeks, try to time your travel with the tides and your paddling can be a lot easier.

In the northern half of the Everglades paddling area, especially closer to the Gulf, watch out for oyster bars. These are huge clumps of oysters growing in a mass beneath the water. Their sharp shells are often exposed or lie just below the surface at low tides. Exercise caution with your craft and your feet. Oyster shells can cut through your foot or a folding kayak before you realize what's happening. Wear shoes when you get out of your boat, and carry duct tape for temporarily sealing tears in your boat.

One of the biggest potential problems is actually little. Mosquitoes, no-see-ums, and even deer flies can dominate an outing. If you can't stand being bitten by bugs, don't come here! I have been on trips where I was bitten less than once a day, and I have been on trips where—even wearing full clothing and a head net on land—I retreated to the tent every night an hour before dark. Mosquitoes can take your breath away at ground sites and no-see-ums can drive you to tears on the beach. Clothes are your best defense: shoes, socks, long pants, long sleeve shirt, bandanna around your neck, and hat. But by all means bring good bug repellent—with DEET—a high-quality tent with fine mesh netting, and a head net. One thing about a head net: when you want one you really want one, and when you don't have one there is usually no way to get one. Plan to have cooked your supper and cleaned your plates by sunset, or you'll be speed cooking in a mosquito-driven frenzy. Or wait an hour or so after dark to start cooking.

Choose your campsite wisely; read the winds and locate a spot where you can catch a breeze. When erecting your tent, place it with the tent door facing the wind. Mosquitoes are less apt to stay on the windward side of a tent, so this way you will bring fewer mosquitoes with you when you enter and exit the tent.

There are two poisonous trees in the Everglades paddling area: manchineel and poisonwood. Pictures of them can be found online, so you might want to familiarize yourself with their appearance. You probably won't encounter the manchineel—it is an uncommon coastal tree up to 30 feet tall with leathery, light green, shallow-toothed leaves on long yellow stems. Its sap will burn you, and its green to reddish fruits are deadly if eaten. The other tree is poisonwood, in the same family as poison ivy. Its shiny, dark green, compound leaves have five leaflets with irregular black spots on them. The sap of this tree is toxic, too. Be reasonably careful and covered when walking through tree hammocks.

Powerboaters are much like the winds and tides; they can either help you or hinder you, depending on the speed and direction they are going. Paddlers and powerboaters share the water, so let's share the best we can. *Powerboaters are not the enemy.* It is not us versus them. Powerboaters can help you determine your direction and give aid in an emergency. But they can also speed by without consideration. It all depends on the driver. Be a defensive paddler: watch and listen for motorboats, then exercise the same courtesy toward powerboaters that you would expect from them.

Now, what about those alligators? And snakes? And scorpions? Alligators pose little problem except for those that hang around campsites waiting for handouts of fish guts and other yummy leftovers. These food-habituated alligators will approach anything thrown in the water. Keep out of the water in such situations, and never feed an alligator! You have nothing to fear from snakes. They are typically shy and do whatever they can to avoid humans. Consider yourself lucky if you see two—then you will have matched the total number of snakes I've seen in the paddling country of the Everglades. No Florida scorpions are considered poisonous, but all of them pack a painful sting. Small scorpions can lurk inside deadwood. Be on the watch for these critters when breaking up firewood at beach sites.

Planning Your Trip

You want to paddle the Everglades, but where to begin? All the information you need is included in this book. However, to access official park information call (305) 242–7700 and ask for a Wilderness Trip Planner. Or go to park service Web site at http://www.nps.gov/ever.

With the rules, routes, and campsite descriptions at your fingertips you can plan a trip. But planning is *all* you can do from home. *Wilderness permits, required for all overnight camping, are available only in person at the Flamingo and Gulf Coast ranger stations. You can pick one up—in person—up to 24 hours in advance of a trip during the winter paddling season, November through April.* Phone permits are available for trips originating in the Florida Keys and going to the North Nest Key and Little Rabbit Key campsites in Florida

Bay. During the off-season, May to November, phone permits aren't available, and you must register in person at the Flamingo or Gulf Coast Ranger Station. If you are planning to head into Ten Thousand Islands National Wildlife Refuge and Rookery Bay Preserve from the Everglades City Ranger Station, you must file a float plan there. At present, permits aren't required to camp overnight at these areas north of the park. This could change, however, so check the Web sites of Ten Thousand Islands National Wildlife Refuge, Collier-Seminole State Park, Fakahatchee Strand State Preserve, and Rookery Bay Preserve to find out the latest.

In the park, head to the permit desk at the Flamingo or Gulf Coast Ranger Station and make a backcountry trip request with park staff. Have alternate trips planned; that way, if campsites are already reserved, you have a backup ready. Once your permit is issued and park regulations have been explained to you, you must pay a modest permit-processing fee, plus a daily camping fee of $2 per person per day. The fee is $10 for parties up to 6; $20 for parties of 7–12; and $30 for parties of more than 12. Everglades National Park gets to keep 80 percent of the fees for park maintenance projects, including those on backcountry campsites and chickees. The other 20 percent goes to parks that don't charge fees.

Heavy-Use Periods

The general paddling season in Everglades National Park runs from November through April. Insects, thunderstorms, and potential hurricanes combine to keep the Everglades backcountry nearly deserted May through October. When the first north breezes cool and clear the air, reducing insect populations, paddlers turn their eyes southward to the Everglades. A few campsites begin to fill on weekends. But the crowds really come around Christmas. The period between Christmas and New Year's is the Everglades' busiest. Expect full campsites and plan alternative trips. After January 1, weekends can be busy, but you can nearly always get on the water and find a campsite in the general vicinity of where you want to go. For the most solitude, plan your trip for weekdays. The next big crowds come around Martin Luther King Day weekend in late January and Presidents' Day weekend in February. The last big hits come during mid-March, when college kids flock to the Glades for overnight trips. Again, get to the ranger stations early and you can get some campsites. As the weather warms up in April, visitation tapers and then dies off by the end of the month.

Wilderness Waterway

For uninformed or novice paddlers, the only route to take in the Everglades is the Wilderness Waterway, which runs from Everglades City to Flamingo. Though combinations of more challenging routes make for more fulfilling experiences for seasoned trippers, the Wilderness Waterway can be a rewarding endeavor for all paddlers. If you decide to trace the Wilderness Waterway from beginning to end, use the following routes. The campsites mentioned are not necessarily the most appropriate places to stay but are included as points of reference.

From the Gulf Coast Ranger Station in Everglades City, take the Causeway Route to Lopez River Route to Hurddles Creek Route to Sunday Bay chickee. From Sunday Bay chickee, take Last Huston Bay Route to Darwins Place Route to Lostmans Five campsite. From Lostmans Five campsite, take the Willy Willy Route to Rodgers River Bay Route to the Broad River Route to Broad River campsite. From the Broad River campsite, take the Nightmare Route to Harney River chickee to the Harney River Route. Paddle up the Harney River Route to Tarpon Bay and the Shark Cutoff Route. Take the Shark Cutoff Route to Oyster Bay chickee. From Oyster Bay chickee, briefly take the Cormorant Pass Route to Whitewater Bay Route to the Buttonwood Canal Route and on to Flamingo.

Paddlers' Waterway

If you want a route that goes from the north all the way to the south and is friendlier to self-propelled craft than the Wilderness Waterway, take what I call the Paddlers' Waterway. If you take the Paddler's Waterway, you will encounter less motorboat traffic and see the best of the Everglades, from the freshwater to the Gulf to shell mounds and on around fabulous Cape Sable.

To travel the Paddler's Waterway, start on the Turner River Canoe Trail off the Tamiami Trail and paddle to the Hurddles Creek Route to Sunday Bay chickee. From Sunday Bay chickee, take the Last Huston Bay Route a short distance to the Huston River Route. Take the Huston River Route to Mormon Key in the Gulf. From Mormon Key, take the Turkey Key Route to Hog Key. From Hog Key head south to Lostmans River, and take the Lostmans River Route to Toms Creek Route. Take the Toms Creek Route to Rodgers River chickee. From Rodgers River chickee, take the Cabbage Island Shortcut to Broad River Campsite. Take the Broad River Route up to Camp Lonesome. From Camp Lonesome, take the rugged Wood River Route to Highland Beach. From Highland Beach, take the Nightmare Route to Harney River chickee. From Harney River chickee, take the Harney River Route a short distance east to the North Harney River Route. Take the North Harney River Route to Canepatch campsite. From Canepatch campsite, take the Harney River Route to the Shark Cutoff Route in Tarpon Bay. Take the Shark Cutoff Route to Oyster Bay chickee. From Oyster Bay chickee, take the Big Sable Route to Northwest Cape campsite. From Northwest Cape, take the Little Sable Creek–Lake Ingraham Route to East Cape campsite. From East Cape campsite, take the East Cape Route to Flamingo.

Rules and Regulations

All plants, animals, and artifacts in the Everglades are protected; do not collect or disturb them. Unoccupied shells may be gathered—up to 1 quart per person.

Closed Areas—All keys (islands) in Florida Bay are closed to landing, except Bradley Key (sunrise to sunset) and those designated as campsites. In Florida Bay, the mainland from Terrapin Point to U.S. 1 is closed to landing.

Fires are allowed only at beach sites along the Gulf Coast, below the storm surge line, using only dead or downed wood. **No fires** are allowed at ground or chickee sites.

Search and Rescue—File a trip plan with a friend or relative before leaving. If you do not return home on time, that person should call Everglades National Park dispatch, which operates 24 hours a day, at (305) 242-7740. If you are overdue, the park service will not search for you without being notified first.

Trash must be packed out. Please help make everyone's wilderness experience enjoyable; leave campsites cleaner than you found them.

Human Waste—Use toilets where provided. At campsites without facilities, bury human waste in a hole at least 6 inches deep. Burn toilet paper in the hole or pack it out with your trash.

Food—Remove all food particles from dishes before washing. DO NOT dump food scraps in the water; pack them out with your trash.

Water—One gallon per person per day is the minimum recommendation.

Weather conditions change frequently and rapidly. Be prepared for intense sun, rain, strong winds, and cold.

Winds and Tides—Check conditions before you depart and carry a weather or transistor radio. Current weather reports are indispensable for overnight Everglades trips.

Nautical charts and compass are necessary for most trips. A GPS is also recommended.

Designated Site—You must stay at the site listed on your permit unless safety factors require otherwise.

Noise—Be considerate of other visitors, especially when in close proximity to other groups. Noise-producing machinery such as generators and bug sprayers is prohibited.

Weapons—Carrying or using weapons is prohibited.

Fishing—State fishing license regulations apply. You are responsible for adhering to size and daily bag limits for Everglades National Park.

Pets are not permitted.

Wildlife—DO NOT feed or harass alligators and other wildlife. Animals habituated to human food can be dangerous.

Equipment

Outdoor adventurers get to choose their own equipment, and they sink or swim with their choice. Hopefully no one will really sink, but good equipment choices can go a long way in making or breaking an Everglades trip.

Canoe or Sea Kayak?

The first choice for Everglades paddlers is which type of boat to take. Canoes have been the mainstay for years, but sea kayaks are really on the rise. Each type has its own advantages and disadvantages. Canoes can carry more equipment and allow more freedom of movement than kayaks, yet kayaks are faster and are safer in big waves. Canoes are easier to load and unload, but sea kayaks keep their loads stored away from the elements. Canoes are more maneuverable in tight spaces, but sea kayaks track better. The comparisons can go on and on, so choose the boat that works for you. I use both and enjoy each on its own terms.

Sea Kayaks

So you have decided to use a sea kayak. Now, what type of sea kayak? There are numerous makes and models on the market. Sit-on-top kayaks are being used more and more in the Everglades, because staying dry is a less important issue here than in colder climates. The sit-on-tops are more comfortable and easier to get in and out of, but expect to get wet in the waves. I do not recommend them except for short trips in favorable weather. Otherwise, big waves and cold weather will leave you wishing you'd opted for a sit-in model. Folding kayaks are convenient for visitors flying to the Glades from far away, but I wouldn't want to be in one around the sharp oyster bars of the Ten Thousand Islands.

Touring kayaks are deservedly the most popular. These have ample room for storing camping gear, food, and water. They are stable and durable but can be hot on a sunny day if the spray skirt is on. I

Touring sea kayaks with a spray skirt can handle the varied waters of the Glades. Photo by author.

keep my spray skirt around my waist, ready to slip around the lip of the kayak if big waves come up. (Bring a sponge to remove unwanted water from your cockpit and storage compartments.)

I prefer models with a rudder. Tides, currents, and winds are easier to negotiate with a rudder. Be prepared to pop the rudder up in the shallow waters of the Glades. Two-person and even three-person sea kayaks are catching on more and more. Sharing responsibility makes paddling and navigating easier for both parties, and someone unable to navigate can travel with an experienced sea kayaker.

Paddles are a matter of personal choice. Kayakers almost always use double-bladed paddles. Each paddler must determine the right length and blade width for their needs. Most kayakers prefer a feathered paddle—a paddle with blades at 90 degree angles to one another. Consider buying a quality paddle, and always bring an extra paddle that breaks down in case you lose your primary paddle.

Canoes

With so many makes and models of canoes out there, which one is right for the Everglades paddler? I like to consider length, depth, volume, and durability when choosing a canoe. Tandem canoers want a boat at least 17 feet long for ample room. Find one that tracks well and has plenty of volume but can still turn sharply enough to handle narrow Glades creeks. A canoe should have adequate depth and volume for gear storage and water displacement. The larger canoes are safer in the Gulf, and remember that paddlers here must carry all their own water, which adds to the load.

Oyster bars, sand bars, shell and beach landings can be rough on a boat. Old-time aluminum canoes are durable but slower than models made from synthetic materials. If your boat is made from synthetics, it's going to wear the scars of Glades travel. Live with it. This is no place to baby a canoe.

Solo paddlers should use a smaller boat. I used a 17-foot Old Town Penobscot in the Everglades for years. It is scarred on the bottom but has served me well. It has no keel, which makes for tracking problems but greater precision in paddling. There's a lot of open water in the Glades—you may be better off with a keel, especially if you're a less experienced paddler.

I have never used a spray cover in the Everglades, but I have wished for one in big water on the Gulf. If you have one, bring it. A bailer made from an old gallon milk jug can remove water from your canoe. Find the canoeing paddle you like best and bring an extra one for each person in the boat.

Life Vest

Not only is it sensible to carry a personal floatation device, but Coast Guard–approved life vests are required for Everglades paddlers. Life vests can also keep you warm on cool days.

Storage

Quality rubber and plastic storage bags and dry boxes come in a dizzying array of sizes and strengths for sea kayaks and canoes. The sea kayak models are shaped to fit in the kayak. They can be a pain to load and unload, but they do the trick. Take the extra moment to close them properly after you put your gear inside.

Other general waterproof bags can be strapped onto a sea kayak or set in a canoe. Strap your gear in your canoe when entering big water. If you capsize, your gear will stay with the boat. I trusted my laptop computer and various other electronic devices to dry bags while working on both editions of this book, and I didn't have a problem. Consider distributing your gear among several bags of medium size—that way you don't have all your eggs in one basket in case of a wetting. Models with shoulder straps can be handy for hauling your gear from the water to island campsites at low tide. These "Everglades portages" can be surprisingly long. Absolutely keep a small waterproof bag close by for personal items such as sunscreen, bug dope, lip balm, and so on. Even though your charts should be waterproof, I recommend using a waterproof map holder to keep your compass and maps together.

Repairs

Keep duct tape on hand for making temporary repairs to your boat and waterproof bags. So that the tape will adhere properly, thoroughly dry the damaged item, brushing away any sand and other debris, then apply the duct tape.

Shelter

The advantage of boat camping over backpacking is the increased equipment capacity paddlers have: you can bring a bigger shelter. For two campers, I prefer four-person tent models with a vestibule. When bugs are bad and the January nights long, you will be happy for the extra room, even though it will make chickees a little more cramped. Freestanding tents are a necessity for chickees. Make sure your tent has a bug screen with mesh tight enough to keep out no-see-ums. Also, make sure the packed size of your tent will properly fit inside a waterproof storage bag. Sand stakes are a good thing to have when you're camped on the beach on a windy day. Large screen shelters are a great option during buggy times, but be careful setting them up in high winds. By all means bring a tarp and rope. After paddling all day in the sun to a beach campsite you're going to want some shade. Use paddles for poles and rig the tarp across them to make a sun shelter.

Cooking Gear and Food

Campers in the Everglades must bring a portable stove, as fires are not allowed on chickees or ground campsites. Bring more than enough fuel for the duration of your trip. I like to grill over a fire, so a foldable, portable grill is part of my kit when I head to a beach campsite. With extra room, boaters can upgrade their cook kits somewhat. No matter how meticulous you are, expect to chew on a few grains of sand when eating your meal on the beach. Many campers like to spread a sheet of plastic over their cooking area to minimize this unpleasant but typical Everglades experience. Bring more than enough matches and lighters—campers often drop things between the cracks in the boards of chickees or lose items in the sand at beaches. My best knife lies beneath the Sweetwater chickee and a super cigar lighter under the Roberts River chickee.

Campers must bring not only all their food but their own water. *Bring 1 gallon of water per person per day.* There are few freshwater sources in the paddling area of the Everglades. Canoers can upgrade their food by using coolers; use dry ice to make it last more than a few days. If you don't use dry ice, convert your melted ice to drinking or cooking water, and consider using brackish water for cooking if you are low on freshwater. Where food is concerned, keep in mind the probable sun and heat of the Everglades. Provisions will spoil quicker there than in cooler, shadier forested wilderness areas. Keep food out of the sun during the day. Because many ground and beach campsites have persistent raccoons, store your food and water in hard-sided containers and tie them shut with rope or bungee cords.

Clothing

When packing their clothes, Everglades novices often go heavy on shorts and T-shirts. But the opposite kind of clothing is better. Though the weather is generally warm, shorts and T-shirts are bad for two Everglades situations: sun and bugs. Bring the summery clothes, but expect most often to wear long-sleeved shirts and long pants. They will protect you from both intense sun and biting insects. Make sure the clothing you bring is light colored and tightly woven. Salt marsh mosquitoes are very persistent and will bite through overly thin clothing. Thick socks and foot-covering shoes also protect against bugs and come in handy during cool weather. And cool weather can strike. Have several layers of clothing with you, culminating in a waterproof rain jacket and rain pants. These will keep your warm and dry. Gloves can protect your hands against blisters and sunburn.

Hats are a must for the Everglades traveler. The sun shining in your eyes and off the water will burn and blind you. Consider wide-brimmed hats and flats fishing hats with neck protection. Bandannas will also protect your neck. Visors and ball caps are more comfortable but don't provide as much overall sun protection. By all means bring sunglasses. Get a strap attachment for around your neck to prevent loss, and bring a spare pair. Your eyes will thank you. Invest in a head net. When the bugs are bad you'll appreciate it, and there is no substitute for a head net if you don't have one. A bug suit can protect your body much as a head net does your head.

Other Items

The four musts for navigators are a waterproof nautical chart, compass, GPS with map downloading capability, and a tide chart. Get the tide chart when you get your backcountry permit. Keep all four items handy at all times. You will need them. And just in case, stow away a spare compass. Binoculars will help you find markers and discern shorelines. A first-aid kit, knife, rope, flashlight, timepiece, and weather radio will support your day-to-day activities. While cellular phones only offer hit-or-miss coverage in the Everglades, a weather radio will help you make daily paddling decisions and can be a lifesaver in the event of big storms. Don't leave home without one! A timepiece will help you calculate the tides. So will your GPS. The first-aid kit will enable you to handle minor injuries until you can flag down aid. Bring flares in case you need to signal for help. Also, bring a flashlight strong enough to shine brightly at night.

Do not enter the Everglades without sunscreen and bug dope. I've seen campers so sunburned they could hardly paddle. Use sunscreen! Bug dope will make life much more bearable when the swamp angels are stinging. Bring creams for your skin and sprays for your clothing to keep the bugs at bay. Don't forget personal items such as your toothbrush. Also, bring toilet paper and a trowel for burying human waste. Not all campsites provide toilets—dispose of your waste properly.

Backcountry Pastimes

Once in the backcountry, there are many other things to do besides paddle. Most folks don't want to navigate and stroke the blade all day, fall into camp, eat some grub, and immediately hit the bag. Fishing, birding, photography, nature study, and beachcombing are among the most popular activities Everglades explorers undertake.

Anglers will have a hard time finding more varied waters to fish than the Everglades. To fish in Everglades National Park, you must have a valid Florida state license for fresh- or saltwater species or both. Check on the latest size and bag limits. Bring more salt-tolerant and heavier tackle than you would normally use from a self-propelled craft. The fish here can be enormous, and if you hook one you will want to land it!

Freshwater bass and bluegill ply many of the interior creeks, such as the upper North River near the beginning of the Hells Bay Canoe Trail and upper Lostmans Creek. Some of the richest waters are where fresh- and saltwaters meet. Snook, Jack Crevalle, ladyfish, and

Fishing is a popular pastime for Everglades paddlers. Photo by Constance Mier.

mangrove snapper will take a well-presented lure. Paddlers will be in for a big fight if they hook a tarpon. It happened to me. I was almost thankful the giant got off the lure—I didn't know what I was going to do if I got it to the boat! Sea trout, reds, and other fish inhabit the rivers and coastlines of the Everglades. Many anglers like to use live bait, though it is harder for paddlers than for motorboaters to keep their bait fresh. Consider trolling with lures on long paddling days. It breaks up the stroking, and you just may catch dinner.

Birders flock to the Everglades just as birds once flocked to the park. Birds still inhabit the Glades, just not in the numbers they once did. Day to day, though, birds are the most prevalent wildlife you'll see. Often, you can stay quietly in one location and let the birds come to you. Invest in one of the many birding books available at park visitor centers. Otherwise you'll be caught in an endless guessing game. Binoculars are a big help in making accurate identifications.

One of my personal interests is trees. Though most of the Everglades paddling area is mangroves and water, there are many trees to identify. Years ago, before I became well-acquainted with the state, I was amazed at the sheer number of Florida's palm tree species. Plant and tree identification is especially challenging here, where differing environments subtly blend into one another. Again, with their stock of native plant and tree guides for sale, the visitor centers can help you.

Beachcombing is fun on Everglades beaches and keys, and identifying shells adds interest. You can gather up to 1 quart per person of unoccupied shells. Remember that all keys in Florida Bay are closed to landing, except for Bradley Key and those designated as campsites. Similarly, in Florida Bay the mainland from Terrapin Point to U.S. 1 is closed to landing. Follow park rules and my suggestions above, and you can have a fun, safe outing that treads lightly on the park. Enjoy your adventure. I hope you make memories that last a lifetime!

The Routes

Florida Bay

Dildo Key Bank Route

Begin: Flamingo	End: Little Rabbit Key
Length: 14 miles	Time: 7 hours
Potential tidal influence: 5	Potential wind influence: 5
Navigational challenge: 3	

Highlights: Wildlife in Florida Bay; clear waters

Hazards: Motorboat traffic; big winds and strong tides in Florida Bay

Campsites: Little Rabbit Key

Connections: Snake Bight Route, East Cape Route, Buttonwood Canal Route

This first leg of the Florida Bay loop is a minimum two-night, three-day loop paddle that traverses west and central parts of Florida Bay, from the shallows of several banks—havens for birds at low tide—to deep basins where the grassy sea floor shines up through several feet of water. This loop is one of the most rewarding in the Everglades. On the other hand, it means a full 44 miles of paddling, and if the winds and tides are against you, it can be downright exhausting and possibly dangerous. The route's long distances and open water favor sea kayakers. Canoers can make it only when the weather is perfect. No matter which craft you choose, be sure you have a favorable weather forecast before embarking on this journey.

This leg of the loop takes you past several islands and shallows where there will be birds aplenty and fish swimming all around, too. Leave Flamingo Marina and the adjacent murky waters to enter Florida Bay, aiming for the west tip of Joe Kemp Key. If the tides are low, you may have to follow the marina channel out a distance. Either way, begin heading in a southeasterly direction for the channel between Frank Key and Palm Key. The shallows around both islands are extensive. Frank Key was named for Frank Erwin, who homesteaded the island in the early 1920s. The waters deepen somewhat beyond the south end of Palm Key, but shallows are not uncommon. Begin aiming for the Pelican Keys, which from the distance will look at first like a single island. Stay generally east of the Pelicans where the water is deeper. Dildo Key Bank, containing Dildo Key and Cluett Key, is a massive shallow to be avoided. (Dildo Key is named for a native cactus of South Florida that has long thorny three-angled stems.)

Ahead, massive sea grass beds, including turtle grass, sway in the clear waters. Arrive at the Pelican Keys at 6.5 miles. As you pass, these twin islands will be easier to identify, because of the channel that cuts between them. From here, curve nearly due east, heading for an unnamed island a mile and a half away. The Rabbit Keys will be visible to your south. You are still working around Dildo Key Bank. Keep following around the east side of the unnamed island, then begin a nearly due south course for the Rabbit Keys. Beware of shallows around the Rabbit Keys: keep to their east side and you will stay in deeper water.

As you near them, the separate islands will look more distinct. Little Rabbit Key and its campsite are your destination. Deep channels surround the key, and it also has a water-monitoring station. Reach the dock and the opening in the mangrove on the island's northwest side at 14 miles. From here, it is 20.5 miles to East Cape Sable via Sandy Key on the First National Bank Route.

East Cape Route

Begin: Flamingo   End: East Cape campsite

Length: 10 miles   Time: 5 hours

Potential tidal influence: 5   Potential wind influence: 5

Navigational challenge: 2

Highlights: Lots of beach camping; most southerly point of mainland U.S.

Hazards: Motorboat traffic; shallow water; big winds and strong tides in Florida Bay

Campsites: East Clubhouse Beach, Clubhouse Beach, East Cape

Connections: First National Bank Route, Northwest Cape Route, Snake Bight Route, Buttonwood Canal Route, Dildo Key Bank Route, Little Sable Creek–Lake Ingraham Route

---

East Cape Route—third leg of the Florida Bay loop and the main route to Cape Sable from Flamingo—takes you along the most southerly piece of mainland real estate in the country. You'll leave Flamingo and civilization behind for a mangrove shoreline that becomes sandier and beachier. Take your pick along this route of one of three quality campsites to do some serious beach camping. How close you stay to shore will depend on water levels, which change dramatically out here with the winds and tides. This is the open water of Florida Bay, on the "outside" of the Everglades, so keep apprised of any changes in the weather.

Flamingo Marina has a canoe and kayak launch to the right of the motorboat ramps facing Florida Bay. Leave the marina and head west, hugging the shoreline. Look for the osprey nest on channel marker #15. Continue to trace the shoreline, passing the park visitor center and the Flamingo Campground. Stay on the outside of the narrow island that parallels the campground. If the tide is up, take the route between Bradley Key and the mainland. The tall mangrove forest, pocked from hurricane damage, will provide an interesting

Paddler spots porpoise just off Bradley Key. Photo by Constance Mier.

contrast to the bay and help you can mark your progress better. If the tide is out, stay outside Bradley Key and several hundred yards offshore, as the shoreline waters can be boat-stoppingly shallow.

Pass diminutive Curry Key at mile 2.5. Continue west and come to East Clubhouse Beach campsite at mile 4. This is a good place to stop and camp or just stretch your legs. East Cape Sable appears on the horizon just after you pass the first point beyond East Clubhouse Beach campsite. Sandy Key and Carl Ross Key are visible to your left, way out in Florida Bay. The Middle Ground Buoy is visible as well.

Pass Slagle Ditch at mile 6. Back in the early 20th century Model Land Company dug this ditch as part of an effort to drain Cape Sable to make it more fertile and appealing to potential land buyers. The intermittent slender beach continues until you come to the Clubhouse Beach campsite at mile 7. This marked campsite has a longer stretch of beach than average for this section of the park and is backed by a sizable marl prairie.

Beyond Clubhouse Beach, stay the course west, passing House Ditch, then East Cape Canal at mile 9, which runs to Lake Ingraham.

This is the southeasterly terminus of the Little Sable Creek–Lake Ingraham Route, which leads 13 miles to Northwest Cape—a viable alternative if big winds are blowing on the Gulf. East Cape Canal is over 100 feet wide and very straight.

Pass one mangrove creek, then a second shortly thereafter. The second creek marks the beginning of the East Cape campsite. End your route at the rounded East Cape, which curves northwesterly at mile 10. Middle Cape is visible just as you swing around East Cape. The Middle Cape Route leads north 10.5 miles to Northwest Cape. The First National Bank Route leads 20.5 miles to Little Rabbit Key via Sandy Key.

First National Bank Route

Begin: Little Rabbit Key	End: East Cape campsite
Length: 20.5 miles	Time: 8 hours
Potential tidal influence: 5	Potential wind influence: 5
Navigational challenge: 3	

Highlights: Solitude; open waters

Hazards: Motorboat traffic; big winds and strong tides in Florida Bay

Campsites: Little Rabbit Key, East Cape

Connections: Dildo Key Bank Route, East Cape Route, Middle Cape Route, Little Sable Creek–Lake Ingraham Route

This route is the second leg of the Florida Bay loop and perhaps the most challenging paddling covered in this guidebook—if conditions are adverse. It heads first for Sandy Key and Carl Ross Key, then turns south for the mainland and East Cape Sable. Sandy Key is a preserved nesting site that often draws hundreds of birds. Carl Ross Key, formerly a backcountry campsite, was closed due to storm damage and is now part of the greater Sandy Key nesting area, off limits to landing.

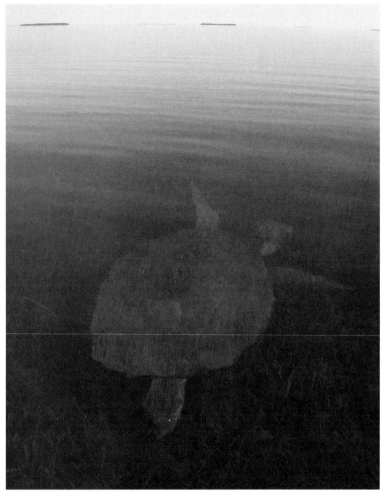

A sea turtle swims the clear waters near Iron Pipe Channel. Photo by author.

From Little Rabbit Key dock, Sandy Key is visible on the western horizon. Man of War Key lies closer to the north. Before leaving Little Rabbit Key, consider the tides; the waters around the Rabbit Keys are notoriously shallow. If the tide is out, take the marked Rabbit Key Pass channel south of the island to reach the deeper waters of Rabbit Key Basin. Enjoy the clear, deep waters of Rabbit Key Basin, while shooting for the Iron Pipe Channel. Between Little Rabbit and Sandy keys, you'll find some of the most open water in the park, so hope for flat water. The mainland around Flamingo is barely visible and the string of Florida Keys extends southeast.

Reach Iron Pipe Channel at 5 miles. Man of War Key still lies to your north. Keep aiming for the south side of Sandy Key, keeping the shallows of First National Bank to your right. The low-growing vegetation of Carl Ross Key will soon become visible. Next, you will begin to see the sands of these two islands. Flocks of birds often wade in the shallows around First National Bank. Work around the Gulf side of these keys, after reaching the south end of Sandy Key at 12.8 miles. Enjoy observing the bird life here, but don't land, despite the tempting beach crowned with coconut palms and gumbo limbo. Interestingly, Carl Ross Key (named for a former Flamingo resident) and Sandy Key were one island until Hurricane Donna separated them in 1960. The 2005 hurricanes seem to have thrown sand into the breach, a step toward merging the two islands as one again. After making the curve, begin aiming northwesterly for the point of East Cape Sable, visible in the distance.

Pass the marked Rocky Channel at 14.4 miles, and the most southerly mainland in the United States, your destination, becomes clearer. The East Cape sands eventually appear, as does the distant curve of Middle Cape. Pass near the red channel marker #4—part of the marked channel into Flamingo from the Gulf—at 17.5 miles. Beyond here, the waters deepen significantly, and if the winds are high you may encounter big waves. Reach East Cape at 20.5 miles. This is a fine backcountry camping area with sites facing southeast and southwest around the bend of the cape. From here, it is 10.5 miles to Northwest Cape on the Middle Cape Route and 10 miles back to Flamingo via the East Cape Route.

North Nest Key Loop

Begin: Key Largo   End: Key Largo

Distance: 16 miles   Time: 8 hours

Potential tidal influence: 4   Potential wind influence: 5

Navigational challenge: 3

Highlights: Colorful ocean waters; camping on a key on Florida Bay

Hazards: Motorboats near Key Largo; open water in Florida Bay

Campsites: North Nest Key

Connections: None

This isolated loop offers some of the best paddling in Florida Bay and the Florida Keys. Start your loop on Key Largo, then enjoy the colorful waters for which the Keys are known. Paddle across large sounds, small creeks, and open bay waters to North Nest Key, where a swim beach and campsite await. Here, you can while away the day or spend the night. Camping is recommended, as the entire loop is a long one-day paddle, though it is more doable on long summer days. The return route is more sheltered, part of the Intracoastal Waterway. The civilized Keys are never far away, and motorboats will be with you the entire route. Even so, the scenery in Florida Bay is hard to beat.

Your jumping-off point is Florida Bay Outfitters, (305) 451-3018. They are located at mile marker #104 on the bay side of U.S. 1. This is your headquarters for canoeing and sea kayaking the Keys. The outfitters offer everything from guided tours to gear for rent or sale. Start your paddle here, at the rear of the outfitters. Head west into Blackwater Sound between channel marker #40 and Bush Point. (This paddle is part of the Intracoastal Waterway.) Once past marker #40, you have entered Everglades National Park waters.

Continue through the clear waters of the sound, bearing toward The Boggies, which is marked with a buoy. Enter The Boggies and

Paddler's-eye view of Florida Bay on a calm day. Photo by author.

traverse the 20-foot-wide creek lined with mangrove and emerge into wide-open Florida Bay at mile 4. Bear west for the island nearest you, Duck Key. Once in the bay, begin to bear more southwesterly past a sandy shoal marked with PVC pipe. The Nest Keys will appear as two long low islands on the horizon. The sea beneath you will have taken on that aquamarine green characteristic of the Keys. The ocean bottom is easy to see. The waters change to other attractive hues with the changing depths, distances, and shades.

Aim for the northern point of North Nest Key, then swing around the west side of the island. A low-slung shore of mangrove parallels the sandy shoreline. Pass a swim beach marked with buoys before rounding another point of the island and coming to the island's campsite at mile 7.5. Here lies a dock, beach, and shaded camping area. Pull up your craft to eat lunch or to spend the night.

Continue your loop by circling North Nest Key past a few other small beach and mangrove areas to split the channel between the Nest Keys. You are now paddling southeast, back toward Key Largo. Shoot for Porjoe Key, an island in the making, and arrive there at mile 11. Small mangrove trees are growing on the edges of the island, attempting to mature and enlarge the key. Keep southeasterly, entering Little Buttonwood Sound via some small islands that make a broken southern border of the sound. Find the short channel leading to Grouper Creek and channel marker #52 at mile 13. You are now on the Intracoastal Waterway. Keep appropriate watch for motorboats on the waterway.

This waterway forms the border of Everglades National Park. Follow the markers northeast; the numbers will be declining as you enter Dusenberry Creek. This deep, warm creek is a wintering area for manatee. You may see one of these gentle giants in the Dusenberry. Leave the stream and head into Blackwater Sound. Bear east for the populated shoreline of Key Largo, and return to Florida Bay Outfitters at mile 16.

Snake Bight Route

Begin: Alligator Creek campsite	End: Flamingo
Distance: 12 miles	Time: 6 hours
Potential tidal influence: 4	Potential wind influence: 5
Navigational challenge: 2	

Highlights: Paddling in Florida Bay

Hazards: Shallow water and big winds on Florida Bay

Campsites: Alligator Creek, Shark Point

Connections: West Lake Canoe Trail, Dildo Key Bank Route, East Cape Route, Buttonwood Canal Route

Wide-open Florida Bay can be a place of exceptional beauty, but if the wind and tides turn on you, paddling can be very tough. This route leaves the quiet and remote Alligator Creek to enter shallow Garfield Bight, then heads south out of Garfield Bight to skirt Shark Point, where there's a backcountry campsite. Depending on the tides, you can take the route across Snake Bight either via the shallows or via the Tin Can Channel back to Flamingo. Combine this route with the 9.5-mile West Lake Canoe Trail for a little-used one-way overnight trip encompassing myriad Everglades environments.

Depart Alligator Creek campsite and paddle south, following the left (east) bank of Garfield Bight. The bay's mud bottom gives the shallow water a brownish tint. Pass a water-monitoring station. Soon you will be able to see the Flamingo tower to your west around Porpoise Point. Continue along the shore to Shark Point and the former Shark Point campsite. A tiny landing on the southwest end of the point allows you to beach your craft along the otherwise heavily wooded shoreline at this former camp. This is your only convenient stopping point along this route.

From here you have two choices for crossing Snake Bight. If the tide is rising or up, it is possible to shoot directly west for Flamingo. But if the winds shift (water depths in Florida Bay are as heavily influenced by wind as by tide) or the tide heads out, you could be slogging through the mud or worse. Not only is this a literal drag, it is ecologically unsound for the bay. Your other choice is to head southwest from Shark Point toward Buoy Key and the Tin Can Channel. The water will be plenty deep here, and if the tide is going out it will be flowing in the direction you want—west. Make the northern tip of Buoy Key at mile 4.5. Pick up the marked Tin Can Channel heading west. Watch out for motorboats.

Proceed across the open waters of Florida Bay, passing Cormorant Key and Palm Key to the south. As you near Flamingo, make sure to go around the outside of Joe Kemp Key, avoiding shallow waters. Veer north and cross Joe Kemp Channel. The visitor center will be visible as you near Flamingo. Stay west of the marked bird-nesting island to enter the cut to Flamingo Marina and the end of your route at mile 12.

Cape Sable, Whitewater Bay, and the South

Big Sable Route

Begin: Northwest Cape campsite   End: Oyster Bay chickee

Length: 13 miles   Time: 8 hours

Potential tidal influence: 5   Potential wind influence: 5

Navigational challenge: 2

Highlights: Diverse waterways on route

Hazards: Big waves in the Gulf of Mexico; strong tides in Little Shark River

Campsites: Northwest Cape, Oyster Bay chickee

Connections: Middle Cape Route, Little Sable Creek–Lake Ingraham Route, Cormorant Pass Route, Shark Cutoff Route

This is a long but doable route. No matter which direction you paddle this waterway, you will most likely end up fighting the winds or the tides or both. Expect a little bit of everything: wide-open ocean, a river, an inland bay. Start early and plan for a full day at the outdoor office. There are virtually no convenient locations to stop at and get out of your boat, so plan on tying up to some mangrove roots to eat lunch or relieve yourself.

So why traverse this route? It provides an important and scenic connection between the "inside" and the "outside." The "outside" is the Gulf of Mexico and the "inside" is everything else paddleable in Everglades National Park. Why else? Because it's challenging!

Leave Northwest Cape and its white beaches behind and head north. Parallel the shoreline and soon pass Little Sable Creek, once the only way in and out of Lake Ingraham, and now the north end of the Little Sable Creek–Lake Ingraham Route, which leads 14 miles to East Cape campsite. The point in the northern distance is the south tip of the Big Sable Creek inlet. Look closely at the mangrove seacoast here. It was stripped by the 2005 storms but has young mangroves rising in the shadow of sun-bleached skeleton trees.

Come to the south end of the Big Sable Creek inlet at mile 3.5. The inlet here extends nearly a mile across. Once you're at the bay, the tip of Shark River Island is visible, as is the balance of the Everglades coast extending northwesterly. The tall mangrove shoreline continues north of Big Sable Creek, but the seashore is more jagged because of numerous tidal creeks forming little coves of their own.

The bay between Shark River Island and the main coast narrows to the Little Shark River channel. Continuing north at mile 7, pass an elaborate light marker at the mouth of the Little Shark River. If you continue north up the Gulf Coast, it is 4 miles across Ponce De Leon Bay to the Graveyard Creek campsite via the Ponce De Leon Bay Route. From this point forward the Big Sable Route is blazed with the customary green and red Coast Guard markers all the way to Oyster Bay, making navigation easy. Negotiate a sharp curve and continue easterly up the Little Shark River.

A lot of water moves up and down the Little Shark River channel, so be prepared for a strong tide. The river is a couple hundred feet wide and is bisected by several small creeks that run perpendicular to it. There are no more channel markers until Little Shark River splits off to the northeast between channel markers #69 and #70 at 9 miles. The channel is much narrower here; watch for motorboats. This channel continues for a quarter mile until it connects with the multiple channels that are part of the Shark River complex, which drains much of the freshwater Everglades. But the water is all brackish to salt this close to the Gulf.

Stay with the channel markers, leaving the Little Shark River at marker #65. Head southeast toward Oyster Bay, still following the markers as their numbers decrease. Make the west end of Oyster Bay at marker #53, 12 miles from Northwest Cape. Head east across Oyster Bay, passing a lone, storm-ravaged island, into a group of islands on the opposite shore. The Oyster Bay chickee is backed against the far (east) side of one of these islands. Paddle into these islands and find the chickee in a little lagoon, ending your route at mile 13. The channel markers continue on another half mile to the Wilderness Waterway. From Oyster Bay chickee it is 4.5 miles north to Shark River chickee via the Shark Cutoff Route. It is 4 miles south to Joe River chickee and 8 miles east to Watson River chickee via the Cormorant Pass Route.

Buttonwood Canal Route

Begin: Flamingo Whitewater Bay	End: Coast Guard Marker #10 at
Length: 5 miles	Time: 2 hours
Potential tidal influence: 2	Potential wind influence: 2
Navigational challenge: 1	

Highlights: Important route connecting Whitewater Bay and Florida Bay

Hazards: Motorboats and tour boats on artificial channel

Campsites: None

Connections: Snake Bight Route, East Cape Route, First American Bank Route, Dildo Key Bank Route, Joe River Route, East River Route, Whitewater Bay Route

---

There are two primary departing points for Everglades paddlers, Flamingo and Everglades City. The Buttonwood Canal Route is the primary "inside" departing route for the Flamingo area. Even if you don't use the canal to leave Flamingo, you will likely use it to get back to Flamingo. This is also the last segment of the Wilderness Waterway, which links Flamingo and Everglades City. It is the necessary pathway for boaters to get to Whitewater Bay and points north. And this means all types of boats, from sea kayaks to skiffs to houseboats. Also, tour boats use this route, so expect a lot of company. Expect your picture to get taken by tourists on the tour boats as they pass your gear-laden craft.

Load up at the Flamingo boat ramp near the fish-cleaning station, then head north from the marina on the Buttonwood Canal. This artificial waterway was dug between 1956 and 1957 by the park service so boaters could access Whitewater Bay without having to go via the Gulf. Here, the shores of the canal are primarily forested by mangrove, but also by mahogany, gumbo limbo, Jamaica dogwood, Brazilian pepper, cactus, and, of course, buttonwood. Paddle under the bridge that is Main Park Road. Look left to observe the limestone rocks and cement placed to keep the canal banks solid. Running parallel to the canal is Bear Lake Road.

The forest shoreline resumes, and the canal continues its southerly course until more limestone rock appears on your left just as you come to the former Bear Lake Canoe Trail at 2.2 miles. There is a dock here, and a portage trail goes to an automobile access and the beginning of the old canal route that once headed west to Bear Lake and beyond. Silt, hurricanes, and mangrove overgrowth did it in. There is talk of reopening the trail between here and Bear Lake, so check with the visitor center for the latest on this.

With the Buttonwood Canal, turn northeasterly toward Coot Bay, arriving there at 3 miles. Coot Bay is the only place on this route where there may be wind problems. Follow the channel markers northwest across Coot Bay to reach Tarpon Creek at 4.5 miles. Upon entering Tarpon Creek, you will see a "Please Watch for Manatees" sign; watch out also for boaters, even though Tarpon Creek is a no wake zone. The creek is about 50 feet wide, banked with mangrove and a challenging paddle if the tide is going against you. It meanders north to Whitewater Bay, which you will probably hear before you see it. Just ahead is the wide-open bay and the end of the Buttonwood Canal at Coast Guard marker #10 at 5 miles. From here, it is 6 miles to Hells Bay chickee via the East River Route. It is 12 miles to Coast Guard marker #40 at Cormorant Pass via the Whitewater Bay Route. It is 6 miles to the South Joe chickee via the Joe River Route.

Cormorant Pass Route

Begin: Joe River chickee   End: Watson River chickee

Length: 12 miles   Time: 6 hours

Potential tidal influence: 3   Potential wind influence: 4

Navigational challenge: 3

Highlights: Island-studded narrows of Cormorant Pass

Hazards: Motorboats through Cormorant Pass

Campsites: Joe River chickee, Oyster Bay chickee, Watson River chickee

Connections: The Labyrinth Route, Joe River Route, Big Sable Route, Whitewater Bay Route, The Cutoff

---

When the Joe River Route leaves the narrows of Joe River and enters Oyster Bay, it then crosses a key portion of the Wilderness Waterway, Cormorant Pass. This part of the route is marked, but beyond Cormorant Pass you must leave the channel markers and skirt northeastern Whitewater Bay to arrive at Watson River chickee. Unfortunately, there is the possibility of motorboat traffic most of the way, except near Watson River chickee. The paddle path provides vital connections to the Gulf of Mexico, the east side of Whitewater Bay, and all points north in the Glades. The cormorant, prevalent throughout the park, is a black and graceful gooselike bird, also called the "snake-bird" for its habit of swimming with only its long neck and head above the water.

Leave the cove of Joe River chickee and paddle the final northerly section of Joe River. As you leave Joe River there will be a "Please Watch for Manatees" sign on your right. Mud Bay will be on your left. Enter the ever-widening Oyster Bay and continue north, keeping a set of islands to your east.

Two miles beyond the Joe River chickee, Oyster Bay widens and the islands to your east have petered out. Almost due north in the middle of the open bay is a lone, storm-damaged island. The Oyster Bay chickee is set in a group of islands on an east–west line parallel to the lone island. Head northeast in the open bay toward a seemingly continuous shoreline. Individual islands will show themselves as you paddle closer. Oyster Bay chickee faces east in a lagoon among these islands. Arrive at this chickee at 4 miles. From Oyster Bay chickee it is 6 miles to the Gulf at Shark River Island via the Big Sable Route. It is 4.5 miles to Shark River chickee via the Shark Cutoff Route—if you run into some channel markers you have paddled too far north beyond the chickee.

Leave Oyster Bay chickee and paddle north past Shark River chickee, heading for the markers north of it. Spot marker #50, then veer southeast to follow the channel markers of Cormorant Pass through the many pint-size islands. Make sure the channel marker numbers are decreasing; if they are increasing, you have gone the wrong way and are heading north on the Wilderness Waterway.

Make a southerly traverse through Cormorant Pass to Coast Guard marker #40. From this marker it is 12 miles southeast to Tarpon Creek at the south end of Whitewater Bay via the Whitewater Bay Route. On the Cormorant Pass Route, leave the Wilderness Waterway to skirt the northeastern edge of Whitewater Bay, passing a few very large mangrove islands. Follow a clear but unmarked open course toward Watson River chickee. After swinging around the largest mangrove island between Cormorant Pass and the Watson

River chickee, you will spot the chickee. It faces north between two keys at mile 12 of your route. From here, it is 7 miles southeast to Roberts River chickee on The Cutoff Route. It is 7.5 miles to Shark River chickee via The Labyrinth Route.

The Cutoff Route

Begin: Roberts River chickee	End: Watson River chickee
Length: 7 miles	Time: 4 hours
Potential tidal Influence: 3	Potential wind influence: 3
Navigational challenge: 3	

Highlights: Some solitude; good camping

Hazards: Big water on Whitewater Bay

Campsites: Roberts River chickee, North River chickee, Watson River chickee

Connections: Roberts River Route, North River Route, The Labyrinth Route, Cormorant Pass Route

The Cutoff is a route that provides a necessary connection for traversing the wild rivers east of Whitewater Bay. The route hooks together three backcountry chickees for some good camping. Powerboat traffic is minimal until you get to Whitewater Bay. On the rivers you really get a sense of the untamed Everglades. And one short section of this route reveals three Everglades environments within a stone's throw of each another.

Whitewater Bay is an environment all its own, and depending on wind conditions you can skirt your way through mangrove keys or take to the open water north to Watson River chickee. The chickee seems really small in all that water, even though it's tucked away among several mangrove keys.

From the Roberts River chickee turn right and head north up the Roberts River. The low mangrove banks of the river resume beyond the chickee, then get taller on river right near The Cutoff proper. The Cutoff connects the Roberts River and the North River without boaters having to traverse further up their headwaters, where their waters intermingle as well. These days it isn't possible to cross watersheds above The Cutoff, as the creeks connecting the Robert and North rivers are impassably clogged with mangrove.

The Roberts River has narrowed considerably by the time you see a confluence of two streams; bear left (northwest) on the stream with the lower banks. You are now on The Cutoff. (There is another Cutoff connecting Lostmans and Rodgers rivers farther north from here.) On river right just before the confluence is an old shell mound grown into a hammock. This used to be a campground for Everglades travelers in the pre-park days.

Beyond the hammock on The Cutoff, look over the low mangrove to your right to see the sawgrass prairie that makes up so much of the Everglades interior. Continue on The Cutoff for a mile. The route widens from stream inflow until it ends at the North River. When

The North River chickee—a place of almost-total solitude. Photo by author.

leaving The Cutoff, pay undivided attention to your position. Do not take the natural course down the North River. The correct route will end up heading due west in a channel much wider than the North River proper. This unnamed channel has irregular, jagged banks of low mangrove that funnel southwest to the North River chickee, which isn't actually on the North River. It should be called the river north of the North River chickee. As if the place weren't confusing enough without adding confusing names!

Anyway, at 3 miles, this unnamed channel narrows and runs directly into the North River chickee, which backs up against the east side of a small mangrove island. It is a single chickee of older make and oozes solitude. This is a good spot for a break or to camp.

Swing south around the tiny island against which North River chickee is set and paddle southwest on this 50–90-foot waterway. The deep channel meanders down to the first and only island beyond the chickee. Past this island, the channel widens as it enters Whitewater Bay at 4.7 miles. Running north to south, a key of high mangrove lies between you and the bulk of Whitewater Bay.

Make your decision about which way to go around the key based on wind and experience. If a manageable wind is blowing from the south, head into the big water and catch a ride alongside the scattered keys to Watson River chickee. In Whitewater Bay, look north for a white manatee warning sign at the mouth of the Watson River to help guide you toward the Watson River chickee. This sign is actually north of the chickee. Alternatively, if the wind is not favorable or you like a more intimate setting, zigzag through the channels on the east side of the bay to the Watson River chickee.

No matter your path, Whitewater Bay will offer wide-open water and accompanying wide-open views of mangrove islands and shores that undulate on the horizon. From the Watson River chickee it is 12 miles to Oyster Bay chickee via the Cormorant Pass Route. It is 7.5 miles to Shark River chickee via The Labyrinth Route.

East River Route

Begin: Coast Guard marker #10
at Whitewater Bay

End: Hells Bay chickee

Length: 5.5 miles

Time: 3 hours

Potential tidal Influence: 2

Potential wind influence: 4

Navigational challenge: 3

Highlights: Varied waters big and small

Hazards: Big water on Whitewater Bay

Campsites: Hells Bay chickee

Connections: Buttonwood Canal Route, Whitewater Bay Route, Joe River Route, Hells Bay Canoe Trail

---

This route is easier to trace from Whitewater Bay to Hells Bay than vice versa, because getting on the right channel leading to the East River from Hells Bay can be very tricky.

Start at Coast Guard marker #10 at the south end of Whitewater Bay, then paddle northeasterly from here along the bay's southeast shoreline. The water is fairly open here, so paddlers may encounter some wind problems. Generally hug the shoreline; you will see more wildlife, be safer, and not get turned around.

At 3 miles, the route shoots between the southeast shore of Whitewater Bay and a north-south-aligned key that shields the headwaters of the No Mans and East rivers. Watch for the sign that reads "Please Watch for Manatees, Operate with Care," and head easterly up the East River, where mangroves of varying heights border each side. Here, potential wind influence diminishes, just as potential tidal influence increases. This river stays generally true to its name for about a mile, with little bays and creeks splintering off it.

Then the East River veers generally north and stays about 60 feet wide before coming to a diminutive bay with two distinct narrow outlets. The smallest outlet is to the left (north). Take the right outlet and head east northeast for about a quarter mile, where the channel splits once more. Both channels immediately lead into Hells Bay. Veer southeast in Hells Bay, entering the Gates of Hell, which is a pass between two peninsular mangrove fingers. Beyond the Gates about 200 yards is a white PVC pipe, the last marker of the Hells Bay Canoe Trail. The trail runs 6.8 miles between this point and its beginning at Main Park Road. Head east for the PVC pipe; the Hells Bay chickee will be on your right just before you come to the pipe marker. From here it is 2.5 miles to Lane Bay chickee via the Lane River Route.

Hells Bay Canoe Trail

Begin: Main Park Road	End: Hells Bay chickee
Distance: 6.5 miles	Time: 3.5 hours
Potential tidal influence: 1	Potential wind influence: 2
Navigational challenge: 1	

Highlights: Marked canoe trail leading through headwaters of East River

Hazards: Completely confusing landscape

Campsites: Lard Can campsite, Pearl Bay chickee, Hells Bay chickee

Connections: East River Route, Lane River Route

In my early days of exploring the Everglades, I used to think I could find my way to Hells Bay from the Main Park Road even if the paddle path wasn't marked. Now, I laugh at my ignorance and thank the park service for placing the numbered PVC pipe markers to guide the way. This place is really confusing, even for very experienced navigators! The area is not on the nautical charts, although you could theoretically use USGS quadrangle maps or aerial charts to get around.

In any event, the Hells Bay Canoe Trail, according to old-timer and *Gladesmen* author Glen Simmons, "twisted and turned worser than any snake." He is right. The trail doubles back and curves generally northwesterly through countless small streams that connect ponds, eventually leading to Hells Bay, which got its name because it "is hell to get into and hell to get out of."

The park service cut out and marked this tedious track in the 1960s. It traced an old trail that rough-and-tumble alligator-hunting gladesmen such as Simmons used to explore the headwaters of the East River, which connects Hells Bay to Whitewater Bay. Back then, this trail was reopened each year by following the flow of water between the mangroves and looking for previous signs of trail clearing, such as sawn limbs.

Leave the dock and the Main Park Road behind as you follow the markers. Travel is slow with all the turning, especially in a loaded boat. The trail is especially tortured beyond marker #40. Sounds of the road will still be with you at first, but those will probably be the last engines you hear, as no boat motors are allowed on the trail until Lard Can campsite. A place to get out and stretch your legs is off to the right just before marker #47.

Touch your paddle down where you can see the whitish creek bottom. The hard surface is limestone marl, which underlies much of the Everglades. On drier clumps of land, there are patches of wax myrtle and coco plum. There is a dry landing at maker #80, where you can stand up for a minute. At marker #114 you'll find a patch of paurotis palm. Notice how the stream can be as deep as 5 feet, but the shallow bays are made shallower by hydrilla, an invasive aquatic weed growing below the water's surface.

At marker #154, the trail leaves a stream and enters the biggest bay yet. Look to your right (east) between marker #155 and #156 across a small bay for the Lard Can backcountry campsite. It is 120 yards distant and is marked by two PVC poles near the shoreline. Stop here for a break and enjoy the tropical hammock with large ferns, palms, coco plums, and other hammock vegetation. The word "hammock" is derived from the Indian word "hamas," meaning shady place. Since Lard Can is natural ground, it has been camped on for hundreds of years, first by Calusa Indians, then gladesmen, and now ecotourists. You are now 3.8 miles and 2 hours from the Main Park Road.

Continue following the sequentially marked poles beyond Lard Can. Begin trying to correlate your position on the nautical chart even though the trail is marked—this will help you learn to navigate when there are no markers to rely on. The direction stays northwest as the poles lead you through a small creek to Pearl Bay at 4.6 miles. The Pearl Bay chickee comes into view to your left at the north end of the bay. This is a two-party, handicapped-accessible chickee. The distance to Pearl Bay chickee is 1 mile and about a half-hour paddle from Lard Can.

Head southwest from Pearl Bay then enter another intimate creek. This one is longer and emerges into an unnamed bay surrounded by low mangrove. Another short, small creek connects the unnamed bay with Hells Bay. As the waterway widens at marker #177, look to your right and you can see Hells Bay chickee just beyond a few tiny islands. This is a two-party chickee and your destination. It takes a little over an hour to get to the chickee from Pearl Bay. From here it is 6 miles to Coast Guard marker #10 at lower Whitewater Bay on the East River Route. It is 2.5 miles to Lane Bay chickee and 5 miles to the Roberts River via the Lane River Route.

Joe River Route

Begin: Coast Guard marker #10 in Whitewater Bay

End: Joe River chickee

Length: 12 miles

Time: 6 hours

Potential tidal influence: 3

Potential wind influence: 3

Navigational challenge: 2

Highlights: Good starter paddle for Everglades novice

Hazards: Motorboats on Joe River; open water

Campsites: South Joe River chickee, Joe River chickee

Connections: Buttonwood Canal Route, Cormorant Pass Route, East River Route, Whitewater Bay Route

---

In pre-park days, Flamingo residents called this the South River instead of the Joe River. Some of these Flamingoites used to come up here to hunt, fish, and camp. Nowadays, this route is used as a good way to head north from Flamingo without getting into too much big water in Whitewater Bay along the Wilderness Waterway. The fishing and camping are still good. The Joe River varies in width, seeming at first like a bay before it settles down and becomes more riverine. Two chickees are set along the river, and this route makes up part of two overnight loops, one around Whitewater Bay and the other around Cape Sable.

Enter Whitewater Bay from Tarpon Creek at Coast Guard Marker #10. Paddle west, staying with the western shore of the big bay. This leads you into the Joe River. If you stay with the shore to your left, you will have no problem navigating up the Joe River. There will be big views of Whitewater Bay. As you continue west, the bay begins to shrink. Finally, on a north turn at mile 5, the Joe River narrows to riverlike proportions, around 200 feet wide. Here, on river right, there's a "Please Watch for Manatees" sign.

Stay with the southwest shore and watch for a meandering channel leading left. Take this channel into the bay of the South Joe chickee, which will be dead ahead as you enter the bay at mile 6. This double chickee makes a good destination for a first day's paddle from Flamingo or just a good resting spot.

Leave the South Joe chickee and swing around the corner, taking the other creek out of the bay. This creek leads north back into the Joe River. Continue northwest up the river, passing around a large island that splits the Joe. After the island, the Joe resumes a 200-foot width and a northwesterly course. The mangrove shorelines vary from 4 to 40 feet in height. The depth of the river is fine for all craft, which makes it an easy route for motorboaters.

As the Joe takes on a more northerly direction, pass three channels leading off to your right into Whitewater Bay as you continue upriver. The first and third of these channels offer views into the big bay. You will find yourself cutting point to point across the river's meanders. At 12 miles, look for a small cove on your right and end your route at the Joe River chickee. From here it is 4 miles to Oyster Bay chickee via the Cormorant Pass Route.

The Labyrinth Route

Begin: Shark River chickee   End: Watson River chickee

Distance: 7.5 miles   Time: 4 hours

Potential tidal influence: 2   Potential wind influence: 1

Navigational challenge: 5

Highlights: Intricate navigating challenge; solitude; no motorboats

Hazards: Getting lost in The Labyrinth

Campsites: Shark River chickee, Watson River chickee

Connections: The Cutoff Route, Cormorant Pass Route, Graveyard Creek Route

---

The Labyrinth is one of the most challenging routes in the Everglades. It is also one of the most rewarding. You must paddle your way through a literal maze of small streams connecting the Shark River to northern Whitewater Bay, choosing the correct streams to get through. There are no markers to point the way, and no motorboaters are going to be passing by to help guide you. You'll need strong map-reading skills and a steely nerve to make the hours-long trek without knowing for certain that you are where you think you are. Of course, a GPS downloaded with nautical charts makes navigating the route a lot easier. Even so, while passing through The Labyrinth you must eyeball the nautical chart and keep fixing your position on it.

So why traverse The Labyrinth? For the navigational challenge, for solitude—there will be no roaring motors here—and for the shortest route between Shark River chickee and Watson River chickee. I paddled The Labyrinth for the first time when I had gotten off my course due to unnavigable high seas in the Gulf. I was behind schedule and trying to get caught up. Sitting at the Shark River chickee, I traced the route on the chart with my finger and dared myself to try it. Then I took the plunge into The Labyrinth (not knowing at the time it was called The Labyrinth) and made it. I was one happy paddler upon seeing Whitewater Bay! (If you traverse this route from Whitewater Bay to Shark River, the creek mouth indicated on the map at the back of this book makes the best entry, because it opens directly into the bay. But there are numerous routes through The Labyrinth as the Map #11 shows.)

There are no directions for getting through The Labyrinth, only hints. Check the tidal flow at the chickee and the tide charts. If the tide is just turning, then tidal direction will remain the same throughout your paddle. Make certain of where you are as you paddle. If you aren't sure where you are, don't just plunge ahead and hope. Take your time. Look back every now and then as you paddle. This may help you if you have to backtrack. Good luck. This is paddling the Everglades at its finest.

After opening into Whitewater Bay, keep southeast past some large keys to your southwest. The north-facing Watson River chickee will appear in the distance, backed against some other islands. Once at Watson River chickee, it is 7 miles to Roberts River chickee via The Cutoff Route.

Lane River Route

Begin: Hells Bay chickee	End: Confluence of Lane River and Roberts River
Distance: 5 miles	Time: 3 hours
Potential tidal influence: 2	Potential Wind influence: 3
Navigational challenge: 3	

Highlights: Bird life on Lane River

Hazards: Confusing section between Hells Bay and Lane Bay chickees

Campsites: Hells Bay chickee, Lane Bay chickee

Connections: Roberts River Route, Hells Bay Canoe Trail, East River Route

---

The Lane River Route stays in the intimate east side of Whitewater Bay, forming a dogleg connection between Hells Bay and the Roberts River. Leave Hells Bay and head north to Lane Bay, passing the single-occupancy Lane Bay chickee, then veer southwest entering the Lane River proper. The low mangrove allows sweeping vistas, yet the very modest size of the river never overwhelms you. This general area is where small ponds, bays, and rivers form a complex of paddle routes that are preferable when brawny winds are blowing on Whitewater Bay. The commanding plant life in the Everglades paddler's realm, the mangrove with its attendant fish and bird life, is all around you.

Head north from Hells Bay chickee, noting that there are more tiny islands here than are shown on the navigational charts for northern Hells Bay. Here you must fight the urge to head to the largest section of open water and catch the 40–50-foot-wide creek connecting Hells Bay to a small, island-dotted, unnamed bay. Continue northwest through the unnamed bay, then merge into The Funnel, a slightly wider creek that leads into Lane Bay. Continue north through Lane Bay, taking time to inspect some of the islands for West Indies mahogany. Identify this tropical tree by its compound leaves and its hard, brown fruit about the size of a pear.

Up ahead is the Lane Bay chickee, backed against a tall wooded hammock on the north side of Lane Bay. Arrive at this older chickee at 2.5 miles. Take the opportunity to stretch your legs here. The trickiest navigational section of this route comes when you leave Lane Bay chickee and dogleg southwest into the Lane River. Pay close attention to the chart and keep westerly. The mangrove on the Lane River is low, sometimes only 3 feet high, the bleached skeletal trees emerging from the greenery making ideal avian roosts. Bird life in this area can be abundant. The mud-bottomed river is deeper than your paddle and runs clear with a tannish tint. The width averages about 80 feet but narrows to as little as 50 feet, such as when it splits around an island to your left about a mile from Lane River chickee.

On down, the river widens considerably as a fair-sized creek merges from the north. Downriver, you can see the high tops of healthy mangroves in Whitewater Bay. Just before its confluence with the Roberts River, Lane River veers southwest and narrows again, ending at a sign warning about manatees in the area. To your left, it is 2.5 miles to the Wilderness Waterway and the Whitewater Bay Route at marker #18. To your right (northeast), it is 3 miles up the Roberts River to the Roberts River chickee.

Little Sable Creek–Lake Ingraham Route

Begin: Northwest Cape campsite	End: East Cape campsite
Length: 14 miles	Time: 5 hours
Potential tidal influence: 4	Potential wind influence: 5
Navigational challenge: 4	

Highlights: Seldom traveled creeks and ponds; high wind route around Cape Sable

Hazards: Strong tides in Mid Cape Canal; winds on Lake Ingraham

Campsites: Northwest Cape, Middle Cape, East Cape

Connections: Big Sable Route, Middle Cape Route, East Cape Route

---

This route is a back way from Northwest Cape to Florida Bay and can be a lifesaver if winds are high in the Gulf or a cold front is blowing from the northwest. (I first used it during such conditions.) In times of calmer winds, it can be an adventurous route that lets you explore the streams and ultra-shallow ponds north of Lake Ingraham. Lake Ingraham is a large but shallow water body, so paddling it, even during big blows, is better than paddling a windy Gulf. From Lake Ingraham, the route takes you into the East Cape Canal, which can have very strong tides. East Cape Canal opens into Florida Bay, where the East Cape campsite is a mile west. Tides are very important to traveling this route. Ideally, you would take Little Sable Creek on an incoming tide; make it to Mid Cape Canal *with* the incoming tide; then reach East Cape Canal on an outgoing tide.

Leave Northwest Cape going northbound, then curve right, southeasterly, into the first creek north of Northwest Cape. Be careful not to overshoot into the creek north of Little Sable Creek. Once, when I was fighting waves out in the Gulf, I somehow overshot Little Sable Creek, which is about 60 to 80 feet wide, uncanopied, and has storm-damaged mangrove at its mouth. More live trees, especially black mangrove, line the creek shore away from the Gulf. Sea purslane grows in the scattered clearings and under standing tree skeletons.

The first mile twists and turns but keeps a generally southeasterly direction. Feeder creeks come off Little Sable, but the primary route is clear. Little Sable Creek narrows, canopied by overhanging trees that grow out of the pungent water. At 3 miles, numerous mud flats and small channels extend from the main stream which, though shallow, is tidally influenced. After half a mile, the creek narrows again to open onto a long linear lake, very shallow, which is almost a mud flat. Passing through here on a falling tide is an iffy proposition.

Make your way south through this lake, but don't take the most southerly channel. Instead, take the southwesterly channel at 5 miles. If the tide has been with you to this point, it will likely turn against you here, as this channel is connected to the wide Mid Cape Canal.

Jog southwest down the stream into the next small lake, which is also shallow. The west-facing side of this small lake is storm damaged, as the Gulf is but a short distance west. Aim for the channel that leaves southeast from this lake. This channel will be strongly influenced by tides.

This area can be confusing, and nautical charts don't show the correct creek connecting to Mid Cape Canal. Aerial maps do, though, and clearly indicate the route. (Consult Map #13 in the back of this book.) The nautical chart *does* show a different creek connecting to Lake Ingraham, and if you head for it, you will be on the right track and reach the lake. If in doubt, follow strongest tidal current. The uncharted creek soon separates from the charted stream heading to Lake Ingraham and makes its own way, passing around a couple of small islands before emerging at the Mid Cape Canal at 6.5 miles. To your right, it is but a short distance to the Gulf and a campsite beside the canal that was opened up after the hurricanes.

From here, the route heads away from the Gulf and down the Mid Cape Canal. Originally 16 feet wide, Mid Cape Canal has been gradually widening ever since it was constructed in the 1920s. An incoming tide on the more-than-200-foot-wide canal will push you into Lake Ingraham, but woe to paddlers having to fight their way into the lake against the tide. A channel through the middle of Lake Ingraham has been staked for motorboaters, and during low tides or strong north winds it's best for paddlers to stay with the staked channel, too. Under calmer conditions, paddlers can take a different tack. If you decide to take the staked channel, be aware that motorboaters, especially in low water, will be traveling fast and staying on plane. They cannot get out of your way without getting stuck in the mud, so it is up to you to avoid them.

At 8 miles, pass the one lone island in Lake Ingraham. As you near the lake's southeast corner, following the staked channel, the canal at the southeast corner of Lake Ingraham becomes visible. The south end of the lake is very shallow, so stay with the staked channel. When you reach the canal at 11.3 miles, it will be 150 to 200 feet wide.

The nautical charts incorrectly show this canal entering a second smaller lake. Keep with this canal as it bears southeasterly until you hit the East Cape Canal at 12.4 miles. On your left, a different canal leads to the overgrown and silted Homestead Canal, which was part of the silted and closed-up Bear Lake Canoe Trail. The tides will be strong in the East Cape Canal.

Emerge onto Florida Bay at 13 miles. To your right, westerly, the nearest part of the East Cape campsite is a half mile distant, whereas the point of the cape and the main camping area is a mile away. From East Cape, it is 10 miles to Flamingo via the East Cape Route. It is 20 miles to Little Rabbit Key, deep in Florida Bay, via the First National Bank Route. It is 10.5 miles to Northwest Cape via the Middle Cape Route.

Middle Cape Route

Begin: East Cape campsite	End: Northwest Cape campsite
Length: 10.5 miles	Time: 5 hours
Potential tidal influence: 5	Potential wind influence: 5
Navigational challenge: 2	

Highlights: Lots of beach camping; natural beach

Hazards: Big waves and strong tides in the Gulf of Mexico

Campsites: East Cape, Middle Cape, Northwest Cape

Connections: East Cape Route, Big Sable Route

This route connects the three points of Cape Sable: East Cape, Middle Cape, and Northwest Cape. Cape Sable has been called one of the finest pieces of real estate in North America. I have to agree. This is a preserved piece of natural Florida coastline that will leave you coming back for more—miles of shell-laden beach backed by natural native vegetation. No glaring high rises or phony landscaping here. And the camping on the cape is superb. Come see it for yourself.

The author stokes the fire at Middle Cape. Photo by Mark Carroll.

When the winds kick up, the Middle Cape Route can become impassable. Thankfully, there is a back door route connecting East Cape and Northwest Cape—the Little Sable Creek–Lake Ingraham Route.

Start your route by heading northwest in the Gulf from the East Cape campsite. Middle Cape is the point visible to your left as you round East Cape. The beach narrows somewhat beyond East Cape, but the shoreline of sand, grass, and varied trees—as opposed to uninterrupted mangrove—continues. The beach lines the water's edge all the way to Middle Cape. Overall, the shoreline is very attractive, with gumbo limbo, cabbage palms, and a few scattered coconut palms increasing as you near Middle Cape. This landscape gives way to a grassy, palm-and-cactus-studded prairie and the beginning of the Middle Cape campsite.

The shore turns almost due west before coming at mile 5 to the Middle Cape itself, which culminates in a very sharp point, especially in contrast to the more rounded East Cape. The point was once the site of Fort Cross, established in the 1850s as a base for U.S. soldiers attempting to eradicate Seminoles far back in the Glades. Once beyond Middle Cape, the shore resumes a more north-south orientation.

Around Middle Cape, a coconut farm was established in the 1880s: the Waddell Plantation. The owners soon left it to caretakers, and the place never had much of a plantation's appearance. Coconuts were harvested off and on through the years, until the palms were blown away by a hurricane in 1935.

Pass the Mid Cape Canal at mile 7.2. The beach ends for a stretch, and the shore is nothing but mangrove skeletons until the Mid Cape Canal. Most signs of civilization in the area have been obliterated by time and the elements, but this canal that connects Lake Ingraham with the Gulf keeps growing with the incessant action of the tides. Be careful when paddling by: the tides are very strong at the mouth of the canal, and sand shoals extend into the Gulf. A friend and I once got sucked in by the strong tides and were stuck in there for several hours before we finally pulled ourselves and our canoe out by grabbing mangrove roots on the shore, one after another, until we were back in the Gulf. The Mid Cape Canal is your connection point for the Little Sable Creek–Lake Ingraham Route. From here, it is 6.5 miles to the Northwest Cape via Little Sable Creek and 7.5 miles back to East Cape via the Little Sable Creek–Lake Ingraham Route.

Beyond the canal, the shore is sporadic mangrove growing out of the sand. But as the land turns more northwest, a palm prairie begins. This large prairie goes back from the sea a good half mile or more. Some Jamaica dogwood, cactus, and a few wooded hammocks break up the grass and palm field that extends to Northwest Cape and beyond. End your route at 10.5 miles at the gently curved Northwest Cape—an attractive camping area of its own. From here, it is 6 miles north to Shark River Island via the Big Sable Route.

Mud Lake There and Back

Begin: Main Park Road	End: Main Park Road
Length: 8 miles total (4 miles each way)	Time: 4.5 hours
Potential tidal influence: 2	Potential wind influence: 3
Navigational challenge: 2	
Highlights: Paddling in no motor zone	
Hazards: Insects in narrow creeks	
Campsites: None	
Connections: Buttonwood Canal Route	

This paddle gives you a good taste of some open water, some confined water, and, more important, quiet water. You'll also get the chance to work in a hike if you want. Half of this paddle is for hand-propelled craft only. The first portion of the route can be used as a shortcut to Whitewater Bay and points beyond.

Start your paddle on Coot Bay Pond, then pass beneath a mangrove tunnel to Coot Bay. Connect briefly to the Wilderness Waterway and the Buttonwood Canal Route before following a small creek to Mud Lake—a more appealing place than its name suggests. Enjoy the quiet of Mud Lake, then take another creek to Bear Lake and a landing, located at the west end of the 2-mile Bear Lake Hiking

Trail. Bear Lake Canoe Trail used to lead paddlers back to Buttonwood Canal in a paddling loop, but because the trail has grown over and silted in (partly a result of the 2005 hurricanes), this is now an out-and-back paddle only. Work is being done, however, to clear the Bear Lake Canoe Trail between Bear Lake and Buttonwood Canal, so check with the park service to see if the trail has reopened.

Set out from one of the small landings on Coot Bay Pond, paddling north to a small tunnel-like opening. From a distance, the passage is hard to see, but this man-made cut, barely wide enough for a kayak, will lead you to Coot Bay. The passage was dug in the mid-1940s to access Whitewater Bay from what is now Main Park Road. The spoils of the cut create land areas upon which drier plant species grow, such as palm. Open up into Coot Bay and paddle west for Coast Guard marker #3 and the Buttonwood Canal Route. Continue to follow the channel markers north for the shortcut to Whitewater Bay, but for this loop stay with the south shore of Coot Bay to a PVC pipe marker at 2 miles that points out the creek leading to Mud Lake. This begins the part of the route reserved for hand-propelled craft.

Enter this shady slender waterway, made even tighter by hundreds of fallen trees, sawn off just enough for your passage. Expect to slide over a few logs. Live mangrove hovers over you until, after a quarter mile, you emerge onto Mud Lake in a group of small circular islands. Follow the PVC pipe markers south and west across this shallow and scenic lake. Its copper-colored waters contrast handsomely with the green shores. The markers lead to the lake's most southwesterly corner and a short creek at 3.8 miles. Follow this creek to the old Homestead Canal and the parallel dike that is now the Bear Lake Hiking Trail. Cut for fill dirt, the Homestead Canal was dug in the 1920s beside a road meant to connect Florida City to Cape Sable. The road has reverted to trail, the canal is now silting in, and the waters here are rich with the pungent smell of decay.

Still following the creek, you will shortly reach the now-closed Bear Lake Canoe Trail, which runs east to west, tracing the Homestead Canal. This canoe trail soon may be reopened toward the Buttonwood Canal. Check with the park visitor center in Flamingo to be sure. If the trail is open, keep east to the end of the canal, then portage your boat to Flamingo Canal and head north back into Coot Bay to make a loop. Otherwise, turn right here, on the westbound portion of the old Homestead Canal/Bear Lake Canoe Trail, and paddle a short distance into Bear Lake at a small landing. From this landing, you can look southwest at the expanse of Bear Lake. If you want more exercise or a different perspective, trace the Bear Lake Hiking Trail about 2 miles to an automobile-accessible trailhead. From the landing, energetic paddlers can explore Bear Lake then backtrack through the narrow creek that returns to Mud Lake and on to Coot Bay Pond.

Nine Mile Pond Loop

Begin: Main Park Road	End: Main Park Road
Distance: 5.7 miles	Time: 3.5 hours
Potential tidal influence: 1	Potential wind influence: 3
Navigational challenge: 1	

Highlights: Marker trail through diverse flora; no motorboats

Hazards: Confusing landscape; sawgrass

Campsites: None

Connections: None

The name Nine Mile Pond leads you to believe this paddle is 9 miles. This day trip is actually 5.7 miles of multiple Everglades environments packed into one loop. It received its name because the pond was 9 miles from the original park visitor center at Coot Bay Pond. The trail is marked with sequentially numbered poles to help you navigate among the mangrove islands, prairies, and tree islands of the region. Prairies here are vastly different from those in the Midwest. Everglades prairies are open, treeless wetlands, with sawgrass emerging from the water. The water levels often change, depending on the season (wet or dry), and the prairies can dry up completely at times. The water here is clear and very shallow; check with the park visitor center to see if there is enough water to float your boat. In some areas you will be paddling through sawgrass that can slow your craft down considerably. Be advised, too, that there is no easily accessible dry land where you can land to stretch your legs.

From the Flamingo Visitor Center, drive east on Main Park Road to Nine Mile Pond parking area at 11.2 miles. Start your trip at Nine Mile Pond, a water-filled pit originally dug for road fill. (Don't be surprised if the water is cloudy.) Paddle directly across the water to the farthest inlet of the pond. This inlet lies east, between two sawgrass stands. Here, the sequentially numbered poles begin. Keep your eyes peeled because Nine Mile Pond is a good place to see alligators. Pass through a mangrove tunnel and emerge onto a small prairie. The mud bottom gives a brownish cast to the otherwise clear water, where you can see small fish and minnows darting from your path.

The mangrove and sawgrass environments alternate. Here, the sawgrass on the trail is sparse and doesn't seriously slow your travel. Enter a wide-open prairie of sawgrass just beyond marker #42. Sawgrass is the most common plant in the Everglades; to many people sawgrass *is* the Everglades. Across the prairie are palm-topped tree islands, also known as bayheads.

At 1.5 miles, just after entering the prairie, follow the numbered poles sharply to the right into a mangrove tunnel to continue the entire loop. If you want to shorten your loop, do not take the sharp right turn, but rather continue forward past marker #44 to #44A and across the prairie to marker #82. Then turn left and complete your shortened loop.

The full trail opens into another prairie where the sawgrass is thicker and can slow you down. Take time to examine the microcosm of life that flourishes below you. Your direction has been primarily east and north until marker #73. Here the trail turns sharply to the left and begins heading westward back toward Nine Mile Pond. Tall hammocks dotted with palm extend beyond the sawgrass on both sides of the trail. You pass closely by a few palms at marker #80, reaching the other end of the shortcut at 4 miles. Leave the sawgrass behind and enter small mangrove islands leading to a few dense palm thickets.

Emerge onto a murky alligator pond and veer left through an opening in a line of sawgrass onto another pond. Beyond this pond is yet another opening in the sawgrass, through which you can see the parking area. Paddle through this opening and the parking area is on your right across Nine Mile Pond, completing your loop.

Noble Hammock Loop

Begin: Main Park Road	End: Main Park Road
Distance: 2.3 miles	Time: 2 hours
Potential tidal influence: 1	Potential wind influence: 2
Navigational challenge: 1	

Highlights: Sheltered, often-shaded, and marked canoe trail; tree hammock

Hazards: Completely confusing landscape

Campsites: None

Connections: None

The marked Noble Hammock Loop offers quiet quality once you leave Main Park Road behind. An intimate narrow canoe path winds through a mangrove maze, looping past Noble Hammock, a haven for moonshiners in the early 20th century. Many fish will stir the waters beneath your boat. Take this trail if the wind is howling or if you only have time for a short trip. And paddle slowly here—the sudden twists and turns of the trail demand it. Full-size sea kayaks are not maneuverable enough for this trail. A canoe and utmost cooperation between bow and stern paddlers will enhance your pleasure here. Bring insect repellent along with you in these bough-covered waters. Also, check with the park service to see if there's enough water for canoeing, especially from February until paddling season ends in April.

From Flamingo, drive east on Main Park Road for 10.2 miles to the signed Noble Hammock put-in, on the right-hand side of the road. Depart the small dock away from the Main Park Road and shortly turn right, following the first of 124 sequentially numbered poles. Don't let these markers detract from the scenery, for you would soon be lost in that scenery if it weren't for the upright white PVC pipes. The waters of the Noble Hammock Trail have a coffee-colored tint caused by the decomposition of plant matter on the bottom.

Passageways barely wide enough for a canoe give way to tiny bays where openings draw you toward them—but don't go. Follow the poles. Just as quickly, the trail leads into tiny creeks over which

A paddler hops out of his canoe at Noble Hammock. Photo by author.

hangs shade-casting mangrove. And so it goes. After marker #45, pass a clump of paurotis palms where you can get out and stand for a moment. There is very little dry land around here.

Continue on through the dense growth. Soon, on your right, there's a sign marking Noble Hammock. You can get out at the small landing, but exploring Noble Hammock and finding the remains of Bill Noble's prohibition-era brick moonshining furnace requires some serious bushwhacking. It was this very growth and available buttonwood for burning that that led to this tree island's becoming a moonshiner's asylum, along with many others.

Don't be surprised when the water stirs as you round a corner on this trail. Many fish ply these waters, including such native species as bluegill, largemouth bass, and the distinctive long-snouted Florida gar. Unfortunately you will also see tilapia, an exotic breamlike fish that is too successfully reproducing here.

The moving cars along the park road will signal the end of the trip. Surprisingly, you will end your paddle at a small dock beside the park road about 100 yards away from where you started. Walk onto the road and your vehicle will be up the road to your right (east).

North River Route

Begin: Coast Guard marker #30 in Whitewater Bay   End: The Cutoff at North River

Distance: 4.5 miles   Time: 2.5 hours

Potential tidal influence: 2   Potential Wind influence: 3

Navigational challenge: 2

Highlights: Good connector route

Hazards: Big water on Whitewater Bay

Campsites: None

Connections: The Cutoff Route, Whitewater Bay Route

The North River Route is used primarily by travelers in the White-water Bay area to make loop paddles. Paddlers often stay at some of the chickees on the perimeter of Whitewater Bay and return toward Flamingo via North River. This route was part of my first trip into the Everglades. The navigation is easy, but the waves can get big in Whitewater Bay. Once in North River proper, you need concern yourself only with the direction of the tides.

From Coast Guard marker #30 in the middle of Whitewater Bay, make your way easterly through a couple of lonely keys, then enter a wide channel that marks the beginning of the North River. This channel shrinks to a couple hundred feet, then seems to be blocked by a wall of mangrove. This "wall" is actually an island that splits the mouth of the North River. Directly in front of this island on the side facing Whitewater Bay is a "Warning, Manatee Area," sign.

At 3 miles, proceed either way around the island on the North River to yet another sizable island that splits the river. Beyond this second island, it is clear sailing down an easily recognizable deep channel banked by mangrove. The river widens to more than 300 feet at points but narrows to as little as 100 feet while meandering northeasterly for another mile and a half to intersect The Cutoff Route. The Cutoff proper is a quarter mile to your right (northeast). To your left on The Cutoff Route (west), the unnamed river north of the North River leads 1 mile to the North River chickee. The actual North River continues for another three-quarters of a mile before it splits off into smaller branches and melds into the sawgrass of the Everglades in a freshwater network of feeder streams.

Roberts River Route

Begin: Coast Guard Marker #18 in Whitewater Bay	End: Roberts River chickee
Distance: 5.5 miles	Time: 3 hours
Potential tidal influence: 2	Potential Wind influence: 4

Navigational challenge: 2

Highlights: Solitude on Roberts River; hammock right by Roberts River chickee

Hazards: Wind on Whitewater Bay

Campsites: Roberts River

Connections: Whitewater Bay Route, Lane River Route, The Cutoff Route

---

The Roberts River Route encompasses multiple environments. Leave the Wilderness Waterway and wide-open Whitewater Bay for a somewhat calmer channel heading northeast. This channel narrows further as gets upriver from Lane River. The actual Roberts River begins here and continues northeasterly as a very intimate waterway with little navigational hazard. It widens a bit before ending at Roberts River chickee, one of the best camping spots in the southern Everglades paddling region.

Head northeasterly from Coast Guard marker #18 for a strait between a series of keys that form a channel leading to the mouth of the Roberts River, passing a couple of isles at the mouth of the channel. The passageway that you have paddled northeasterly continues to narrow until it jogs right and bottlenecks to about 50 feet in width just past the Lane River, marked by a manatee area warning sign. The Lane River Route leads east 5 miles to the Hells Bay chickee. You have now paddled 2.5 miles.

On the Roberts River Route, continue up the deep channel, now the Roberts River in name and body, where you will experience solitude more often than not. Gorgeous sun-bleached snags rise above the low mangrove, often providing perches for osprey. Soon you will come to a confluence of two creeks of nearly the same size. Stay left (north); the river is now less than 50 feet wide and mostly remains that width for around a mile. Then the Roberts River widens into an elongated bay with finger peninsulas jutting into the bay, between smaller creeks meandering into the mangrove. At the head of this elongated bay is the Roberts River chickee. Backed against a tall hammock, the chickee lies on your right in a small cove, well protected from the elements. This hammock, just a few feet north of the chickee, has some dry ground and freshwater plants and ferns. From the Roberts River chickee, it is 1.5 miles to the North River proper via The Cutoff and 3 miles to the North River chickee via The Cutoff Route.

West Lake Canoe Trail

Begin: Main Park Road	End: Alligator Creek campsite at Florida Bay
Distance: 9.5 miles	Time: 4.5 hours
Potential tidal influence: 2	Potential wind influence: 2
Navigational challenge: 3	

Highlights: Less-used trail; no motorboats on last 5 miles of trail

Hazards: Extremely shallow water; excessive mosquito potential

Campsites: Alligator Creek

Connections: Snake Bight Route

The West Lake Canoe Trail uses a mix of lakes and small creeks to take you to some of the Everglades' least used backcountry. Once you pass West Lake, you'll see no motorboats as you work your way in winding fashion to Florida Bay. West Lake was the site of a hunting and fishing camp from 1916 to the 1930s. Both before and after this time, alligator and plume hunters used this very canoe trail to access these creeks and adjoining lakes for their rich wildlife. Laws against certain animal merchandise eventually had to be passed, because the hunters were so excessive in their slaughter that they drove many animals, especially wading birds, to the brink of extinction. Day paddlers can turn around at any point in the round-trip route of 19 miles. Overnight campers can enjoy the little-used Alligator

Creek campsite and return to West Lake or head into Florida Bay to Flamingo and beyond.

Leave the dock on an arm of West Lake and head south into the main lake, where there are many downed trees strewn along its shores. The official canoe trail follows the right bank south, then east. It is marked by very occasional plastic PVC pipes. Otherwise, you can just paddle for the extreme southeastern corner of the lake, where a creek links West Lake to Long Lake. There is a marker and a buoy at the entrance to this creek at 4.5 miles. No motors are allowed beyond this point.

Head south into this canopied creek that is only 10 to 15 feet wide and interspersed with branches. Be prepared for mosquitoes in this and all creeks on this trail. Open into shallow Long Lake after a short distance. Keep east through small islands, ending up in the most southeasterly portion of this lake, where marked Mangrove Creek begins.

Mangrove Creek is broken up by two small ponds that open up the otherwise shady creek, where prop roots of red mangrove drop into the water, along with their branches. Thousands of aerial roots of black mangrove line the shore. The final of three sections of Mangrove Creek feeds into The Lungs, a lake shaped vaguely like human lungs. Keep south through this slender cove of The Lungs and emerge into the main part of the lake. The marked beginning of Alligator Creek, at 8.2 miles, will be on the west shore.

Alligator Creek, about 20 feet wide, does have alligators. Their flattened mud lounging spots can be seen along the creek's edge. A couple of ponds break this creek up, too. Mangrove lines the creek, but in the final section, shrubby prairies open up behind the tree-lined bank. Scattered black mangrove and the bleached skeletons of trees past offer an eerie contrast to the tawny green prairies.

Pass some old pilings of a road bridge, built in the 1930s. This road was used by government employees who were attempting to eradicate tree cotton. This cotton, native to the Everglades, was thought to be blighted and therefore a threat to commercial cotton operations

Camper rests inside tent at Alligator Creek campsite. Photo by author.

to the north. Soon after the bridge pilings, come to the Alligator Creek campsite on your right and Garfield Bight, a part of Florida Bay, at mile 9.5. This is the end of the canoe trail. From here it is 12 miles to Flamingo via the Snake Bight Route.

Whitewater Bay Route

Begin: Coast Guard marker #10 in Whitewater Bay	End: Coast Guard marker #40 at Cormorant Pass
Distance: 12 miles	Time: 6 hours
Potential tidal influence: 2	Potential wind influence: 5
Navigational challenge: 1	

Highlights: Marked route for less experienced navigators; multiple route connections

Hazards: Big waves and motorboats

Campsites: None

Connections: Joe River Route, East River Route, Roberts River Route, North River Route, Cormorant Pass Route, Shark Cutoff Route

---

This is the shortest and most direct route north through Whitewater Bay. It encompasses a significant leg of the Wilderness Waterway, but this segment is seldom trekked by paddlers on the waterway because there are no campsites in Whitewater Bay. The route is used in its entirety primarily by powerboaters navigating their way north through Whitewater Bay.

There is a reason for the name Whitewater Bay. This is by far the most open stretch of water on the "inside." The waves can become high here, and powerboaters make more waves. But inexperienced navigators can benefit from the marked route, especially in accessing the rivers east of Whitewater Bay and making other route connections. Keep an eye out for powerboats at all times while paddling this route. I have paralleled the route, staying off to one side a bit, giving powerboaters the main route right beside the markers. If the winds are high, get behind some of the scattered islands in the bay to rest along the way.

Leave Tarpon Creek and come to Coast Guard marker #10 and the open bay. Paddle north, looking ahead from marker to marker. Pass between a couple of islands, turning northwesterly, and come to marker #18 at 3 miles. Northeast from here is the Roberts River Route. Proceed up Whitewater Bay through the Midway Keys to marker #30 at 6.5 miles. Northeast from here is the North River Route.

Now, enter the most open stretch of water. It is 3 miles northeast to the Watson River chickee from marker #34 at 8 miles. Ahead of you are myriad islands that look like one continuous shoreline. As you paddle closer, the individual islands begin to stand out. The marked path leads through Cormorant Pass, which slices through these islands. The current can be strong going in and out of the pass. The pass begins at marker #40 at 12 miles, the end of the Whitewater Bay Route. Intersect the Cormorant Pass Route here. The Watson River chickee is 3 miles east from marker #40. Oyster Bay chickee is 1 mile distant through Cormorant Pass. You can continue on the Wilderness Waterway via the Shark Cutoff Route.

The Central Rivers Area

Broad River Route

Begin: Gulf of Mexico	End: Camp Lonesome
Distance: 12 miles	Time: 6 hours
Potential tidal influence: 4	Potential wind influence: 3
Navigational challenge: 2	

Highlights: Varied Everglades environments

Hazards: Motorboat traffic in Broad River

Campsites: Highland Beach, Broad River, Camp Lonesome

Connections: Highland Beach Route, Wood River Route, The Nightmare Route, Cabbage Island Shortcut, Rodgers River Bay Route

The Broad River Route traces Everglades waters from the salty Gulf to the freshwater near Camp Lonesome. The varied waters and changing vegetation keep the scenery interesting. Along the way you'll pass from beach to bay to an old shell mound along the upper Broad River. Part of this route is on the Wilderness Waterway. These are popular fishing waters, so expect to hear the motorboat engines roar. The deep and wide river makes for strong tidal flow upstream and down, so factor the tides into your travel.

Leave the Gulf, following the marked channel into the Broad River to avoid the many oyster bars that crop up at low tide. Hand-propelled craft shouldn't have any problems entering the island-studded bay on a rising tide. Work your way east among the islands, being careful not to accidentally enter the Rodgers River. The Broad River stays true to its name, stretching nearly 250 feet across as it intersects the Wilderness Waterway at marker #25 at 2 miles. Here, the Wood River and The Nightmare converge into the Broad. From this point, the Wood River Route leads east 11 miles to Camp Lonesome on the upper Broad River. The Nightmare Route leads 8.5 miles south to the Harney River chickee. Just east of marker #25, on the south bank of the Broad River, is the Broad River campsite. This notoriously buggy ground campsite has a dock and is a convenient stopping point.

Continue up the Broad, which has contracted to around 200 feet in width. Pass a water-monitoring station on the south bank, a half mile past the campsite. There is much more than mangrove and buttonwood on the shoreline. Palms and poisonwood indicate drier land. Unfortunately, there is also an excessive amount of Brazilian pepper, an exotic invasive bush with red berries that birds spread and that the park service simultaneously tries to eradicate. A major cause of habitat loss in Florida, invasive plants crowd out the native species that animals depend on for food and cover. It's disheartening to see the pepper literally line the Broad. In other places copses of palms rise skyward.

At 6.5 miles, come to The Cutoff at a particularly sharp bend in the river. This channel is at the northern outer edge of the bend and connects the Broad River to the Rodgers River. Don't confuse this channel with the other Cutoff, down south near Whitewater Bay, that connects the Roberts River with the North River. One hundred and fifty yards east of The Cutoff, on the same north bank, the Cabbage Island Shortcut leads 3.5 miles to Rodgers River Bay. This channel is only half as wide as The Cutoff. A water-monitoring station is located about 150 yards east of the Cabbage Island Shortcut.

A half mile east of The Cutoff, the Broad River enters Broad River Bay. The shoreline is nearly all mangrove and buttonwood. As you paddle up the bay, you can use shoreline undulations and points to mark the distance paddled. Reach Wilderness Waterway marker #26 at mile 9. Here, the Wilderness Waterway turns north for Rodgers River Bay. The Rodgers River chickee is 4 miles north via the Rodgers River Bay Route. The Broad River Route, however, continues easterly toward Camp Lonesome. Broad River Bay constricts, passing a conspicuous island in the middle of the channel, and then the riverine characteristics of the Broad resume. Just beyond this island, come to a water-monitoring station on the north bank.

The waters now are clear and somewhat fresh, depending on rainfall and tides. The bottom is clearly visible, and the river varies between 50 and 60 feet in width. An occasional palm and wax myrtle pop out of the now-lower mangrove edges. Come to the confluence of four waterways, including the one you are on. The Wood River flows in from the right. Dead ahead is an unnamed channel, and to your left is the continuation of the Broad River. Take the Broad River left. Notice above the mangrove line the tall Jamaica dogwood and gumbo-limbo. Follow the left shoreline to reach the Camp Lonesome dock, tucked away amid some trees and brush at mile 12. This is an old shell mound that has been occupied, going back centuries, by the Calusa, Seminoles—and now you. From here, the Wood River Route leads 11 miles west back to the Broad River at The Nightmare.

Cabbage Island Shortcut

Begin: Rodgers River chickee Broad River Bay	End: Broad River just west of
Distance: 3.5 miles	Time: 2 hours
Potential tidal influence: 2	Potential wind influence: 2
Navigational challenge: 3	

Highlights: Quality creek paddling

Hazards: Choosing wrong creek from Broad River

Campsites: Rodgers River chickee

Connections: Rodgers River Route, Broad River Route, Rodgers River Bay Route

---

The Cabbage Island Shortcut offers the best in Everglades creek paddling. The waterway is small but not enclosed; it is grown up but not overgrown. There are just enough twists and turns and dodgeable tree limbs to keep the paddling lively without its becoming tiresome. There is only one channel, so the route doesn't become a guessing game as to which way to go. Logistically speaking, Cabbage Island Shortcut is the quickest way to Broad River from the Rodgers River chickee.

Start your route by paddling southeast from the Rodgers River chickee toward Cabbage Island. Aim for the channel along the west side of Cabbage Island. There is a conspicuous palm tree at the point for which you should aim. Take this slender channel and head for the extreme southwest corner of a small bay southwest of Cabbage Island. Where the bay splits at its end, take the south creek, which is about 20 feet wide and plenty deep. Begin your southwesterly course toward the Broad River. Notice the preponderance of buttonwood on this creek.

Every now and then you'll have to sneak past some roots and limbs, but the paddling never becomes an ordeal. Keep south and west before coming out at a big bend in the Broad River at mile 3.5. Just 100 yards west is the entrance to The Cutoff, which also connects Broad River to Rodgers River. This is not to be confused with The Cutoff that connects North River and Roberts River near Whitewater Bay.

If you're paddling this route from Broad River to Rodgers River Bay, make sure *not* to take The Cutoff. The Cabbage Island Shortcut is *east* of The Cutoff from the Broad River. Once on Broad River, it is one-half mile east to Broad River Bay. Southwest 4 miles down Broad River is the Broad River campsite via the Broad River Route.

Graveyard Creek Route

Begin: Shark River chickee	End: Graveyard Creek campsite
Distance: 7 miles	Time: 3.5 hours
Potential tidal influence: 4	Potential wind influence: 3
Navigational challenge: 3	

Highlights: Mature mangrove forest; good camping at Graveyard Creek

Hazards: Strong tidal flows upriver and down

Campsites: Shark River chickee, Graveyard Creek

Connections: Highland Beach Route, Shark Cutoff Route, The Labyrinth Route

The Graveyard Creek Route gets you from the "inside" to the "outside," or vice versa. Starting at the Shark River chickee on Little Shark River, the route goes a short distance to the Shark River, then heads west toward Ponce De Leon Bay. From the Shark River, several connecting tributaries bring you toward the bay. You will paddle among some of the tallest mangroves in the park, as your route winds through these channels to end up in the northern end of Ponce De Leon Bay. From here it is but a short paddle in the Gulf to the Graveyard Creek campsite, which has characteristics of both beach and ground campsite, though it is officially classified as a ground campsite.

Leave Shark River chickee and make a few strokes north to the Little Shark River. Turn right (northeast) up the Little Shark River just a short distance to Wilderness Waterway marker #6. At this point, you can see far up the waterway above the confluence of the Shark and Little Shark rivers. At marker #6, take the north channel,

Sea kayakers set up camp among barren mangroves at Graveyard Creek.
Photo by author.

which shortcuts to the Shark River. Soon, turn left (west) on the
Shark River and make your way downriver. The mangrove shoreline
here rises from the waterway; the trees growing taller beyond the
bank create the illusion of hills rising from the Shark.

The waterway is generally around 150 feet wide as it flows into
the central part of Ponce De Leon Bay. Before continuing too far
downriver, consider taking some of the many interconnecting channels that run parallel to the Shark. Paddling the Shark into Ponce De
Leon Bay will necessitate a paddle across big water to reach Graveyard Creek, and the going may be very rough on windy days. Also,
more powerboats use the Shark than they do the interconnecting
east-to-west-running channels north of the Shark. These channels
also offer a more intimate view of the mature mangrove woodland,
and they empty into the northern part of Ponce De Leon Bay, closer
to the Graveyard Creek campsite. If the wind is really fierce, you can

use these channels and side creeks to avoid the bay altogether, arriving at the campsite via Graveyard Creek. The channels also present a good low-tide paddling option. All in all, I recommend using them.

Be advised that tides run very strong in the Shark and its tributaries. Paddling against the tide here can be slow and exhausting. Try to time your paddle with the flow of the tides. Also, pay strict attention to the nautical charts: the interconnecting pattern of these channels can be confusing, though their east-west orientation and common destination of Ponce De Leon Bay make mistakes more forgivable.

After you choose your exact route among the channels of the Shark, hug the northern shore of Ponce De Leon Bay. Note the sporadic storm damage to the islands facing the bay. Beach and mangrove intermingle as the coast turns north and overlooks the Gulf of Mexico. Come to the small inlet of Graveyard Creek at mile 7. The Graveyard Creek campsite is on the north side of the inlet, with the best landing up Graveyard Creek. Here, a small beach and relatively deep water allow paddlers their best access to the campsite, which can be hard to reach at low tide.

Harney River Route

Begin: Canepatch campsite	End: Gulf of Mexico
Distance: 13.5 miles	Time: 7 hours
Potential tidal influence: 4	Potential wind influence: 3
Navigational challenge: 2	

Highlights: Route extends from freshwater to saltwater

Hazards: Strong tides up or down river

Campsites: Harney River chickee, Canepatch campsite

Connections: Highland Beach Route, Shark Cutoff Route, The Nightmare, Little Banana Patch Route

The Harney River connects the salty Gulf to the freshwater Glades on its east-west course. The river was named for Colonel William Harney, who used the river for passage to the Gulf in 1840, after crossing the Everglades westward from the Miami River. This Gulf passage took place after Harney pursued and killed the Indian Chekika, who had conducted his own deadly raid on some white residents at Indian Key during the Seminole Wars. Your passage on the Harney River will be less dangerous of course. From freshwater creeks, the route passes through Tarpon Bay to enter the Harney River. The river splits and widens, then reaches the Gulf beyond an island-dotted bay just north of Ponce De Leon Bay.

Leave Canepatch campsite and paddle south a short distance to Avocado Creek, passing a "No Wake" sign. Proceed westerly down Avocado Creek. Though this creek is narrow, it is deep enough and the vegetation kept back enough to allow small motorboat passage. The upper creek was opened by Hurricane Andrew in 1992. Broken and low trees, punctuated by surprising amounts of sawgrass and other freshwater vegetation, occupy the shore, which varies in width from 15 to 40 feet. For a creek of this diminutive size, the views are unusually wide. Closer to Tarpon bay, the shore crowds in on your sea kayak, though there are few canopied sections.

Pass an "End No Wake" sign and enter the arm of Tarpon Bay created by Avocado Creek at mile 1. Continue westerly in the arm along a shore of mangrove with scattered sawgrass and palms, traveling into the south arm and then into the heart of Tarpon Bay. Tarpon Bay is several hundred feet wide at this point. Stay along the south shore, coming to Wilderness Waterway Marker #9 at 4 miles. To your south is the commencement of Shark River and the Shark Cutoff Route, which follows the Wilderness Waterway south. The Harney River Route, however, picks up the Wilderness Waterway as it heads northwest along the beginning of the Harney River.

Paddle west along the Harney River, where the passage contracts to around 120 feet. Watch first for a feeder stream to the North Harney River at mile 5.5, then for a water-monitoring station on river north. Merge with the North Harney River by Wilderness Waterway marker #11 at mile 9. Northeast from marker #11, the North Harney River Route heads 10.5 miles back toward Canepatch. The Harney River is a good 200 feet wide here. Pass around an island, and the Harney River chickee stands at marker #12 at mile 9.5, where the Wilderness Waterway heads north to Broad River via The Nightmare Route. The Harney River chickee is an important staging area for paddling The Nightmare Route because of tidal considerations.

To continue the Harney River Route, leave the Harney River chickee and paddle almost due west, leaving the Wilderness Waterway behind. Continue west, staying with the south bank of the river as it turns south and passing by a channel on the right that also heads to the Gulf. A second, smaller channel splitting the south bank leads back to the Harney River chickee. The river resumes a westerly course, more than 100 feet wide and several feet deep.

Beyond the split in the river, watch the south bank for high places with perpendicular banks that are high enough to support salt-intolerant species such as palm. Part of this was once a farming area known as Ellis Fields. The river continues to broaden as it nears the Gulf, becoming over 200 feet wide when the Harney enters a bay enlarged by a merging river coming in from the south. The Gulf side of this bay seems to be blocked by multiple islands, but as you get closer you will see that three distinct channels enter the Gulf at mile 13.5. From here it is 7 miles north to Highland Beach and 2 miles south to Graveyard Creek backcountry campsite via the Highland Beach Route.

Highland Beach Route

Begin: Mouth of Lostmans River	End: Graveyard Creek campsite
Distance: 13 miles	Time: 7 hours
Potential tidal influence: 4	Potential wind influence: 5
Navigational challenge: 2	

Highlights: Highland Beach; many river mouths

Hazards: Big Gulf water and winds; being stranded at low tide

Campsites: Highland Beach, Graveyard Creek

Connections: Lostmans River Route, Rodgers River Route, Broad River Route, Harney River Route, Shark River Route, Ponce De Leon Bay Route, Turkey Key Route

---

The shoreline of the Highland Beach Route is as wild as the Florida coast gets in this era. This route covers the less-traversed central Everglades' Gulf coast, which was slammed by the 2005 hurricanes. Getting here takes more paddling than the time constraints of most trips allow. The Gulf paddle is varied and scenic with mangrove and beach coastline. Both campsites on this route offer quality experiences. In pre-park days, much of this land was settled, first by the Calusa and later by a family of Hamiltons and other settlers. Out here, it is just the mainland and the wide-open Gulf. There are no islands to hide behind or skirt between. The Gulf feels big, and when the waves come up, these waters can be downright treacherous.

This paddle starts at the mouth of the Lostmans River, where a high shell mound overlooks the landscape. (The abandoned Lostmans Ranger Station used to stand on this mound, but station and tower are now gone.) Pass Lostmans Key, then Little Creek, and swing around Highland Point, coming to Highland Beach. The beach here is airy and impressive, stretching for miles. Next, the route takes you to the river mouths, cycling the daily flow of the tides in and out of the Gulf. The paddle ends just south of Shark Point at Graveyard Creek and its campsite.

Leave the Lostmans Mound, where dock pilings mark the ranger station site, and paddle south, crossing the channel that enters Lostmans River and then paddling parallel to Lostmans Key with its abundant standing mangrove snags. Notice the sloping beaches on

Lostmans Key as you pass the island and the south entrance to Lostmans River.

Come to the inlet of Little Creek, then pass the small beach backed by freshwater trees that mark the old Leon Hamilton Place. Opened up by the recent hurricanes, this site is now more visible than it used to be. Make your way around Highland Point with its barren mangroves and now-exposed beach, and at 3.5 miles come to the long and attractive Highland Beach. The camp here has been shaped by hurricanes past and present. Palm trees sway atop the tall sand bluff, formed by wave action, which slopes back to a grass prairie studded with gumbo-limbo, Jamaica dogwood, and strangler fig. In pre-park days, this high land was farmed by the Rewis family. This is a great campsite, but be aware that low tide will leave you stranded on the beach until the water rises again later.

Continue south, reaching the wide bay of Broad and Rodgers rivers at 6.5 miles. The Broad River and Rodgers River routes lead into the interior Everglades from here. The channel markers in the bay guide boaters from the Gulf into the Broad River between the sand and mud bars so numerous here. Pass the mouth of Broad Creek at 9 miles, then reach the Harney River and the Harney River Route at 11 miles. In this section between the Broad and Harney rivers, you may have to paddle a mile or more from shore to avoid the numerous sand, mud, and oyster bars that extend into the Gulf here.

Past the Harney River, the Gulf gets deeper closer to shore. Pass around Shark Point, and the shoreline veers southeasterly at the northern end of Ponce De Leon Bay. At mile 13, come to Graveyard Creek campsite in the small inlet where Graveyard Creek enters the Gulf. Your best campsite access is up Graveyard Creek and to the beach area on the north side of the inlet. From here, it is 4 miles across Ponce De Leon Bay to Shark River Island and the Big Sable Route on the Ponce De Leon Bay Route. It is 7 miles to Shark River chickee on the Graveyard Creek Route.

Little Banana Patch Loop

Begin: Canepatch campsite	End: Canepatch campsite
Distance: 8.5 miles	Time: 4.5 hours
Potential tidal influence: 2	Potential wind influence: 2
Navigational challenge: 3	

Highlights: Remote freshwater Everglades creeks; Little Banana Patch Mound

Hazards: Narrow overgrown streams of "the Jungle"

Campsites: Canepatch

Connections: North Harney River Route, Harney River Route

The Little Banana Patch Loop explores part of the remotest paddling area in the Everglades—although it can be and is accessed by motorboats. The route makes a loop in the headwaters of the Shark River, where Glades freshwater flows east out of the sawgrass and into the mangrove creeks that ultimately empty into the Gulf of Mexico. Starting from Canepatch campsite, the route explores the uppermost reaches of Avocado Creek, then passes Little Banana Patch, a historic mound used by past Gladesmen—from the Calusa to the Seminoles to the conservationists protecting the rookeries here in the heart of the Glades. Beyond the mound, the route turns to join North Prong for a stream run before briefly entering Tarpon Bay. The return stretch travels through what paddlers have named "the Jungle," an overgrown set of creeks that emerge very near the Canepatch campsite.

Start at the Canepatch dock, paddling left (northeast) on Avocado Creek. Travel a short distance on Avocado Creek through a narrow channel before opening into a tiny bay, where a water-monitoring station is located. The narrow creek to your left is your return route and also the end of the North Harney River Route. Continue up Avocado Creek, passing the water-monitoring station. On the other side of the primarily mangrove shoreline, Squawk Creek runs generally parallel to Avocado Creek. Watch for occasional coco plum and wax myrtle. Air plants, such as wild pine, find homes in the trees where they attach to branches. At 1.1 miles, a creek leads left (northwest) into a slough of small streams that eventually connect to Tarpon Bay. Avocado Creek continues northeast. Small overgrown streams connect south to Squawk Creek.

After a long northeasterly straightaway, Avocado Creek meets Rookery Branch at 3 miles. Rookery Branch is a large stream that extends northeasterly, deep into the heart of the freshwater Glades. Down this long, wide stream, Rookery Mound awaits the determined paddler; but for now, continue north. Just beyond the Rookery Branch turnoff, Little Banana Patch lies to the left. It can be easily spotted by the banana trees clustered along the shore. Little Banana Patch, used for centuries by Gladesmen, is likely to be so overgrown as to be nearly unexplorable, but you can try.

To continue the loop, take the smaller channel, northbound, beyond Little Banana Patch. Pass a "No Wake" buoy on a 50-foot-wide stream lined with mangrove and freshwater trees such as palm. Stay with the wide stream, curving westerly. Merge into the much smaller North Prong, now heading southwesterly, and pass a second "No Wake" buoy. At 5.2 miles, North Prong curves northwest, narrows, and the shoreline becomes less uniform. Reach a four-way confluence at 6.3 miles. Keep southwesterly to enter Tarpon Bay at 6.9 miles. Immediately curve sharply southeast to enter a narrowing bay and join the North Harney River Route. Paddle to the very end of the bay, staying with the south shore to keep on the correct track. Do not take the tiny creek at the very end of the bay—it is overgrown. Instead, take the 10-foot-wide creek, the "Jungle route" portion of the North Harney River Route, leaving northeast just a few paddle strokes distant from the tiny creek at the very end of the narrow bay.

Follow the uncanopied waterway until it appears to dead-end. Two very small creeks split off here. Take the overgrown, canoe-

Relaxing at Canepatch after paddling the Little Banana Patch Loop. Photo by author.

width creek flowing in from the south. The mangrove is very low here (look for saw marks on the bigger branches), but the water is deep and passable. The creek is alternately open and overgrown. Merge into a tiny bay, where a creek flows in from the east and where there's a water-monitoring station in view. You have been here before. Paddle south through a slender channel, immediately coming to the dock of the Canepatch campsite on your right at mile 8.5.

Lostmans River Route

Begin: Wilderness Waterway
marker #52 near Second Bay
in Lostmans River

End: Mouth of Lostmans River

Distance: 6 miles

Time: 3 hours

Potential tidal influence: 4

Potential wind influence: 3

Navigational challenge: 2

Highlights: Shell mound at Lostmans Ranger Station site

Hazards: Strong tides in Lostmans River

Campsites: None

Connections: Willy Willy Route, Turkey Key Route, Highland Beach Route, Toms Creek Route

---

Lostmans River Route connects the Wilderness Waterway to the Gulf on the history-laden Lostmans River. Modern farmers, homesteaders, hunters, and fishermen followed the Calusa, who for hundreds of years enjoyed the natural bounties of this river and the Gulf. The upper Lostmans is made up of bays; the middle Lostmans is more riverine in character. Another bay opens up by the Gulf, near Lostmans Key. The Calusa's presence endures in the impressive mound at the mouth of the Lostmans, site of the abandoned Lostmans Ranger Station that was finally destroyed by Hurricane Wilma in 2005. Storm surge reexposed the shells of the mound, but vegetation is now taking back the hill. For the paddler, the ranger station site is a marker or a place to stop for lunch and stretch your legs.

Leave the Wilderness Waterway and the Willy Willy Route at Wilderness Waterway marker #52. Paddle southwest into wide Second Bay, keeping in the main flow of the current to avoid mud bars. Pass the mouth of Toms Creek to the east at 2 miles. This is the terminus of the Toms Creek Route, which heads east to the Rodgers River chickee.

Enter the riverine portion of Lostmans River, which now flows west. The mangrove shoreline is impressive here, rising high along the water's edge. The tidal flow can be strong in the 200 to 300 feet between the streambanks. This river section lasts a little shy of 2 miles. The river is way over your head here—10 or more feet deep. This is one of the few places in the Everglades with this kind of depth, and thus with powerful tides.

Pass a pair of water-monitoring stations on the south bank, half a mile west of Toms Creek. There are pilings from an old dock on the north bank across from the water stations. The dry land behind the pilings is the old homesite of Walter Hamilton, who resided here in the early 1900s. Stay with the north bank as you enter First Bay. The water is broken by oyster bars farther westward. Lostmans Key blocks most of First Bay, but there are Gulf access channels north and south of the key. Head for the north channel.

Pass the north side of Lostmans Key through the north channel and soon come to the Lostmans Ranger Station site at a point on the north shore. The remains of a dock mark the end of your route at 6 miles. The ranger station site occupies an extensive Calusa shell mound, scoured by storm surges from the Gulf. Note the sea grape, coconut palms, and extensive grasses that adorn this high sand perch. At one time, this mound was also the site of a fish house and a small community of palmetto shacks. The access at the pilings can be muddy and mixed with oyster bars at low tide. The best access nowadays is from the Gulf, around the corner to the north, where a small beach has opened up. To the north, it is 2 miles to Hog Key on the Turkey Key Route. To the south, it is 3.5 miles to Highland Point and the beginning of Highland Beach on the Highland Beach Route.

The Nightmare Route

Distance: 8.5 miles	Time: 4 hours
Begin: Broad River campsite	End: Harney River chickee
Potential tidal influence: 2	Potential wind influence: 2
Navigational challenge: 4	

Highlights: Canopied creeks; bird life

Hazards: Fallen and overgrown trees; low tide

Campsites: Broad River, Harney River chickee

Connections: Harney River Route, North Harney River Route, Broad
River Route, Wood River Route

The Nightmare is the stuff of Everglade legend. This is the only paddling route not on the Gulf to connect the northern and southern
Everglades. This makes it an essential link for those traveling the
Wilderness Waterway from end to end, especially if the wind and
waves are high on the ocean. Many of the linked creeks, pungent
with decaying vegetation, are overgrown with mangrove in places.
And if the tide is low, this route can be risky—too shallow to paddle
for a time. But you only have to wait for the tide to rise, then resume
your course. Otherwise, you can always paddle out the Broad River
to the Gulf and rejoin the Wilderness Waterway up Broad Creek.
The Nightmare should be an interesting paddle; there is much bird
life along the route's quiet creeks where a paddler rarely if ever sees a
motorboat. I presume this segment of the Everglades is so named for
the disagreeable situation of being stuck here at low tide, especially
when the mosquitoes are buzzing.

Leave the Broad River campsite and paddle west down the Broad
River a few hundred feet to Wilderness Waterway marker #24 and
the Wood River. Turn left (south) on the Wood River and trace it a
short distance to Wilderness Waterway marker #23. From here, the
Wood River Route heads left (east) 11 miles to Camp Lonesome on
the upper Broad River.

Turn right (southwest) at marker #23 and begin a convoluted paddle that will take you in all compass directions. This route is partly
canopied and partly open overhead. There is much deadwood in the
water, along live trees—limbs and roots—to paddle around. There
are also a few open shrubby areas. Other creeks spin off here and
there, but the main channel is usually obvious. If you are in doubt,
look for limbs sawn and branches broken by other paddlers to keep
The Nightmare passable. The creeks here are also a little deeper than
indicated on the chart. You can run them not only at high tide, but
also on a rising tide or a high falling tide from the Broad River camp-

site. Just don't run the route at absolute low tide. The tides flowing in and out of here scour the creek bed and keep The Nightmare runnable.

Come to Wilderness Waterway marker #23 at mile 2.8. To your right is a channel to the Gulf. Stay left. Here, the creek opens up somewhat, then narrows as it snakes among mangrove roots. Stay left again at marker #21 at 3.6 miles, which is off to the right in another channel leading to the Gulf. Coming from Broad River, you may miss this marker and see marker #19 next. Here, the creek is no longer canopied. Merge with Broad Creek at marker #17 at 4 miles. This is where the low-water Gulf alternative rejoins the Wilderness Waterway.

Paddle east up the rich waters of Broad Creek, which remains broad for 5.5 miles until it seems to dead-end in mangrove. The creek doesn't stop; it's just overgrown here. At this point, stow your gear and fishing rods below the gunwales of your canoe and batten down any gear strapped on your sea kayak. Through this section of Broad Creek expect to be ducking and darting amid the growth of some large red mangrove. Be prepared for a few spider webs, too. Water depth is no problem here. Often, water extends far into the mangrove beyond the main channel, creating a swamp effect.

Emerge from the tangle of Broad Creek just before reaching marker #16, 7 miles into the route. Leave Broad Creek and head southwest down a much more paddler-friendly creek to marker #14. Here, pick up a mud-bottomed stream winding southeasterly to merge with the Harney River at Wilderness Waterway marker #12. The marker is attached to the Harney River chickee, dead ahead at mile 8.5 and the end of the route. To the west, it is 4 miles to the Gulf on the Harney River Route. To the east, the Harney River Route leads 5.5 miles to Tarpon Bay and the Shark Cutoff Route. The North Harney River Route starts one-half mile east on the Harney River.

North Harney River Route

Begin: Wilderness Waterway marker #11 at Harney River

End: Canepatch campsite

Distance: 10.5 miles

Time: 6 hours

Potential tidal influence: 4

Potential wind influence: 3

Navigational challenge: 4

Highlights: Multiple types of waters

Hazards: Tiny creek near Canepatch

Campsites: Harney River, Canepatch

Connections: Harney River Route, The Nightmare, Little Banana Patch Loop

---

Are you looking for the route less traveled? Are you looking for a route that encompasses bays, rivers, streams, and creeks, with a little navigational uncertainty thrown in for good measure? Then paddle the North Harney River Route. It starts innocuously enough as it splinters off the Harney River, traveling east and getting a little smaller as time goes on, until it is but 20 feet wide just before meeting big Tarpon Bay and its mixture of fresh- and saltwater flora. Then comes the finale—a trip through tiny, deep creeks of the "Jungle route." Through here, you will have to trust your chart and your compass, especially at the end where these freshwater streams seem overgrown. They will prove passable, though, getting you to your destination: Canepatch campsite. This campsite is a historic shell mound that is still growing the plant descendants of its final farming incarnation. Don't expect to see any motorboats except, maybe, on Tarpon Bay.

Start your route at Wilderness Waterway marker #11, half a mile east of the Harney River chickee. Paddle north from the marker, then east to get on the North Harney River, which veers east to parallel the much more heavily traveled (by boaters of all stripes) Harney. The North Harney is a good 150 feet wide but soon shrinks to just under 100 feet. Tributary streams splinter off the north bank. Watch for occasional fern patches on the shore.

At mile 3.5, meet your first navigational challenge. About 120 yards after the river has made a sharp southeasterly jog, come first to a small inlet and creek on the south bank, then to a place where the river splits into two channels of roughly equal size. The southerly channel meets the Harney, while the easterly channel is the continuation of the North Harney. Take the east channel.

The river is now only 40 feet wide, but the effective paddling area is only 15 to 30 feet. There is no canopy, but the shores are lush with mangrove. The North Harney winds in all directions, but keeps an easterly inclination. This is great paddling—a clear meandering stream with no serious obstructions and few if any motorboats. The mangrove shore lowers and is punctuated with fern patches and bare mud banks where alligators sun themselves.

Leave the serpentine stream and enter a series of tapered bays that continue easterly and finally open into Tarpon Bay at mile 8. Notice the appearance of sawgrass, mahogany, palm, and wax myrtle—indicators of fresher water and bits of higher land.

Stay on the primary northeast arm of the bay until it veers southeast toward the Canepatch campsite. Paddle to the very end of the bay, staying with the south shore to keep on the correct track. Do not take the tiny creek at the very end of the bay—it is overgrown. Instead, take the 10-foot-wide creek, the "Jungle route," leaving northeast just a few paddle strokes distant from the tiny creek at the very end of the bay. The correct creek is plenty deep, with fingerlike roots of trees floating in the water. Follow the uncanopied waterway until it seems to dead-end. Two very small creeks split off here. Take the overgrown, canoe-width creek flowing in from the south. The mangrove brush is very low, but the water is deep and passable. Look for saw marks on bigger branches.

The creek's fresher water is accompanied by the appearance of less salt-tolerant tree species, including coco plum and fig. From here, the creek is alternately open and overgrown. Merge into a tiny bay with a creek flowing in from the east, where a water-monitoring station comes into view. You, however, paddle south through a slender channel, immediately coming to the dock of the Canepatch campsite on your right at mile 10.5. This campsite, an old shell mound, has been in use since humans first lived in the Everglades. The Harney River Route has come into Canepatch via Avocado Creek to the southwest, where you see a "No Wake" sign.

Ponce De Leon Bay Route

Begin: Shark River Island	End: Graveyard Creek campsite
Distance: 4 miles	Time: 2 hours
Potential tidal influence: 4	Potential wind influence: 5
Navigational challenge: 2	
Highlights: Open Gulf paddle	
Hazards: Big water and strong tides	
Campsites: Graveyard Creek	
Connections: Highland Beach Route, Big Sable Route, Graveyard Creek Route	

Ponce De Leon Bay Route is a short connector route for travelers paddling north and south along the Gulf margin of the Everglades, on the "outside." Ponce De Leon Bay is the single largest bay on the Everglades' Gulf coast. This significant stretch of water divides Cape Sable to the south from the central Glades and the Ten Thousand Islands to the north. You will feel the tides as they push and pull out of the bay, which drains the Shark River and Whitewater Bay. The relatively deep water of the bay means big waves if the wind is blow-

White ibis stalks the shallows for supper. Photo by Constance Mier.

ing. In that case, you will have to circumvent Ponce De Leon Bay via the many channels of the Shark River system.

Start your route at the oversized flashing buoy just southwest of Shark River Island at the mouth of the Little Shark River. South of you is the continuation of the Big Sable Route, which swings around Cape Sable. For the Ponce De Leon Bay Route, paddle north around Shark River Island almost due north across the bay. The water becomes shallower on the last half of the bay. Graveyard Creek flows into the north end of the bay. The campsite is marked by a couple of coconut palms. Your best bet for accessing the campsite is to paddle into Graveyard Creek about 50 yards and then land on the sandy north side of the creek. Here, the water is deep and access is possible regardless of the tides, which can leave the Gulf side of the campsite high and dry. From Graveyard Creek, the Highland Beach Route heads north up the Gulf 13 miles to Lostmans River.

If the winds are high, you can alter the Ponce De Leon Bay Route. Paddle up the mouth of the Little Shark River, following the Coast Guard markers to #64. Veer north into the Shark River's system of channels and islands, circumventing Ponce De Leon Bay. You can even work your way around to enter Graveyard Creek campsite via Graveyard Creek. This will obviously add time and mileage to your paddle, but I was very glad the option was available to me one blustery day when it was dangerous to cross the bay in an open canoe.

Rodgers River Route

Begin: Gulf of Mexico   End: Rodgers River chickee

Distance: 11.5 miles   Time: 6 hours

Potential tidal influence: 3   Potential wind influence: 3

Navigational challenge: 3

Highlights: Old homesites; solitude

Hazards: Oyster and mud bars at the river's mouth

Campsites: Highland Beach, Rodgers River chickee

Connections: Highland Beach Route, Broad River Route, Cabbage Island Shortcut, Rodgers River Bay Route

---

The Rodgers River Route is a good connector—and much quieter than the nearby Broad River—for those heading for Rodgers River chickee and the "inside" from the Gulf. The Rodgers River is seldom used by motorboats. It is challenging to enter from the Gulf, and the many mud bars at the river's west end make navigation difficult unless you are in a shallow-draft hand-propelled craft.

Once beyond the many islands at the river's entrance, the route passes a surprising amount of high ground, accompanying vegetation, and an old homesite, too, before the river narrows and changes course. The upper half of the Rodgers is slender and winding before opening up into Rodgers River Bay, where the route ends at Rodgers River chickee.

Leave the Gulf of Mexico near Highland Beach and enter a maze of islands inhabiting a large bay formed by the confluence of the

Rodgers and Broad rivers. This area can be confusing. Use the flow of the tides to help you through the islands, making sure you are paddling northerly into the Rodgers River and not easterly into the Broad River.

Leave the bay and islands behind as the Rodgers River turns easterly. Note the mud bars on the inside bends of the waterway at lower tides. The Rodgers constricts to less than 100 feet wide as high ground appears on both sides of the river, harboring a palm or two and way too much Brazilian pepper, an invasive exotic. Three miles from the Gulf, note the proliferation of hammock species such as fig, gumbo-limbo, and tamarind on the north bank. Traditionally used for shade and decoration, the tamarind tree, with its spreading branches of tiny compound leaves, is an indicator of old homesites. The homesite here is most likely that of Shelton Atwell. On this property in the late 1800s, in the cleared fields behind his home, Ashton grew sugarcane for sale along with assorted vegetables for sustenance. As you paddle upriver, look for other palm-studded lands. They ordinarily show up on the outside bends of the Rodgers, which has further contracted to around 80 feet and is more uniformly deep. Also watch for alligators, which seem to inhabit the river in inordinately large numbers.

Come to The Cutoff at 6.5 miles. This waterway connects the Rodgers to the Broad River. The Cutoff here is not to be confused with another Cutoff that connects Roberts River to the North River near Whitewater Bay. The Rodgers River turns sharply southwest at The Cutoff and heads in that direction for three-quarters of a mile before resuming a northeasterly bearing. The dry land is all but gone here, and the shoreline is mostly mangrove, buttonwood, and occasional fern patches. The waterway maintains a 40-foot width before widening and twisting around to arrive at Rodgers River Bay at mile 10.

Paddle east through a narrow neck of the bay, which afterward opens up. Begin to look for Rodgers River chickee in an inlet on the north side of the bay, coming to the chickee at mile 11.5. The chickee lies west of where it is shown on the nautical charts. The Rodgers River Bay Route and the Wilderness Waterway are 1 mile east. The

Cabbage Island Shortcut leads southwest 3.5 miles to Broad River. The Toms Creek and Lostmans routes lead 11.5 miles to the Gulf at the mouth of Lostmans River.

Rodgers River Bay Route

Begin: Willy Willy campsite	End: Wilderness Waterway marker #26 at Broad River Bay
Distance: 7 miles	Time: 3.5 hours
Potential tidal influence: 2	Potential wind influence: 3
Navigational challenge: 3	

Highlights: Nearby freshwater creeks

Hazards: Motor boats on Wilderness Waterway

Campsites: Willy Willy campsite, Rodgers River chickee

Connections: Willy Willy Route, Toms Creek Route, Rodgers River Route, Cabbage Island Shortcut, Broad River Route

The Rodgers River Bay Route leaves the Willy Willy shell mound and heads south on Rocky Creek to Lostmans Creek, to rejoin the Wilderness Waterway through Rodgers River Bay, making a side trip to Rodgers River chickee. Paddlers come back to the Wilderness Waterway and skirt Cabbage Island to enter a twisting channel that emerges onto Broad River Bay. This is one of three routes heading south from Rodgers River Bay, and it is the preferred route if you are heading for Camp Lonesome on the upper Broad River. Freshwater creeks flow into the bays from the marshy glades to the east, making for good side explorations.

Leave Willy Willy campsite and paddle a scant 50 yards east up Rocky Creek Bay to Rocky Creek. Turn south on Rocky Creek and punch the dark objects below the crystal clear water with your paddle. These rocks gave the creek its name. The shore here is fraught with hammock tree species—palm is the easiest to identify. Rocky

Creek widens. Turn right at the first side creek. It comes into Rocky Creek at an acute angle from the northwest. This is not Rocky Creek, but it too has a rocky bottom. The stream quickly circles southwest, opening into a bay that runs north-south.

Paddle to the south end of the bay into Lostmans Creek, which at this point is an east-west arm of Big Lostmans Bay. Steer toward the distant western shore of the bay. Dead ahead is Wilderness Waterway marker #39. Join the Wilderness Waterway, but instead of doubling back around the slender island in front of you, take the south channel before the marker and paddle south to marker #37. This marker is currently not shown on the charts.

Enter Rodgers River Bay and paddle southeast from marker #37 to marker #36. This area can be confusing, because the Wilderness Waterway has been rerouted away from the openest part of Rodgers River Bay. Stay south past marker #35 into an 80-foot-wide channel with mangrove and buttonwood banks. Marker #34 is gone, though it is still on the charts. Keep south and come to marker #32 at 4 miles. To your west 1 mile, not visible from here, is the Rodgers River chickee. To reach this chickee, paddle west along the north shore until coming to a shallow inlet. There you'll see the chickee, perched about 40 feet from the north shore. From here, it is 3.5 miles to Broad River Bay on the Cabbage Island Shortcut, 11.5 miles to the Gulf on the Rodgers River Route, and 11.5 miles to the Gulf on the Toms Creek and Lostmans River routes.

Return to Wilderness Waterway marker #32 on the Rodgers River Bay Route. Stroke south, skirting the east side of Cabbage Island and marker #31. East of marker #31 is Indian Camp Creek, another good freshwater paddle. For the Rodgers River Route, stay south past marker #29 into a winding channel that leads to Broad River Bay. Come to Broad River Bay and Wilderness Waterway marker #26 at 7 miles. To the east, it is 3 miles to Camp Lonesome on the Broad River Route. To your west, it is 7 miles to the Broad River campsite on the Broad River Route.

Shark Cutoff Route

Begin: Wilderness Waterway
marker #9 at Tarpon Bay   End: Oyster Bay chickee

Distance: 9 miles   Time: 4 hours

Potential tidal influence: 4   Potential wind influence: 2

Navigational challenge: 2

Highlights: Big trees on Shark River

Hazards: Tidal flow on Shark River

Campsites: Oyster Bay chickee, Shark River chickee

Connections: Big Sable Route, Shark River Route, The Labyrinth Route, Whitewater Bay Route, Harney River Route, Cormorant Pass Route

---

The Shark Cutoff Route forms part of the primary "inside" connector for north-south Everglades paddlers using the Wilderness Waterway. The Shark Cutoff Route follows the Shark River from its beginning at Tarpon Bay down to its confluence with the Little Shark River, coming to the Shark River chickee. Next, following the Little Shark River, this route turns south at the Shark Cutoff, entering the northern reaches of Oyster Bay. After leaving the Wilderness Waterway, the route enters a small group of mangrove islands, coming to the Oyster Bay chickee in a lagoon among the islands.

Start your route at Wilderness Waterway Marker #9, 4 miles west of Canepatch campsite and 5.5 miles east of Harney River campsite. Paddle south on the Shark River, bordered by young, small mangrove and buttonwood. Larger, taller patches of mangrove look like hills off in the distance. Arrive at Wilderness Waterway Marker #8 at mile 2. On your left is an unnamed channel coming from the eastern end of Tarpon Bay. This channel is an alternative, windy-day route for those paddling to Canepatch campsite.

Here, the Shark River widens and turns more westerly. The

straightness of the waterway allows for distant views downriver. Pass Gunboat Island at mile 3.5. Someone accurately imagined that this island looks like a warship steaming up the Shark River. Several water-monitoring stations flank the shoreline in this area. The great mangrove forest of the Shark is evident below Gunboat Island. Less than a mile downstream is the confluence of the Shark and Little Shark rivers and another unnamed channel. The southerly channel leads into The Labyrinth. The westerly channel is the Shark River. Straight ahead, southwesterly, is your route, the Little Shark River.

Dead ahead is Wilderness Waterway marker #6. To your north, the Graveyard Creek Route leads 7 westerly miles to Graveyard Creek. Stay southwesterly on the much narrower Little Shark River. On the next channel to your south is the Shark River chickee and the beginning of The Labyrinth Route. The Shark River chickee, about 50 yards up the channel at mile 4.5, is a good place to camp or stop and stretch your legs. There is no dry ground on this route.

Return to the Little Shark River and paddle southwesterly on the Wilderness Waterway, coming to Wilderness Waterway marker #5 and the Shark Cutoff at 6 miles. Turn south on the Wilderness Waterway, traversing the winding shortcut into the northern fringe of Oyster Bay and passing Wilderness Waterway marker #3. The waterway penetrates the bay, heading southeasterly toward a passage between some mangrove islands. Trust your compass; these islands look like one continuous shoreline from afar. Make the passage among the islands and look for Wilderness Waterway Marker #2 at 8 miles.

Leave the Wilderness Waterway at marker #2 and bear southwest toward Coast Guard marker #50. Do not head for Coast Guard marker #48—it leads to Whitewater Bay and points south through Cormorant Pass on the Cormorant Pass and Whitewater Bay routes. Paddle south from marker #50 into a small group of islands. Inside a lagoon amid the islands is the Oyster Bay chickee at mile 9. From the Oyster Bay chickee, it is 4 miles south to the Joe River on the

Cormorant Pass Route. It is 6 miles west on the Big Sable Route to the Gulf of Mexico at Shark River Island.

Toms Creek Route

Begin: Rodgers River chickee	End: Lostmans River at Second Bay
Distance: 7 miles	Time: 3.5 hours
Potential tidal influence: 3	Potential wind influence: 3
Navigational challenge: 3	

Highlights: Shortcut between Rodgers River chickee and the Gulf

Hazards: Winds on Rodgers River Bay

Campsites: Rodgers River chickee

Connections: Cabbage Island Shortcut, Willy Willy Route, Rodgers River Route, Lostmans River Route

The fastest and best way to access Lostmans River from the Rodgers River Chickee is the Toms Creek Route. Plus it's off the motorboaters beaten path. The route runs west out of the Rodgers River Bay into a very shallow bay and then into Toms Creek. Both sections of this little-used waterway, which exudes a feeling of the wild Everglades, meet the east end of the Lostmans River and the Lostmans River Route.

Leave the Rodgers River chickee and paddle west on the south Rodgers River Bay through a neck in the bay to the wider north Rodgers River Bay. Turn north, passing the beginning of the Rodgers River to the southwest at 1 mile. From here, the Rodgers River Route heads west 10.5 miles to the Gulf.

Stay northwest, aiming for the peninsula that extends out from the west shore of Rodgers River Bay. Once around this point, continue your paddle path west through three bays. The west end of the last bay funnels into Toms Creek. This final bay is very shallow, as is evidenced by numerous snags in the water. This is what discourages motorboats from using this route. Palms grace the shore at the origin of Toms Creek at mile 4.5. The stream, about 40 feet wide, is kept deep enough by tidal action, which can be surprisingly swift. Toms Creek starts west but then meanders north for a little less than a mile, where it widens before opening into the Lostmans River. Stay with the west shore of the river and swing around a point, paddling back south into the continuation of Toms Creek. As you swing around the point, watch for a big mud flat—especially at low tide.

Now paddle southerly on the wider second portion of Toms Creek. The mangrove shore is much taller on this winding stretch of stream. You will find yourself shortcutting the bends here, where the tides are less pronounced. Shy gators will slip into the water upon your approach.

Toms Creek opens up near an island on Lostmans River. Stay on the north side of this island and end your route at the south end of Second Bay on the Lostmans River. To your west, it is 4.5 miles to the Lostmans Ranger Station on the Gulf via the Lostmans River Route. It is 1.5 miles to Wilderness Waterway marker #52 and the Willy Willy Route via the Lostmans River Route.

Wood River Route

Begin: Camp Lonesome	End: Wilderness Waterway marker #24 at The Nightmare
Distance: 11 miles	Time: 6 hours
Potential tidal influence: 2	Potential wind influence: 2
Navigational challenge: 2	
Highlights: Much of route is paddler only	
Hazards: Overhanging limbs; brush in the river	
Campsites: Broad River, Camp Lonesome	
Connections: Broad River Route, The Nightmare Route	

Camp Lonesome has been used for centuries—first by the Calusa, then by the Seminoles, and today by paddlers. Photo by author.

In *some* ways, the Wood River route is the most challenging route in the entire park. A significant part of it is overgrown with tropical vegetation and obstructed by fallen trees. Together, these hindrances make for a tough go, which at the same time, makes this a paddler-only waterway. And paddlers alone keep it open. The route needs to be traveled to remain passable. So, don't shy away from this true wilderness experience. The Wood River Route encompasses a variety of exceptional Everglades settings. And favoring the solitude, birds are abundant here. Though extra effort is required to squeeze through some tight spots, the trip is well worth it.

Leave Camp Lonesome and head southeast, immediately coming to the confluence of four waterways, one of which you are on. Paddle west into the smallest of the four. The Wood River seems blocked until you paddle into it and find that it jogs north. The channel is around 30 feet wide, but the effective paddling area is from 5 to 20 feet in width, due to the thick mangrove bank. Come to Wood River

Bay at 1.3 miles, soon passing a creek on your left that leads back toward Camp Lonesome. Pass this skinny bay's only island, dotted with palm, before coming to a split in the bay. Take the western channel; the eastern channel leads deep into the Glades.

The Wood River gently tapers beyond the bay until it's just a slender ribbon of mangrove-lined water snaking westerly through the surrounding marsh. This mangrove-ribbon shoreline is very irregular, with small bushy trees near the water and larger tall trees behind them reaching high for the sky. In contrast, myriad skeletal trees lie above and beneath the pristine creek, a mosaic of life and death in a mangrove wood.

At mile 4, come to the channel leading to the Mud Lakes. This creek meanders north to these shallow lakes. Continue southwesterly on the Wood, which can be busy with bird life in this section. Overgrown sections, pinching in the paddling area, appear irregularly.

On the maps you will see two creeks connecting Wood River to Broad Creek. These are impassable but, depending on the tide, can bring murky, copper-colored waters into the middle part of the Wood.

Around mile 6.5, the river becomes more junglelike in both appearance and disposition: the waterway has narrowed, and the mangrove shoreline has risen and canopies over and into the Wood, mixing with the already-ample number of fallen trees and submerged timber. The paddling here can be challenging. Also, the lower the tide, the more such obstacles you will encounter in the water. This lesser depth, however, can add wiggle room for sneaking beneath low-hanging trees. The waters down here become thick and pungent with the smell of salt and decay, much like those of Broad Creek, which parallels the Wood one watershed south. Just when you're about tired of the tangled stretch, around mile 10 the waterway opens, first to 40, then to more than 60 feet in width, with little in the way to impede your paddling. Occasional shrubby patches break up the mangrove.

Intersect the Wilderness Waterway at marker #24. You have paddled 11 miles. To your left is The Nightmare, which leads south a little over 8 miles toward the Harney River chickee. The Wood River continues north a short distance to meet the Broad River. The Broad River campsite is just a couple of hundred yards east up the Broad River. The Gulf of Mexico and Highland Beach is 2 miles west down the Broad River on the Broad River Route.

Ten Thousand Islands

Causeway Route

Begin: Chokoloskee

Distance: 3 miles

Potential tidal influence: 4

Navigational challenge: 2

End: Gulf Coast Ranger Station

Time: 1.5 hours

Potential wind influence: 3

Highlights: Connector between Chokoloskee and Gulf Coast Ranger Station

Hazards: Low water and strong tides under Halfway Creek bridge

Campsites: None

Connections: Hurddles Creek Route, Lopez River Route, Turner River Route, Rabbit Key Pass Route, West Pass Route, Indian Key Pass Route, Sandfly Island Route, Halfway Creek Canoe Trail

---

The Causeway is a connector route in its purest sense. There is little scenic about this paddle. Much of it parallels the road connecting Chokoloskee Island to the mainland. What you can accomplish with this paddle is getting back to your car at Gulf Coast Ranger Station from Chokoloskee or vice versa. Also, you can avoid big winds in Chokoloskee Bay. Making this connection can be tough at low tide, because the main channel along the causeway can be shallow and the canoe launch at Gulf Coast Ranger Station can be nothing but mud. Time your paddle not to pass through here at dead low tide.

Leave the pay landing at Outdoor Resorts on Chokoloskee Island and paddle north into a slender channel at one-half mile. The channel parallels the causeway. Keep northwest until the channel opens up. The channel is deeper on the right (north) bank. Halfway Creek is off to the east and leads 7.5 miles to the Tamiami Trail on the Halfway Creek Canoe Trail. Avoiding shallows and bars, stay with the road until it opens up at the Halfway Creek bridge. Paddle southwest under the bridge and open into Chokoloskee Bay at mile 2.2. Be careful: tides can power through here. Resume a northwesterly direction, passing a tour boat landing and two brown park service buildings before reaching the canoe launch at Gulf Coast Ranger Station at mile 3, ending the route.

Chatham River Route

Begin: Mormon Key

End: Sweetwater Chickee

Distance: 8 miles

Time: 4 hours

Potential tidal influence: 4

Potential wind influence: 3

Navigational challenge: 3

Highlights: Old homesite; quiet chickee

Hazards: Ghosts at Watsons Place

Campsites: Mormon Key, Watsons Place, Sweetwater chickee

Connections: Pavilion Key Route, Turkey Key Route, Last Huston Bay Route, Huston River Route, Darwins Place Route

---

The Chatham River Route leaves the lower Ten Thousand Islands at Mormon Key and heads into the interior Glades via the Chatham River. This river, with its numerous and shifting sandbars and mud bars, can be a tricky to navigate, but it is much less dangerous for self-propelled craft than for the motorboats you will see. Once beyond the mouth of the Chatham, the waterway weaves its way up to Watsons Place, home of the infamous Ed Watson, who murdered his way into Everglades lore at this very locale. His homesite is now a backcountry camp, and you can explore the ruins of Chatham Bend, as the now overgrown farm was called. But be aware that the bodies of several Watson victims were never found . . . The route continues up the Chatham from Watsons Place to intersect the Wilderness Waterway near Last Huston Bay, then up the hard-to-find but rewarding Sweetwater Creek to Sweetwater chickee, which is off the main traveling routes.

Leave Mormon Key and paddle north into the mouth of the Chatham, passing close to a point of the mainland to your east. Do not go too far west, which would take you up the Huston River and the Huston River Route. The correct route will take you past some shallows into a deep channel flanked by a set of finger islands. Keep northeast between mud flats and oyster bars on this 70-foot-wide channel, surprisingly slim for a river of this volume.

Work your way northeast among the islands until wide-open river lies before you. A continuous mangrove shoreline is broken only by one or two marl flats covered with pickerel weed and scattered mangrove, and by an occasional feeder stream entering the river.

If the tide or winds are against you, the bends in the Chatham, forming breaks in the current, make it easier to paddle up the river. Pass some pilings and concrete of a former dock on the south shore of one such bend. It is obvious by the vegetation that this is dry land. Around this bend on the north bank is a water-monitoring station, then the dock of the Watsons Place campsite at mile 4. Notice the tall gumbo-limbo trees extending above the forest at the old home place.

This cleared area once extended for 35 acres and was a full-fledged cane and vegetable farm. Nowadays, you see a cistern, old farm implements, and a kettle encased in brick for boiling cane juice into syrup. Other remaining artifacts are scattered about the dense woods. Watsons Place is a popular camping spot for paddlers and motorboaters alike.

The story of Ed Watson has been told time and again. He came to the Everglades in the 1890s with a troubled past, then settled at Chatham Bend; but he had a few scrapes in which one man was wounded and two others wound up dead. Neighbors kept an eye on Watson. Other ruffians and drifters joined him from time to time, working on his farm. In 1910, some of Watson's workers were seen in the Chatham River—floating with weights attached to their bodies. The ire of residents on nearby Chokoloskee Island was raised. Some of them gunned Watson down when he landed on their island and attempted to explain the deaths of his workers.

Leave the Watson Place, noting the sheared shell shore just beyond the dock near a tamarind tree. The gumbo-limbo trees continue up the north riverbank. The Chatham widens as it joins an unnamed channel leading to Huston Bay. Here, the Chatham River continues east, then northerly, passing a few more islands and coming to the Wilderness Waterway at marker #99, just short of 6 miles.

To the northwest, the Last Huston Bay Route leads 7 miles to the Sunday Bay chickee. To the southeast, it is 3 miles to Darwins Place via the Darwins Place Route. The Chatham River Route, however, continues almost due east from marker #99, up an 80-foot-wide channel leading toward Sweetwater Creek, Sweetwater Bay, and the Sweetwater chickee. Paddle up this channel and come to an arm of Last Huston Bay.

You cannot access Sweetwater chickee via Last Huston Bay. Do not get sucked into the open-water trap by paddling into Last Huston Bay. Instead, from the end of the channel, paddle northeast no more than 200 feet across the arm of Last Huston Bay to an opening in the shoreline that is the mouth of Sweetwater Creek. The creek immediately turns north, then northeast again, as it widens to more than 40 feet. Pass Sweetwater Bay on your right (east). Stay north into the second segment of Sweetwater Creek. Come to a conspicuous island topped with a few palm trees. Sweetwater chickee, the end of your route, is on the far side of the island, 2 miles from Wilderness Waterway marker #99 and 8 miles from Mormon Key.

Darwins Place Route

Begin: Wilderness Waterway
marker #99 at Chatham River   End: Lostmans Five campsite

Distance: 9.5 miles   Time: 5 hours

Potential tidal influence: 2   Potential wind influence: 4

Navigational challenge: 2

Highlights: Historic shell mounds; varied vegetation

Hazards: Motor boats on Wilderness Waterway

Campsites: Darwins Place, Plate Creek chickee, Lostmans Five campsite

Connections: Last Huston Bay Route, Chatham River Route, Gopher Key–Charley Creek Route, Willy Willy Route

---

The Darwins Place Route passes through a few historic settings while it alternately traverses spacious bays and slender creeks. It traces the Wilderness Waterway through Chevelier Bay, named for an early Everglades plume hunter and naturalist, then come to Darwins Place. This is a park service campsite on a shell mound that has been occupied off and on since the time of the Calusa. The route slips past Cannon Bay and Tarpon Bay into narrow Alligator Creek, which contrasts well with the big water of Alligator and Dads bays. Another intimate paddle follows, on Plate Creek. Then the route opens up on Plate Creek Bay, only to repeat the small-water paddle one more time before arriving at Lostmans Five campsite, another bit of ground that has played host to humanity for a long time here in the Glades.

Start your route at Wilderness Waterway marker #99, where the Chatham River intersects the Wilderness Waterway. Paddle east toward Chevelier Bay. The water is very shallow among the islands as you swing around Chevelier Point and marker #97. This point and bay are named for Frenchman Jean Chevelier. He was a contradictory man. In the late 1800s, acting on his naturalist's bent, he collected and stuffed wild birds, while simultaneously depleting bird stocks by pluming throughout the area from his home base on Opossum Key. He was rumored to have buried a fortune somewhere in the Everglades, and folks have searched nearby islands for his stash ever since. Of course, if Chevelier did bury loot, it must remain where it is as a park artifact, just like any settlers' or Calusa artifacts.

Stay along the south bank of shallow Chevelier Bay, bordered by low mangrove, turning almost due south from Wilderness Waterway marker #93 toward a pass between a lone island and a point on the south shore at marker #89. To avoid confusion, stay with this shoreline to marker #88. Here, you enter a creek and shortly veer south to marker #87, where there is a "No Wake" sign. Soon you'll come to the Darwins Place campsite at mile 2.5. This is a good resting and camping spot. Arthur Darwin, the park's last living resident, was also the last in a long line of people to live in the Everglades, dating back to the Calusa. This shell mound has had huts, houses, and crops on it for a long time. It has grown over a lot since becoming a campsite, especially with the invasive exotic, Brazilian pepper.

Leave Darwins Place and paddle southeast past marker #86, and another "No Wake" sign toward marker #85, barely visible between two islands off in the distance. The bulk of Cannon Bay opens up to the east. To the southwest is the mouth of Gopher Key Creek and the Gopher Key–Charley Creek Route, which leads 8 miles to the Gulf and Turkey Key.

Soon, squeeze into a tapered channel south to Tarpon Bay, much smaller than the other Tarpon Bay by the Harney River. This Tarpon Bay is also the smallest bay on this route. Paddle the length of

Tarpon Bay, tracing the markers, until you reach Alligator Creek at marker #77. It would stand to reason that there would be more than one Alligator Creek in the Everglades, and there is. Do not mix this Alligator Creek up with the Alligator Creek on the West Lake Canoe Trail near Flamingo.

On this Alligator Creek, pass a "No Wake" sign as you enter the 20-foot-wide stream. The shoreline rises high with mangrove but is cleared enough to allow an average skiff to pass. There is only sparse canopy overhanging the deep water. A few palm and buttonwood trees accompany the mangrove at first. The creek widens to a "No Wake" buoy, then narrows again, passing a clump of land on creek left, just before emerging onto Alligator Bay at Wilderness Waterway marker #75.

Keep southeast across the big water, aiming for the channel that connects Alligator Bay to Dads Bay. The shoreline here has much palm and wax myrtle. Stroke it a full mile across Alligator Bay. Look southwest at the bulk of the bay. Pass a north-facing point and gain entry to Dads Bay at mile 6. The bulk of Dads Bay is also to the southwest. Keep along the east shore of the bay, and look for the Gator Bay Canal, which was likely a feeble drainage effort by land developers. Stay in Dads Bay to make a 10-foot-wide channel at marker #68. Turn east toward the "No Wake" sign and enter Plate Creek. Way back, Gregorio Lopez dropped a plate in the water here, giving Plate Creek its name. Buttonwoods reach over the creek as if trying to bridge it. The south bank almost passes for land. It certainly features palm, coco plum, and poisonwood on its shore.

Enter Plate Creek Bay at marker #65. Another canal leaves the bay from the north bank. It is possible to paddle up this creek a ways before it becomes overgrown. The Plate Creek chickee is visible, backed against an island in the bay at mile 8.5. This chickee is built on the pilings of an old land office complex. The larger pilings of the chickee shelter were parts of the water tower for the series of floating buildings. Cross Plate Creek Bay, an especially pretty place, with towering palms swaying over the varied mangrove forest below.

Come to an inlet and another modest creek at marker #63. There are clumps of land along this creek, too. It is but a short distance to Lostmans Five Bay. Paddle southeast across the bay to reach Lostmans Five campsite at the mouth of Lostmans Five Creek at mile 9.5. From here it is 8 miles to the Gulf on the Willy Willy and Lostmans River routes. It is 10 miles to Willy Willy campsite via the Willy Willy Route, using a portion of the Wilderness Waterway.

Gopher Key–Charley Creek Route

Begin: Darwins Place campsite	End: Turkey Key
Distance: 8 miles	Time: 4.5 hours
Potential tidal influence: 2	Potential wind influence: 2
Navigational challenge: 4	

Highlights: Bird life; storm devastation; historic shell mound; tight mangrove creek; alternate route to the Gulf to avoid high winds

Hazards: Bugs on Gopher Key; shallow water bays from Gopher Key to Pelican Bay

Campsites: Darwins Place, Turkey Key

Connections: Darwins Place Route, Turkey Key Route

The Gopher Key–Charley Creek Route is a quiet and seldom-stroked paddle on a small scenic stream that passes an old Calusa mound and roams through open, storm-damaged terrain before entering a narrow creek leading to the Gulf. This route leaves Cannon Bay near Darwins Place campsite and heads down Gopher Key Creek to Gopher Key. From here, the route heads toward the Gulf, nearing Pelican Bay before joining primeval Charley Creek in its winding journey to the ocean. Gopher Key was named after the boat that archaeologist Clarence B. Moore used in his early 1900s explorations of Calusa cultural sites in the Everglades. Once at Gopher Key, you can walk around and explore the hilly shell mound. Numerous birds roost and nest back here. The trees on Gopher Key are larger than those on most other shell mounds, and the storm-stripped landscape on the way to the Gulf contrasts sharply with Cannon Bay's thick mangrove forests. *Remember, mounds like this are protected, so no digging. Leave anything you happen to find. These are special treasures we should preserve for all to enjoy.* Be aware that while this route *can* be traveled at low tide, there may not be any water in the Gulf once you finish Charley Creek. Try to reach the big water on a rising or high falling tide if you want to get from Charley Creek over to Turkey Key.

Depart Darwins Place campsite, paddling south into Cannon Bay. If you look back toward Darwins Place, on the horizon you will see the gumbo-limbo trees towering over the mangrove. To find Gopher Creek, hug the west shoreline of Cannon Bay, passing between the shore and several islands in Cannon Bay. The mouth of Gopher Creek, at one-half mile, lies almost due south as you paddle. Pass a small teaser creek before coming to Gopher Key Creek. Gopher Key Creek's mouth is around 50 feet wide, soon tapering to about 30 feet. A "No Wake" sign was posted here in the past and may be still, so keep a look out. The banks are forested with red and black mangrove, and the water here is plenty deep so fallen trees pose no obstacle to the paddler.

After awhile, the forested banks give way to a shoreline of sea purslane and pickleweed, backed by younger mangrove. Dotting the shoreline, gangly, bleached skeletons of storm-damaged trees make the most striking feature of the landscape. Paddle to the northeastern arm of Gopher Key Bay. Continue southwest through this shallow bay into the main body of Gopher Key Bay at mile 2. Birds abound here, just as they do along the entire length of the creek.

Traverse the wide heart of the bay, keeping a southwesterly course to the continuation of Gopher Key Creek. At more than 40 feet, this second half of the stream is much wider than the first. It is also very shallow in spots. Keep your eyes peeled to the southwest. The taller vegetation of Gopher Key will be visible in the distance, especially the red-trunked gumbo-limbo trees.

Just before you get to Gopher Key at 3.4 miles, the creek splits. (This is the creek the nautical charts show going to the unnamed bay northwest of Rookery Bay.) Follow this creek, heading northwest on what looks like a small bay compared to the Gopher Key Creek channel. Stay with the right bank and look for a canoe-width clamshell landing between two mangrove trees. This is where you leave your craft to explore Gopher Key on foot. Get your bug dope ready! A small mound lies close by your landing site. Narrow "trails" made by previous explorers wind around the mound. These are often overgrown, so keep your compass handy just in case. Check out the fig trees and other vegetation that cloaks the numerous hills here. Imagine the time it took for this mound to accumulate, shell by shell.

As an alternate way to access Gopher Key, head farther up Gopher Key Creek on a high tide and take the east channel at a second split—away from the previously mentioned unnamed bay. Be aware, though, that when the water is low, the mud will be too thick to paddle and too thin to walk.

To continue toward Charley Creek, backtrack to the main artery of Gopher Key Creek, continuing southwest beyond Gopher Key. The stream breaks into shallow bays scattered with small islands. Do not head toward Rookery Bay. Instead, keep generally southwest in the very shallow water, aiming for Pelican Bay. The connecting waterway from here to Pelican Bay is NOT SHOWN on the nautical charts, but it can easily be seen on aerial maps. At 5 miles, Charley Creek splits right, away from the mix of open water and small islands. Most of Pelican Bay can still be seen to the southwest. Charley Creek passes through an open storm-damaged plain, its expanse punctuated by a few trees and many snags. This is the remote Everglades.

Looking south from Turkey Key toward the mouth of Charley Creek. Photo by author.

Charley Creek finally becomes a full-fledged creek. By 5.5 miles, canopy overhangs the water, and the creek narrows to a width of 15 feet or less. At 6 miles the creek splits. Stay right with the larger stream. Crabs by the thousands skitter away from the shoreline. Expect to work around fallen trees. The mangrove rises and the stream widens before reaching the Gulf at 6.7 miles. On a low tide, you may see nothing but a gigantic mud flat scattered with tree snags. Buzzard Key stands to the southwest, and the beaches on the south side of Turkey Key are visible in the distance. Paddle west to reach Turkey Key at 8 miles. The main camping area is around the west side of the island. From here, it is 8 miles south to Lostmans River and 3 miles north to Mormon Key on the Turkey Key Route.

Halfway Creek Canoe Trail

Begin: Tamiami Trail   End: Gulf Coast Ranger Station

Distance: 7.5 miles   Time: 4 hours

Potential tidal influence: 3   Potential wind influence: 2

Navigational challenge: 2

Highlights: Diverse habitats; mangrove tunnels

Hazards: Low water; strong tides under Halfway Creek bridge

Campsites: None

Connections: Halfway Creek Loop, Turner River Route, West Pass Route, Indian Key Pass Route, Sandfly Island Route

---

The Halfway Creek Canoe Trail is a microcosm of South Florida in many ways. It reveals human impact on the land and offers a good view of the land's beauty maintained under park protection. The trip starts with a paddle down a man-made canal, a landscape feature that is definitely part of South Florida today. Next, you'll cross an attractive habitat of sawgrass, cattails, and tree islands, before entering a strange and wonderful mangrove tunnel that turns to a brackish stream beneath a taller shady forest. The paddle exits the park boundary, passes by houses, goes under the bridge of an artificial causeway to emerge in open, busy Chokoloskee Bay, and ends at Gulf Coast Ranger Station. Consider paying for a shuttle from an outfitter in Everglades City to make this a one-way day paddle. Halfway Creek is not on the waterproof charts, but the route is marked most of the way and the Big Cypress National Preserve produces a fine map of this trail for your use. It is available at both the Everglades' Gulf Coast Ranger Station and Big Cypress Oasis Visitor Center.

Start your trip on the Tamiami Trail, U.S. 41. To get there from Everglades City, drive north on C.R. 29 for 3 miles to U.S. 41. Turn right to go east on 41, and drive 2 miles to Sea Grape Drive. Turn right on

Sea Grape Drive and follow it a short distance to the Halfway Creek landing.

Put into the canal and begin paddling southwesterly. Note the limestone banks here. The clear water flows by sawgrass, cattails, and occasional mangrove. Other freshwater plants adorn the dredge spoils of the south bank. Soon, pass the markers of an airboat trail that branches left from the canal. Leave the 40-foot-wide canal and come to the first lake at mile 1.1. Keep southwest. Numerous palms grace the shore.

Pass marker #1 toward the end of the meandering lake, keeping west past marker #2. A beautiful variety of South Florida vegetation surrounds you here, making for some of the most scenic paddling in this entire guidebook. The white PVC markers guide you in the right direction. Paddlers headed toward the Gulf will be looking at the green side of these markers. Paddlers heading away from the Gulf will be seeing the red side of the same markers. Reach marker #3 at 1.7 miles. Look to your right and you will see another PVC marker—L15. This signals the end point for paddlers making the Halfway Creek Loop from the opposite direction.

Continue down Halfway Creek. The trail alternates between small lakes and narrower creeks, keeping a generally southwesterly direction. Stay with the markers. Past marker #6 at 2.4 miles, tree limbs intertwine above Halfway Creek, eventually forming a tunnel that continues for a good distance. Keep a reasonable pace, not going too fast among the twists and turns of the tunnel. The water here is plenty deep, but at times you have to duck your head under vegetation.

You are still in the canopied tunnel when you reach marker #7 at 2.9 miles. A smaller creek branches off to your right, marked by PVC pipe L1. This is the beginning of the Halfway Creek Loop.

Keep paddling straight ahead. As you proceed down the Halfway Creek Canoe Trail, the creek becomes murky and pungent. The 2005 hurricanes have added even more fallen trees and brush to the water. The canopy rises and tidal influence increases as you continue downstream. Come to a major split in the creek at 5.5 miles. To your left (east), a creek leads toward Turner Lake and Left Hand Turner River. To your right (west), Halfway Creek widens and continues toward Chokoloskee Bay. Stay with Halfway Creek.

Leave the Everglades National Park boundary and pass a few houses on your right. Notice the Australian pine, Brazilian pepper, and other invasive exotic vegetation. The Plantation Island community is on your right, before the creek opens into a shallow bay. From here, the Causeway Route leads southeast 2 miles to Chokoloskee Island. Keep southwest on the Halfway Creek Canoe Trail, passing under the Halfway Creek bridge. Watch for strong tides flowing through here. Once under the bridge, turn northwest, passing a tour boat landing and two brown park service buildings to the Gulf Coast Ranger Station and the end of your route.

Halfway Creek Loop

Begin: Tamiami Trail at Sea Grape Drive	End: Tamiami Trail at Sea Grape Drive
Distance: 8.8 miles	Time: 4.5 hours
Potential tidal influence: 3	Potential wind influence: 2
Navigational challenge: 2	
Highlights: Loop paddle through diverse habitats; mangrove tunnels	
Hazards: Overgrown tunnels	
Campsites: None	
Connections: Halfway Creek Canoe Trail	

The Halfway Creek Loop paddle, located entirely within Big Cypress National Preserve, follows the first section of the Halfway Creek Canoe Trail, then spurs away from it in a series of creeks, ponds, and small lakes to make a circuit back to where you started. Leave Sea Grape Drive, taking a canal to Halfway Creek. Paddle this gorgeous waterway through tree-canopied tunnels and ponds before veering off to follow tidal creeks around the loop. The entire route is marked with numbered PVC pipes, which makes it a lot harder to get lost, even though you will be navigating mazelike terrain. Be aware that no matter when you travel, the tide will be with you for a portion of the trip and against you for the other. Winds won't be much of a factor, and this can be a doable paddle when breezes are high in the Glades. Like Halfway Creek Canoe Trail, you won't find this route on waterproof nautical charts, but the Big Cypress National Preserve produces a good map of this loop for your use. You can also go to the back of this book and use Map #2, created from a GPS track.

To start the loop, follow the put-in directions for Halfway Creek Canoe Trail, and begin paddling southwesterly through crystalline water bordered by sawgrass, cattails, and occasional mangrove. Other freshwater plants adorn the south bank, where the canal dredge spoil has created dry ground. Soon, pass the markers of an airboat trail that branches east. Reach the first lake and the end of the canal at 1.1 miles.

Keep southwest. Pass marker #1 toward the end of the lake. Keep west past marker #2. Tall palms rise above the mangrove understory. Reach marker #3 at 1.7 miles. Look to your right across the water and you will see PVC marker L15. This is where you will come out after completing your loop. For now, continue down Halfway Creek.

The trail alternates between small lakes and narrower creeks, keeping a generally southwesterly direction. Stay with the markers. Beyond marker #6 at 2.4 miles, mangrove limbs overhang the slender creek, meshing to form a tunnel that continues a good distance. Keep an unhurried pace among the twists and turns of the tunnel. You may have to duck your head under low-hanging branches, but the water will be plenty deep.

You are still in the canopied tunnel when you reach marker #7 at 2.9 miles. A smaller creek branches off to your right, marked by

PVC pipe L1. Take this right, the beginning of Halfway Creek Loop. From this point on, the PVC pipes are marked with the letter L and sequentially higher numbers, from 1 to 15, as you proceed around the loop. The creek is hemmed in by arching limbs and tree roots, making for a tight but enchanting passage. Numerous ferns along the way indicate that the terrain is a bit drier than that bordering Halfway Creek. The drainage here heads for the Barron River. Be prepared for very sharp convolutions, requiring some fancy steering on your part.

Proceed further into tidal waters, vaulted by the mangroves' stained prop roots, then open onto a small shallow pond at 3.8 miles and marker L3. Soon, open into a big lake, keeping west along its south shore to shortly bisect a strait at 4.2 miles and marker L5. Turn right here, and begin looping northbound into a funneling channel-turned-creek. No canopy will overhang your passage, and the tidal waters will probably shift to a direction opposite the one you have up to this point experienced. Keep northeast at marker L7, then proceed to marker L8 at 5 miles. Keep left here in a slender channel that will soon open into a pond. Follow a northerly course through an alternating pattern of ponds and channels. Some of these channels are bordered by mangrove; some are canopied, while others aren't.

Stay left at marker L12 at 6.2 miles. Enjoy the tea-colored but clear water below which the channel bottom usually shows. A keen eye will spot slow-moving crabs and darting fish. Continue your route of alternating ponds and creeks, watching for the reappearance of palms and buttonwood before reaching marker L14 and a lake at 6.7 miles. Bear southeast here, passing the sawgrass that borders the lake. Reach the end of the lake and your last marker, L15, at 7.1 miles. You have now rejoined Halfway Creek and completed the loop. From here, keep left and backtrack 1.7 miles up Halfway Creek to the put-in.

Hurddles Creek Route

Begin: Chokoloskee	End: Sunday Bay chickee
Distance: 7.5 miles	Time: 3.5 hours
Potential tidal influence: 3	Potential wind influence: 2
Navigational challenge: 3	

Highlights: Calusa shell mound

Hazards: Motorboats in Chokoloskee Bay

Campsites: Sunday Bay chickee

Connections: Turner River Canoe Trail, Lopez River Route, Last Huston Bay Route, Huston River Route

---

Hurddles Creek is the preferred route for southbound paddlers from Chokoloskee using the "inside" routes. There are fewer motorboats on this than on the Lopez River Route, and it also traverses more varied and sheltered waters, in addition to passing a Calusa shell mound on the way. The route begins with a paddle up the Turner River, passing the shell mound, to Hurddles Creek with its tall mangrove. Then, it traverses the Cross Bays to intersect the Wilderness Waterway at Crooked Creek, tracing the Wilderness Waterway a short distance before splitting off to Sunday Bay chickee.

Start your route at the boat ramp on the north end of Chokoloskee Island, near Outdoor Resorts. Leave the ramp and paddle easterly toward the Turner River. Pass a few minuscule mangrove islands just before coming to Wilderness Waterway marker #129, at the mouth of the Turner River.

Cross the Wilderness Waterway and enter the Turner River, hugging the south bank. Mixed mangroves of varying size crowd the river. About half a mile up the south side of the river is an old Calusa shell mound. Look for the nearly vertical bank of shell, dotted with a variety of hammock shrub and tree species. Parts of this mound reach an elevation of 19 feet, a dizzying height by South Florida standards.

Keep paddling up the deep river, passing Left Hand Turner River on the north at mile 1.5. The Turner River veers east and diverges into two channels. The now-smaller Turner River splits easterly, while the wider Hurddles Creek goes southeast. Take Hurddles Creek at 2 miles. Soon, pass a small creek coming in from the east. This creek heads east into Hells Half Acre, a maze of ponds and channels where paddlers get lost. Stay away! Hurddles Creek, meanwhile, is about 50 feet wide and bordered by tall mangrove as it meanders southeasterly to Mud Bay.

Enter shallow Mud Bay, passing a little island on your right. Veer easterly toward the creek that exits Mud Bay. This is the continuation of Hurddles Creek, wider than before. It makes a sharp U-turn south before coming to the first of the Cross Bays at 4 miles. The shallowness of these bays discourages motorboat traffic, especially at low tide. Keep southeast across the bay, traversing a channel to the second of the Cross Bays. Keep southeast across this bay, which narrows into yet another creek. In the creek, stay with the left (northeast) bank, pass an island, then intersect Wilderness Waterway marker #125 at 6 miles. The Lopez River Route and the Wilderness Waterway have come 7 miles from Chokoloskee.

It is another mile to Wilderness Waterway marker #123 in Sunday Bay at 7 miles. Paddle easterly in the direction the arrow on the marker points toward what looks like one island but is actually two. Come to a slight split between the two islands. Look north between the two islands, and you will see Sunday Bay chickee, perched against the mangrove in a small bay of its own at mile 7. The Last Huston Bay Route continues southeast via the Wilderness Waterway. The Huston River Route starts 1.5 miles south of the chickee at Wilderness Waterway marker #119.

Huston River Route

Begin: Wilderness Waterway
marker #119 at Sunday Bay

End: Mormon Key

Distance: 9 miles

Time: 5 hours

Potential tidal influence: 4

Potential wind influence: 3

Navigational challenge: 2

Highlights: Solitude

Hazards: Shoals in Huston River

Campsites: Mormon Key

Connections: Last Huston Bay Route, Chatham River Route, Pavilion
Key Route, Turkey Key Route

The Huston River Route is one of the best lesser-used connectors between the Gulf and the interior bays of the Wilderness Waterway. From its obscure beginning near Sunday Bay to the shallows of House Hammock Bay to the shifting shoals and propeller-eating oyster bars of Huston River, this route naturally repels motorboaters. Such obstacles need not deter paddlers. The sole navigationally challenging section is among the many isles just before the Gulf. The only busy segment is out in the Gulf, from Gun Rock Point to Mormon Key. From Sunday Bay, the route is southerly to House Hammock Bay. Beyond the bay, it follows the Huston River southwest into island-dotted Storter Bay, where the Chatham and Huston rivers meet and flow into the Gulf at Chatham Bend. From the Gulf, it isn't far to the beach campsite at Mormon Key.

Start your route at Wilderness Waterway Marker #119 in the southeastern corner of Sunday Bay. Paddle southerly past some tiny isles, and enter the channel that flows 1.3 miles to open into House Hammock Bay. This bay was named for Dan House who, along with his family, homesteaded an old shell mound in the vicinity. Keep southeast across the bay, entering the Huston River at mile 3. To

Raccoons are sometimes seen digging around riverside oyster bars. Photo by Constance Mier.

your left (east), the river leads half a mile to Huston Bay. To your right (southwest), Huston River leads to the Gulf. Head southwest.

The river is over 200 feet wide here, with an occasional solitary island growing on shallow oyster and mud bars. The preponderance of these bars keeps all but the most intrepid motorboaters from using this river. Stay along the northwest bank and look for a ring of Brazilian pepper bushes fringing a peninsula that juts out from shore. Here, at mile 4, stands another shell mound, built by the Calusa and later known as Camp Huston by local white settlers.

The river widens and turns southeast, broken by myriad shoals. The islands increase in size and number as you enter Storter Bay at 7 miles. If the winds are high, it's possible to cut easterly across Storter Bay to reach the Chatham River here. Stay along the Chatham's shore to reach Mormon Key, avoiding open Gulf water. Otherwise, follow the deep channel of the Huston River—cut by strong tides among these islands—to enter the Gulf at mile 7.5. The peninsula of Gun Rock Point will be to your right. The main beach of Mormon Key will be visible to your left (south), across Chatham Bend. Aim south for the beach at Mormon Key, arriving there at 9 miles. This is an agreeable campsite and a good location for heading in either direction on the Gulf. From here it is 8 miles south to Hog Key via the Turkey Key Route. It is 8.5 miles to Rabbit Key on the Pavilion Key Route.

Indian Key Pass Route

Begin: Gulf Coast Ranger Station   End: Picnic Key

Distance: 7.5 miles   Time: 4 hours

Potential tidal influence: 5   Potential wind influence: 3

Navigational challenge: 2

Highlights: Fastest route to outer Ten Thousand Islands; local culture

Hazards: Commercial fishing boats and recreation boats

Campsites: Tiger Key, Picnic Key

Connections: West Pass Route, Pavilion Key Route, White Horse Key Route, Sandfly Pass Route, Rabbit Key Pass Route, Halfway Creek Canoe Trail, Causeway Route

---

Sometimes, to get to a scenic destination, you travel the shortest distance between two points, even though the route may not be so appealing. Such is the case with Indian Key Pass Route. While it connects the Gulf Coast Ranger Station with the superior camping destinations of Picnic Key, Tiger Key, and areas north of the park, this marked route is a veritable highway of tour boats, recreational motorboats, and commercial fishing vessels. It can be engaging to see all the watercraft, but that may not be your idea of a natural experience. Think of Indian Key Pass as your highway to the Gulf, only this highway has some brawny tides that should be worked to your advantage, if possible. Your first task is to span Chokoloskee Bay to enter marked Indian Key Pass, cruising between the islands while sidestepping boats. Eventually, the route opens into the Gulf, with Indian Key guarding the mouth of the pass. Slicing through a few mangrove islands, the route ends at Picnic Key, where there is a beach and a campsite.

Start your route from the canoe landing at Gulf Coast Ranger Station. Try not to leave here at dead low tide; it's hard to load your boat and harder to paddle in the sloppy, swallowing mud that can be exposed when the water is down. Paddle westerly across shallow Chokoloskee Bay, immediately passing a couple of channel markers connecting Barron River to Sandfly Pass. Stay westerly, aiming for Indian Key Pass. Watch for boats coming out of the pass across Chokoloskee Bay toward the Barron River. (Its mouth is near the ranger station.) A few islands will be off to your right, between you and the marked channel of Indian Key Pass. At 1.5 miles, intersect the pass at channel marker #24 and the welcome sign for Everglades National Park.

Enter the channel of Indian Key Pass. Numerous small mangrove islands here make it easy to see why this area was dubbed Ten Thousand Islands. The dry ground on a few islands represents the spoils from dredging the Indian Key Pass channel to make it deep enough for some of the big boats that travel this way. Continue westerly, as low mangrove islands give way to a taller shoreline with bays splitting off the pass. The channel widens and turns southwesterly at marker #15. Watch for tour boats, pleasure boats, fishing boats, and any other boats you can imagine, as well as a few sea kayaks and canoes.

A little beyond marker #10, at 3 miles, the Gulf opens up before you. Keep your craft aimed for channel marker #6. If the winds are strong, consider cutting between some of the mangrove islands due west of marker #6 and maneuvering the waters to emerge on Gaskin Bay and the east side of Picnic Key. Otherwise, stay with the pass toward Indian Key, swinging northwesterly around the Gulf side of the Stop Keys and their shallows at 6.5 miles. Look for the sandy, Gulf-facing, southwest side of Picnic Key at 7.5 miles. Here, a long beach backed by coastal vegetation makes for a good campsite. The

Tiger Key beach is only 1 mile distant around the far side of Tiger Key. From Picnic Key, it is 7 miles to Rabbit Key via the Pavilion Key Route. It is 9.5 miles back to Gulf Coast Ranger Station via West Pass Route. It is 2.5 miles to Camp Lulu Key via the White Horse Key Route.

Last Huston Bay Route

Begin: Sunday Bay chickee	End: Wilderness Waterway marker #99 at Chatham River
Distance: 7 miles	Time: 3.5 hours
Potential tidal influence: 2	Potential wind influence: 4
Navigational challenge: 2	

Highlights: Paddling Wilderness Waterway

Hazards: Motorboats on channels of Wilderness Waterway

Campsites: Sunday Bay chickee

Connections: Hurddles Creek Route, Huston River Route, Chatham River Route, Darwins Place Route

Last Huston Bay Route traces the Wilderness Waterway as it travels southeasterly through a series of broad bays broken by brief channels. The entire paddle path is marked at strategic points by small brown park service signs. Even though this route is on the "inside," the open bays can get bumpy in big winds, though tidal influence will only be felt in the channels between bays. Motorboats frequent this route while fishing the Glades, so stay alert in the channels.

Leave Sunday Bay chickee and return to the Wilderness Waterway and marker #123. Paddle southerly down the Wilderness Waterway into the end of Sunday Bay as it funnels past marker #121. Slip into and through a few islands, passing marker #120. Shortly, come to marker #119. The channel to the south behind the two small isles is the beginning of the Huston River Route, 9 miles from Mormon

Key. Continue to move through the channel, passing an open bay to your left. Paddle directly to marker #117 where, between two islands, you will see marker #116. Then, turn south to marker #115. (All three markers cover only a short distance.) Proceed southeasterly to marker #114 and the open water of Oyster Bay. This should not be confused with the Oyster Bay near Whitewater Bay. Passing markers #112 and #110, stroke it south across *this* Oyster Bay for a flank of isles. Bisect another flank of isles to open into Huston Bay and marker #108 at 3.5 miles.

Head straight for the island fronted by an old house on stilts and skirt the east side of the island. This is the last built-on inholding in the park. Now paddle for the pass on the southeast end of the bay at Wilderness Waterway marker #103. Beyond this pass is wide-open Last Huston Bay. This bay, like the previous two, is around 2–4 feet deep, with brown-tinted clear water bordered by low mangrove. Stay with the south bank to the south corner of Last Huston Bay.

At the corner, progress beyond marker #101 into a channel. This channel splits at marker #100. To your right (west) is a channel leading to the Chatham River. You proceed left (southeasterly) and come to Wilderness Waterway marker #99 at mile 7. Here, you intersect the Chatham River Route. It is less than 2 miles southwest down the Chatham River Route to the Watson Place campsite, and it is 2 miles northeast up the Chatham River Route to Sweetwater chickee. The Darwins Place Route starts here and heads southeasterly down the Wilderness Waterway 9.5 miles to Lostmans Five campsite.

Lopez River Route

Begin: Chokoloskee	End: Wilderness Waterway marker #125 at Crooked Creek
Distance: 7 miles	Time: 3.5 hours
Potential tidal influence: 3	Potential wind influence: 4
Navigational challenge: 2	

Highlights: Gregorio Lopez homesite

Hazards: Motorboats in Chokoloskee Bay

Campsites: Lopez River

Connections: Hurddles Creek Route, Causeway Route

Lopez River Route is a busy route for all boaters. It is the primary access route into the backcountry from Chokoloskee, tracing the Wilderness Waterway over its entire course. The route begins at the landing on Chokoloskee and crosses open Chokoloskee Bay, fronted by the houses of Chokoloskee Island. It then enters the shoaly Lopez River, passing a homesite turned campsite on the south bank, and continues up the Lopez to Crooked Creek, which winds its way up to an arm of Sunday Bay. Though this route is on the Wilderness Waterway, it is anything but wild. From the houses of Chokoloskee to the heavy motorboat traffic, it feels more like paddling around a marina. But it's the way to go if you plan to camp at Lopez River campsite.

Leave the pay dock of Outdoor Resorts at Chokoloskee. The dock has a launch fee and a daily parking fee. Paddle around the north point of the island, then stroke it southeast across Chokoloskee Bay. The colorful island houses will keep your eyes entertained, but watch for motorboats as you traverse the shallow waters. Aim for the northeast shore of the bay—the mainland—and paddle parallel to it, passing channel markers indicating the deeper water.

Continue along the northeast shore and enter the mouth of the Lopez River. A mud bar extends far from shore here, but it shouldn't present a problem for paddlers. Notice the deep-water channel marker far out in the river. The Lopez funnels to about 140 feet wide. Except for a couple of spots where there are grown-over shell mounds, the shore is dense mangrove before the river makes a couple of sharp bends. Come to the Lopez River campsite at 5 miles, also on a Calusa mound. This land was settled and farmed by Gregorio Lopez, who came to the area from Spain in 1890. The landing here is a shoreline of shell. A cistern lies in view of the river. Water that ran off the roof of Lopez' house was stored in it for his use.

Pass the campsite and continue up the tapering Lopez River before you reach Crooked Creek and Wilderness Waterway marker #126 at mile 6. Turn east up the mouth of Crooked Creek, which joins the Lopez River at an acute angle. The creek winds and curves, building mud bars on its inside bends. Listen for motorboats coming around the sharp bends. Pass a white channel marker just before emerging onto an arm of Sunday Bay and the Wilderness Waterway at marker #125, mile 7. From here, it's 1.5 miles southeasterly to the Sunday Bay chickee on the Hurddles Creek Route. From the Sunday Bay chickee, continue southerly on the Wilderness Waterway via the Last Huston Bay Route. To the northwest, it is 5.5 miles back to Chokoloskee via the Hurddles Creek Route.

Pavilion Key Route

Begin: Picnic Key	End: Mormon Key
Distance: 15.5 miles	Time: 8 hours
Potential tidal influence: 5	Potential wind influence: 5
Navigational challenge: 3	

Highlights: Gulf paddling among the Ten Thousand Islands; good campsites

Hazards: Big winds and waves in the Gulf

Campsites: Picnic Key, Rabbit Key, Pavilion Key, Mormon Key

Connections: West Pass Route, White Horse Key Route, Indian Key Pass Route, Rabbit Key Pass Route, Huston River Route, Chatham River Route, Turkey Key Route

Pavilion Key Route traverses the portion of the Ten Thousand Islands within the boundaries of Everglades National Park. I like to island hop along the outermost keys that extend into the Gulf, but there are as many variations to the route as there are islands to check out along the way. The many campsites on the route make extended stays and explorations of the vicinity possible, and you will be surrounded by fantastic scenery everywhere you look. The route leaves Picnic Key just before Indian Key Pass, which links the Gulf to Chokoloskee. The paddle path is toward Jewel Key, then across open water to Rabbit Key, where you can also camp. The route then turns southerly to arrive at big Pavilion Key, another camping spot. From here, the route crosses Chatham Bend, where Mormon Key, and your final camping option, awaits. The paddling on this route can turn as scary as the trip is beautiful. Unfavorable winds and tides can make the route formidable, especially out near Pavilion Key. More small craft have capsized between Pavilion Key and Mormon Key than anywhere else in the park. Use good timing and better judgment in choosing your exact passage.

Leave Picnic Key and paddle south around the Stop Keys. Stay on the Gulf side of the Stop Keys shallows. Dead ahead is Indian Key, where there used to be a backcountry campsite. Aim for the lighted buoy adjacent to Indian Key, watching for boat traffic through the Indian Key Pass. Make the Gulf and turn southeast, where many other keys lie in the distance to the east. Pass what's left of Comer Key, which was nearly scoured of vegetation in a big storm. It was once the camping ground of fisherman and Alabama governor, Braxton Bragg Comer, for whom the island is named. Jewel Key precedes Chokoloskee Pass. Chokoloskee Pass is marked by a large wooden post. Jewel Key is now a designated backcountry campsite, though its beach is rocky by Everglades standards. The camping area is on the inside of the island, away from the Gulf. From Jewel Key, it is 4.5 miles to the Gulf Coast Ranger Station via the Sandfly Island Route. Watch for shallows on the south side of Chokoloskee Pass.

From here, a direct line for Rabbit Key requires crossing wide-open water. If the waves are imposing, flank the islands closer to the mainland. From Jewel Key, Rabbit Key and the other islands appear to be uninterrupted shoreline. Make a compass bearing for Rabbit

Key and stick with it. While you're in the open water, look beyond Turtle Key for the marked Rabbit Key Pass. It leads to Chokoloskee Bay. The Rabbit Key Pass Route leads 5.5 miles to Chokoloskee Island from Rabbit Key. On the Pavilion Key Route, come to Rabbit Key at mile 7. Approach the island on the north side, shooting for the strait between Rabbit and Lumber keys. The Rabbit Key campsite is in a lagoon near the strait.

Depart Rabbit Key and shoot southerly past Crate Key for Pavilion Key, which is the island farthest out on the horizon's Gulf side. Beyond Crate Key the mainland is hardly visible, obscured by the numerous islands to your east. Keep southerly toward Pavilion Key. As you approach this stripped and sometimes-submerged isle, Little Pavilion Key will look like a dot against the much larger Pavilion Key. Little Pavilion Key is a good birding spot.

As you near Pavilion Key, aim for the sandy spit on the northern end of the island where the spit meets the forest. This is where the main camp lies. At low tide, Little Pavilion Key will reveal a sandbar to paddle around. In the early 1900s, clam diggers lived in small stilt-houses around Little Pavilion Key. They wore canvas "shoes" around their feet that protected them from getting cut yet still allowed them to feel around for clams beneath the sand. A good digger could hand harvest more than 15 bushels of clams a day.

Reach Pavilion Key at 11 miles. This key is a beach camper's dream come true—a long, sloping swath of sand that stretches toward an endless horizon of water. Other campers will be here, having had the same dream. Learn to share this Everglades National Park highlight.

Leave the northern tip of Pavilion Key, paddling toward the mainland, then southeasterly between some mangrove islands toward Mormon Key, which at this distance blends with the main shoreline. Cross open water, being mindful of the history of capsized craft here. Duck Rock is off to your left. This treeless island used to be a rookery until it was stripped of vegetation by Hurricane Donna in 1960. A few small mangroves are now coming back.

Between Pavilion Key and Mormon Key, the coastline turns from southeast running to south running. This coastal turn is known as Chatham Bend, for the Chatham River that flows into the Gulf at the bend. The high beach of Mormon Key will face you, becoming visible as you get closer to the island. A smaller key south of Mormon Key will also have a visible beach.

Reach Mormon Key at 15.5 miles. This island was once home to a man who lived here with his first and second wives, giving the island its name. It is now a fine backcountry campsite. From here, it is 11 miles south to Lostmans Ranger Station along the Gulf on the Turkey Key Route. It is 4 miles east to Watsons Place on the Chatham River Route and 9 miles to Sunday Bay on the Huston River Route.

Rabbit Key Pass Route

Begin: Rabbit Key	End: Chokoloskee
Distance: 5.5 miles	Time: 3 hours
Potential tidal influence: 4	Potential wind influence: 4
Navigational challenge: 2	

Highlights: Short connection to Gulf

Hazards: Motorboats in Chokoloskee Bay

Campsites: Rabbit Key

Connections: Pavilion Key Route, Sandfly Island Route, Hurddles Creek Route, Lopez River Route, Causeway Route, Turner River Route

Rabbit Key Pass Route is marked most of the way. It takes you from the beauty of the Ten Thousand Islands back to the civilized world at Chokoloskee. The route begins on the open Gulf, then enters the deep channel of Rabbit Key Pass to meander among some islands and open into Chokoloskee Bay. Here it passes alongside Chokoloskee Island, where you can observe the still-changing face of this one-time shell mound.

From Rabbit Key campsite, paddle northward around the edge of Lumber Key toward Turtle Key. Just on the sandy east point of Turtle Key at mile 1 is the first marker for Rabbit Key Pass. Though the markers here aren't numbered, each wooden post is painted with a white triangular arrow that points toward the deeper side of the channel. Paddlers need not be as concerned as other boaters with staying on the deep side of the channel, just with going the right direction in the channel.

Look northeast for more white markers. Trace the markers into the deep pass. Don't fall for the open-water trap, but head more northeasterly on the narrower route. Soon the waters open again, and there are two sets of markers at mile 2.7. One set continues easterly into an open bay, while the other set heads left, northerly, through a much smaller channel. Follow the more sheltered northerly route, which splits some islands. The markers confusingly turn back toward the Gulf for a moment, but they are working around some shallows before veering Chokoloskee way again. The mangrove shoreline takes on a hilly appearance here, as the shorter waterside trees give way to taller mangrove away from the water. The channel widens into Chokoloskee Bay—and the civilized world appears before you. There are some shallows ahead, which you will have to paddle around at low tide. Your best bet is to aim for Chokoloskee, then circle the island to the right.

Come to the south tip of the island at mile 4.7. Take in the scenery here, observing evidence of Chokoloskee's evolution from fishing village to tourist, retiree, and snowbird destination. The mouth of Turner River appears on your right before you come to the pay landing of Outdoor Resorts at mile 5.5. From here, it is 3 miles to the Gulf Coast Ranger Station via the Causeway Route; 9 miles to U.S. 41 on the Turner River Canoe Trail; 5 miles to the Lopez River campsite via the Lopez River Route; and 7 miles to Sunday Bay chickee via the Hurddles Creek Route.

Sandfly Island Route

Begin: Gulf Coast Ranger Station

End: Rabbit Key

Distance: 8 miles

Time: 5 hours

Potential tidal influence: 4

Potential wind influence: 4

Navigational challenge: 2

Highlights: Nature trail on Sandfly Island; Gulf connector

Hazards: Motorboats in Chokoloskee Bay and Sandfly Pass

Campsites: Rabbit Key

Connections: Indian Key Pass Route, Pavilion Key Route, West Pass Route, Halfway Creek Canoe Trail, Causeway Route, Rabbit Key Pass Route

---

This route leaves busy Chokoloskee Bay to enter Sandfly Pass after first reaching Sandfly Island. One option is to enjoy Sandfly Island with its nature trail and simply turn around for a 4-mile round trip. Sandfly Island was once inhabited by the Calusa and then by white settlers until the national park era. Before tackling the nature trail, inquire at the ranger station about bug conditions on Sandfly Island. Beyond Sandfly Island, this route takes Sandfly Pass into the island-studded Gulf, where a southeasterly track will lead you to Rabbit Key, a designated backcountry campsite.

Start your paddle at the Gulf Coast Ranger Station kayak and canoe launch. Direct your craft almost due south from the launch into Chokoloskee Bay, passing between markers #5 and #6 and a manatee warning sign. You are now tracing the marked channel of Sandfly Pass. Keep south, passing a series of markers whose numerals decrease and a sign welcoming you to Everglades National Park just before mile 1. Pass marker #1 and #2, then turn southwest to enter Sandfly Pass proper. The channel here is a good 110 feet wide and bordered by high mangrove.

White pelicans gather near Chokoloskee Pass. Photo by Jean S.

The dock of Sandfly Island will come into view not long after you enter the pass. It is also visible from the second floor of the ranger station, where you started. The push and pull of the tide is evident here in the pass. Look for a shell landing beneath the mangrove just before you reach the dock at mile 2. Pull your craft onto the shell and tie up to a mangrove tree. The Sandfly Nature Trail starts near the dock.

The paddle route keeps south beyond the Sandfly Island dock, passing a shell landing below some gumbo-limbo trees. As the pass turns southwest, the water flows among some small islands. Here, at 2.7 miles, motorboaters keep south on an unnamed channel for the Gulf. Sandfly Pass continues between peninsulas and shallow coves, opening into the Gulf at 3.7 miles. To the south you can see the sands of Jewel Key and a few scraggly trees on what is left of Comer Key. Once in the open Gulf, aim for Demijohn Key. You may feel the tidal pull of Chokoloskee Pass before reaching Demijohn Key at 5.5 miles. Rabbit Key stands out on the horizon. If the winds are howling, consider weaving among the mangrove islands. Otherwise, head through open water, crossing Rabbit Key Pass. The beaches of Rabbit Key take shape, and you reach the island at 8 miles. The primary camping area is on the northeast side of the key. From here it is 8.5 miles south to Mormon Key and 7 miles north to Picnic Key via the Pavilion Key Route. It is also 5.5 miles to Chokoloskee via the Rabbit Key Pass Route.

Sandfly Nature Trail

Leave the dock and immediately pass the cistern, foundation, and spring of the Boggess family, who farmed the island, once cultivating more than 30 acres of tomatoes. They came here in 1912. As you walk the island, try imagining it as your permanent home, with no modern conveniences and sparse contact with the outside world. Imagine what the Boggess family would think of their "back of beyond" if they could see it today!

The nature trail splits; take the left fork. The hammock forest here is rich with gumbo-limbo, poisonwood, and pigeon plum. Mangrove drapes low-lying areas. Look for the telltale tamarind trees that indicate a homestead—perhaps another Boggess family dwelling. Swing around to the west side of the island, gaining glimpses of the water beyond Sandfly. Watch for a strangler fig engulfing a cabbage palm right on the path. The final feature of the trail is a boardwalk that extends over a creek and beneath a tall mangrove forest just before you complete the loop.

Turkey Key Route

Begin: Mormon Key	End: Mouth of Lostmans River
Distance: 11 miles	Time: 6 hours
Potential tidal influence: 5	Potential wind influence: 5
Navigational challenge: 2	

Highlights: Beach campsites; historic islands

Hazards: Strong winds and big waves in the Gulf

Campsites: Mormon Key, New Turkey Key, Turkey Key, Hog Key

Connections: Pavilion Key Route, Chatham River Route, Gopher Key–Charley Creek Route, Highland Beach Route, Lostmans River Route

Turkey Key Route encompasses several island campsites and even more keys as it heads down the Gulf to the mouth of Lostmans River.

Many of these once-inhabited islands have reverted to a wilder state. The points of these keys are often sandy, while the bulk of the isles are mangrove. Shallows scattered among the islands may be exposed at low tide, and it can be extremely shallow by the mainland at all times. The mainland along this route is mangrove with an occasional bit of beach. Gnarled bleached trees add to the setting. The wind may play a role in the exact paddle path you choose on this route. There are four campsites along the way, so you can stretch this leg of your journey out for days. Fishing can also be productive in these keys.

Start your route by leaving Mormon Key, where there is a fine backcountry campsite, and paddling around the shallow west side of the island. Start south for a crowded group of keys. At low tide, you will have to stay on the Gulf side to keep from running aground, but bisect the keys if possible for the most scenery.

Once beyond these islands, aim for the channel between New Turkey Key and an unnamed mangrove key closer to the mainland. Tall pilings mark the channel. Watch for motorboats here. The best approach to the New Turkey Key campsite is from the southeast, beyond the pilings. The primary camping area here is on the mainland side of this slender island, 2 miles beyond Mormon Key.

Paddle southeast from New Turkey Key to Turkey Key. The island, 1 mile distant, is visible, and the signed camping area is directly in front of you on the key's west side. I once spent two days here, trapped by gale-force winds. In pre-park days, this was a rendezvous point for fishermen who would turn in their catch to a boat from Chokoloskee and receive supplies. It is now an excellent paddler's camp whose shallow approach discourages motorboaters. From here, the Gopher Key–Charley Creek Route leads 8 miles to Darwins Place campsite.

Leave Turkey Key and paddle south past Buzzard Key into the Plover Keys. At low tide, numerous snags will be exposed along the islands, and the inside way can be impassable for lack of water. This is an attractive group of islands with scattered beach areas among the mangrove. The Gulf-facing points are storm scarred, studded with leafless trees. The southeast side of Plover Key has the most extensive section of beach among these islands. Continue down the coast for Bird Key. The creatures that gave the key its name inhabit it still. The combination of nearby food and relative safety from predators make this an attractive spot for them.

The beach at Porpoise Point on Wood Key is visible from Bird Key. But first will come Boggess Point, facing west into the Gulf. If the winds are strong, you may want to take the inside route by Toms Bight. Either way, pass Wood Key and look for coconut palms on the island's south side. They are a reminder of the days when this island was occupied by several families. There was once even a small school here. Traverse Wood Key Cove to Hog Key, arriving at mile 9. Here is an attractive beach campsite backed by large sea grape. There are still hogs on Hog Key. Also note the storm-scarred tamarind tree. Leave Hog Key and swing southeast beside a long point of land leading into Lostmans River. At some pilings on the point, come to the Lostmans Ranger Station site. The old station tower, a paddlers landmark, is now gone. The shell-covered high ground of the ranger station is fairly extensive. I have seen deer here. End your route at 11 miles. From here it is 3.5 miles south to Highland point on the Highland Beach Route. It is 6 miles east to the Wilderness Waterway at marker #52 on the Lostmans River Route.

Turner River Canoe Trail

Begin: Tamiami Trail	End: Chokoloskee
Distance: 9 miles	Time: 5 hours
Potential tidal influence: 2	Potential wind influence: 2
Navigational challenge: 4	
Highlights: Diverse habitats	
Hazards: Motorboats in Chokoloskee Bay	

Campsites: None

Connections: Hurddles Creek Route, Rabbit Key Pass Route, Lopez River Route, Causeway Route

---

Turner River Canoe Trail may be the most botanically diverse paddle in the Everglades. It starts on the Tamiami Trail in Big Cypress National Preserve amid a freshwater environment dominated by towering cypress trees. It opens into sawgrass, broken by occasional tree islands, makes multiple tight squeezes through eerie tree tunnels, then transforms to classic mangrove-zone environment before intersecting the Hurddles Creek Route at Hurddles Creek. The trail continues down the Turner River as the river opens up and passes a high, historic Calusa Indian mound before arriving at civilized Chokoloskee Island. In the 1950s a canal was dug near the upper Turner, diverting much of its water and altering the ecosystem. Now, the water has been redirected to the Turner in an effort to restore the river.

This is a great day paddle or unconventional starting point for longer trips. (A canoe launch with restrooms and parking adds to paddlers' convenience at the outset.) The paddling on this trail can be tough and very slow. Also, be aware that later in the paddling season, late February or March, the river can be too low to paddle. Early in the route, shallow water and hydrilla, an invasive aquatic plant, combine for slow going. Next, the tree tunnels are very constricted, making steering and paddling difficult at best. Long touring sea kayaks don't work well here, though shorter ones seem to fare slightly better. The double-bladed paddle makes for very hard work in tight tunnels with sharp turns. To best enjoy this trail, take a canoe and consider paying an outfitter to provide shuttle for a one-way trip or to lead you on a guided nature paddle.

Start at the landing just west of the Turner River bridge. To access this landing from Everglades City, drive north on State Road 29 to U.S. 41. Turn right on 41 and drive for 6 miles to the Turner River.

Turn left into the canoe launch parking area. Put in at the launch and briefly parallel U.S. 41 before passing under the low bridge. Begin paddling south on a clear stream filled with hydrilla. The channel soon constricts to less than 15 feet. Your immediate surroundings are freshwater plant species: maple, pond apple, cypress, cattails, willow. Sawgrass-displacing cattails have made a recent appearance due to fertilizer runoff from the farming region north of the Everglades National Park.

This river was named for a guide, Richard B. Turner, who led U.S. forces up the waterway in search of Seminoles in 1857. The force, under John Parkhill, went upriver and destroyed some Indian villages. Later, Parkhill was killed in an ambush, and the bluecoats retreated to the Gulf.

Come to the first mangrove tunnel just a short distance into the paddle. Here, roots of red mangrove form a gauntlet for your craft. Overhead, intertwined tree branches and leaves crowd out the sun, leaving scant room for your canoe. Notice the profusion of epiphytes or air plants that grow on the mangrove branches. The water is shallow and crystalline. The going is slow. Briefly open into a pond at 1 mile. Stay right and reenter the mangrove tunnel to emerge finally into a different environment. Here, cattails, sawgrass, and willows provide an open and bright contrast to the cool shady tunnel.

Intersect an old canal and turn right; the canal is blocked to the left. Continue in the open water, occasionally passing sawgrass-ringed tree islands. One of these islands of palm, on river left at 2.1 miles, provides a dry spot to take a break. The river here varies in width but stays deep enough to paddle with ease as you enter a very short second mangrove tunnel. There will be mangrove on river right and sawgrass on the left. Pay close attention here and look for another tunnel diverging right. This tunnel is marked by a PVC pipe.

Take this tunnel to the right, soon passing an Everglades National Park boundary sign at 2.6 miles. This third tunnel is a little roomier than the first but is still a challenging paddle. After this tunnel opens,

Paddlers ply mangrove tunnels on Turner River. Photo by Constance Mier.

the vegetation becomes more typical of the park paddling zone: red and black mangrove and buttonwood, with a few palms thrown in. The Turner twists and turns and continues to vary in width. Keep your eyes peeled for orange tape tied to tree branches, which help distinguish the main river from side streams. Another clue is the river's stronger tidal flow.

The mangrove shores rise, and the river widens before intersecting Hurddles Creek on your left at 7 miles. To your right the Turner River becomes much wider. The Hurddles Creek Route leads southerly 5.5 miles to the Sunday Bay chickee.

Paddle west on the Turner River, passing Left Hand Turner River on your right. Stay with the left-hand bank, looking for the nearly vertical bank of shell, here indicating a Calusa shell mound that reaches 19 feet at its highest elevation. Come to the mouth of the Turner River at 8.5 miles. The mouth is guarded by a few mangrove isles near Wilderness Waterway marker #129. Paddle westerly toward the park service boat ramp on the north end of Chokoloskee Island, near Outdoor Resort, ending your route at 9 miles. From here, the Rabbit Key Pass Route leads 5.5 miles to Rabbit Key. The Lopez River Route leads 5 miles to Lopez River campsite. The Causeway Route leads 3 miles to the Gulf Coast Ranger Station.

West Pass Route

Begin: Gulf Coast Ranger Station	End: Picnic Key
Distance: 9.5 miles	Time: 5 hours
Potential tidal influence: 4	Potential wind influence: 4
Navigational challenge: 4	

Highlights: Numerous scenic islands; good beach camping

Hazards: Motor boats in Chokoloskee Bay

Campsites: Tiger Key, Picnic Key

Connections: Halfway Creek Canoe Trail, Causeway Route, Indian Key Pass Route, Pavilion Key Route, White Horse Key Route

West Pass Route takes you into the northernmost reaches of the park and into the midst of the Ten Thousand Islands and paddling areas north of the park. Three sorts of waters are represented here: the busy Chokoloskee Bay, the riverine West Pass, and the open water of the Gulf of Mexico. Boat traffic is heavy in Chokoloskee Bay, but it drops off as you paddle north along the mainland to enter West Pass. West Pass opens to the Gulf and Tiger Key, which overlooks the vast western horizon. Just around the corner is Picnic Key, another picturesque and popular camping destination.

Start your paddle at the Gulf Coast Ranger Station and paddle north in Chokoloskee Bay toward Lane Cove. At one-half mile, pass marker #5, which indicates the channel into the Barron River. Keep northwest, crossing the marked channel that leads out Indian Key Pass, proceeding beyond some dredge-spoil islands and markers #29 and #30. Chokoloskee Bay is shallow on both sides of this channel.

Keep northwest in open water, passing a point on your right and paralleling Lane Cove. Scoot past some low-slung finger islands on your left. Note that other islands in the vicinity are comprised of just a single mangrove tree. Veer west, leaving Lane Cove and paddling past the mouth of the Ferguson River at mile 3.5. The river is fronted by more islands, as you would expect in these Ten Thousand Islands. Stay close to the mouth of the Ferguson while making the passage for West Pass Bay. Notice how much stouter the mangrove is along the Ferguson River than on the nearby islands. It seems that mangrove thrives best when exposed to both freshwater and seawater, alternating with the tides.

Clear the straits past the Ferguson River into West Pass Bay. Aim just south of due west for West Pass. A conspicuous island in the foreground makes a good target. Stay just south of the conspicuous island and enter West Pass at 5 miles—it is about 80 feet wide, running south then west. The waters are kept deep by daily tidal flows. Numerous tapered bays splinter off West Pass before it arrives in open waters at mile 6, where the Gulf of Mexico is visible. Fakahatchee Island and its campsite are about 2 miles northwest through some channels and small islands. The northern tip of Tiger Key is also visible on the edge of the Gulf. Continue a southwesterly course beyond a few smaller islands, then swing around the northern tip of Tiger Key and its campsite at 7.8 miles. The waters can be shallow here. Keep south and look for the beach and the signed Tiger Key campsite at mile 8.5. The white sands and Gulf view draw many campers here.

The West Pass Route continues south around the shallow south end of Tiger Key. The sandy camp of Picnic Key comes into view. Paddle east to the sea grape–lined beach, arriving at Picnic Key at mile 9.5. This encampment lures Everglades enthusiasts, too. From Picnic Key, it is 7 miles back to Gulf Coast Ranger Station via the Indian Key Pass Route. It is 7.5 miles to Rabbit Key via the Pavilion Key Route and 2.5 miles to Camp Lulu Key via the White Horse Key Route.

Willy Willy Route

Begin: Lostmans Five campsite   End: Willy Willy campsite

Distance: 10 miles   Time: 5 hours

Potential tidal influence: 3   Potential wind influence: 3

Navigational challenge: 3

Highlights: Historic shell mounds

Hazards: Motorboats on Wilderness Waterway; wide-open bays

Campsites: Lostmans Five campsite, Willy Willy campsite

Connections: Darwins Place Route, Lostmans River Route, Rodgers River Bay Route

---

The Willy Willy Route connects three historic ground sites to one another. It traces the Wilderness Waterway for most of the paddle through a series of big bays linked by channels to pass the east end of Lostmans River. There, it leaves the Wilderness Waterway and crosses Big Lostmans Bay to access a little-used creek leading to the Willy Willy campsite, an old Calusa shell mound adjacent to a freshwater creek at the edge of the marshy Glades. Along the way, it passes Onion Key, another bit of land with a storied past and present.

Start your route at the Lostmans Five campsite. Leave the dock and paddle west around a point to Wilderness Waterway marker #60. Notice how the land of Lostmans Five campsite continues to the point by the marker, as evidenced by the hammock species on the shoreline. Paddle into a tapering inlet and a south-flowing stream, which is a good 50 feet wide and opens into Two Island Bay at marker #59.

There are no more islands in Two Island Bay. They were probably swept away by a hurricane. Head easterly for the peninsula protruding from the northern shore. Near the peninsula, veer southeasterly toward another channel at marker #58. Though the waters are shallow at the entrance to this channel, they should pose no problem to paddlers. Turn almost due south into this channel, which leads to 1-acre-square Onion Key.

Two tales predominate as to how Onion Key got its name. The first says the island was named for a forgotten farmer and his wife who settled here and cultivated onions. The second story states that early Everglades pioneer Gregorio Lopez ate his last onion while camped on this island. Whatever the case, Onion Key's shell shoreline—as opposed to mud and mangrove shoreline—gives it away as an Indian mound. Onion Key is the site of more than 1,000 years of human occupation. Calusa, then Seminoles, were born and died here. In more recent times, the 1920s, the headquarters of the Poinciana Company, a land development business, was based here; it went bust after the 1926 hurricane. The key has also been used as a park campsite. Now it is overgrown by a profusion of the shrubby exotic invasive, Brazilian pepper. Invasive plants are a big contributor to habitat loss in Florida according to the Fish and Wildlife Commission.

Leave Onion Key, heading south, and come to marker #56. From here, enter Onion Key Bay, hugging the west shoreline to the point between the shoreline and the island. The reason the Wilderness Waterway goes the way it does is to provide more sheltered, deeper waters for motorboats, for which it was originally designed. Pass marker #55 and continue southerly, shooting for marker #53, which is barely visible on the horizon. Shoot the channel south, and come to Wilderness Waterway marker #52 at mile 3.5.

Here begins the Lostmans River Route. It heads west, where the Wilderness Waterway marker arrow points, 6 miles to the Gulf and the Lostmans Ranger Station. The Willy Willy Route, however, swings southeasterly for a channel and marker #51. This short channel is riverine in its width, depth, and tidal pull. Follow its steep banks past marker #50 to marker #49. The arrow here points toward Third Bay, but you continue east another 100 yards, then turn south. Do not take the first southerly channel past marker #49—it leads back toward Lostmans River. The correct channel heads south, then turns almost due east into a nameless bay. Paddle almost due east across this bay, first passing marker #47 and then a tiny isle in the bay. Be sure to cross all the way to the far east end of the bay, coming to marker #45. Turn south, then east to marker #44 and Big Lostmans Bay at mile 6.5. Note the large, gnarly buttonwoods here.

Leave the Wilderness Waterway and paddle just north of due east for a V-shaped inlet 1.5 miles across Big Lostmans Bay. Trust your compass on the crossing. At the back of the shallow inlet is a winding creek that heads generally east. The 15-foot-wide creek is plenty deep enough for self-propelled craft. Mudflats line the inside of the creek bends. When you come to a split in the creek, take the south channel. Pass an open sawgrass area before opening into Rocky Creek Bay.

Paddle east up Rocky Creek Bay, skirting a clump of palms on the south shore. Jump over to the north shore, noting the tall trees above the mangrove. Just ahead is the dock of the Willy Willy campsite at mile 10, by the mouth of a summertime freshwater stream entering Rocky Creek Bay from the north. This is an old Indian shell-mound hammock where modern Everglades adventurers can spend a night of their lives and from which they can paddle the freshwater creeks of the interior Glades. From here, it is 5 miles to the Rodgers River chickee and 7 miles to Wilderness Waterway marker #26 at Broad River Bay via the Rodgers River Bay Route.

~~~~~~

East River Route

Begin: U.S. 41 north of
Everglades City (Tamiami Trail)   End: Round Key

Distance: 12.5 miles   Time: 7 hours

Potential tidal influence: 3   Potential wind influence: 4

Navigational challenge: 4

Highlights: Mangrove tunnels; historic island with cemetery

Hazards: Overgrown tunnels filled with deadfall

Campsites: Fakahatchee Island, Round Key

Connections: White Horse Key Route

East River Route, mostly within Fakahatchee Strand State Preserve, travels a series of small lakes and serpentine mangrove tunnels eventually opening into Fakahatchee Bay. These intriguing tunnels and lakes are small enough to prevent all but self-propelled craft from traveling through them until you hit the wider portion of the East River. The route continues in Fakahatchee Bay and aims for Fakahatchee Island, settled by the Calusa more than 1,000 years ago and built up from millions of shells left over from the shellfish that made up part of their diet. Later, white settlers came and farmed the fertile, rolling tract, leaving their mark in the form of old cisterns, home foundations, and even a cemetery that you can visit on the now-forested island. The route next traces Fakahatchee Pass, a deep riverine channel opening to the Gulf and ending at the small island of Round Key.

You can either drive directly to the launch site or go to Everglades City and take a shuttle. I recommend the shuttle, as the launch site parking area is unsafe for unattended vehicles and very small to boot. If you decide to go direct, head north on U.S. 41 toward Naples. Go through the intersection of U.S. 41 and C.R. 29 near Everglades City and travel 5.2 miles. The left turn you need to take to reach the launch is currently unsigned, so hit your odometer at the aforementioned intersection. Drive 5.2 miles, then turn left onto a gravel road that immediately curves right and go less than 50 yards from U.S. 41 before dead-ending at a small pond on the left. If you reach a roadside park on your left, you have gone just a bit too far on U.S. 41.

Put in at the pond and aim southeast for a tapered mangrove tunnel obscured by a tree island. Pass through this first passageway to join an old shallow canal running north-south less than a half mile into the paddle. Head south on this more than 40-foot-wide waterway, which narrows to join a second tree-canopied tunnel—about a boat's width—at the canal's south end.

At 1 mile, this tunnel opens into a pond with sawgrass on the right-hand bank. If you continue forward to reach a channel that curves north and opens into a lake, you have gone the wrong way. Instead, upon reaching the sawgrass area look left for a canopied mangrove tunnel and head southeasterly, passing near a bit more sawgrass. Travel through a small pond just before reaching shallow Lake One at 1.4 miles. Keep a southerly course through this shallow lake to shortly make a curvy mangrove-and-buttonwood tunnel, rich with air plants. This tunnel, like the others, will contain much deadfall that you will have to work around. Tan sands glow beneath the tea-colored water. At 1.8 miles, you will reach a T in the route. Keep left (eastbound) and curve gently around to meet small Lake

Taking a break at the mouth of East River. Photo by Constance Mier.

Two at 2.3 miles. Head southwest in Lake Two to access another mangrove tunnel, this one larger than the ones before. Fallen trees here constrict the paddling area and make for slow going. Thousands of red mangrove prop roots dangle along the water's edge.

Enter Big Lake at 3.4 miles. Keep south in this shallow, relatively large water body as it returns to the uncanopied East River at its south end. Pass a water-monitoring station at 4.2 miles. From here, the way is clear. Tidal influence will increase and you will pass a few small islands just before reaching Fakahatchee Bay at 6 miles. Daniels Point separates you from the Fakahatchee River, which also enters the bay here. Now aim southwesterly toward Fakahatchee Island, crossing a mile of open water before reaching a small line of finger islands at 7 miles.

Continue crossing the bay to reach Fakahatchee Island at 7.7 miles. Scan the northeastern tip of the island for an opening in the mangrove shore and a shell landing. At this high point on the island shell mound, just to the east of the landing, you will find a campsite and an old cistern. If you continue east, curving around the island, you will come to another landing at 7.8 miles. A mangrove-bordered

A paddler explores the old cemetery on Fakahatchee Island. Photo by author.

campsite is situated here, along with the beginning of the trail to the island cemetery.

Leave Fakahatchee Island and its extensive shallows to join Fakahatchee Pass that flows around the northwest tip of the island. Note the old pilings on the edge of the deep channel as it seeks the Gulf. Fakahatchee Pass winds generally west among small islands and extensive shallows. At 10.5 miles, the widening river curves south and the Gulf appears. Round Key stands in the distance. As you paddle toward the island, beware of its extensive shallows. From the Gulf, you'll see the beaches of Panther Key shining white to the west.

Make Round Key at 12.5 miles. This small island, with a rocky beach and shaded by sea grape and mangrove, offers small camping areas that face in nearly all directions. Examine the remains of a foundation on the southeast side of the island. From here, it is a little over 1 mile to Camp Lulu Key to the southeast and 1.5 miles to Panther Key via the White Horse Key Route.

Fish Hawk Creek Route

Begin: Collier-Seminole State Park   End: Gullivan Key

Distance: 13.5 miles   Time: 7 hours

Potential tidal influence: 4   Potential wind influence: 4

Navigational challenge: 4

Highlights: Small creeks and big bays; less motorboat traffic for the area

Hazards: Oyster bars; big winds in Gulf

Campsites: Gullivan Key

Connections: Mud Bay–Goodland Route, White Horse Key Route

Fish Hawk Creek Route, in the northern Ten Thousand Islands, covers many miles and many marine environments en route from Collier-Seminole State Park to the outermost islands facing the Gulf of Mexico. The navigational challenges are varied as well. Start by following a marked channel, then zigzag through shallow bays riddled with oyster bars and tiny islands before joining a relatively small stream opening into the Gulf of Mexico. Once you leave the state park, the route follows a man-made canal before joining the mangrove-bordered Blackwater River, which winds its way into an unnamed bay. From here, the route travels southeast through Buttonwood Bay and finds Fish Hawk Creek, a sheltered alternative to high-wind travel that narrowly splits a peninsula opening into the Gulf. Gullivan Key, a fine campsite, opens into view not far beyond Fish Hawk Creek.

To access Collier-Seminole State Park from Everglades City, take U.S. 41 north for 16 miles to the park entrance, on your left. You must pay a park entrance fee and a modest daily parking fee (if you're leaving your car overnight), and you will need to file a float plan. All of these tasks are done at the park entrance station.

Leave the boat basin and paddle southbound on a 60-foot-wide, mangrove-lined canal for a half mile to reach channel marker #56. Here, join the slender and deep Blackwater River, marked nearly all the way to the Gulf. Note that the numbers on the channel markers decline the closer you get to the Gulf. These markers are strategically located at the side streams splitting off the main river. Tidal influence increases in this area, and the waterway widens as you paddle toward channel marker #47 at 1.9 miles. Here, the Mud Bay–Goodland Route, the other half of the Collier-Seminole Canoe Trail, leads straight through a mangrove tunnel to pass Goodland in 7 miles and make Coon Key in 9 miles. This route traces the still-widening Blackwater, where mud bars form inside the river's bends. At 3.7 miles, pass a water-monitoring station. The river curves southwesterly and opens into an unnamed bay, pocked with small look-alike islands and scattered with oyster bars. Reach channel marker #9 at 6.8 miles. Here, the Collier-Seminole Canoe Trail veers northwest for Palm Bay, while the southeasterly route jitterbugs its way to Buttonwood Bay.

If you're paddling the Collier-Seminole Canoe Trail loop, turn northwest, keeping the mainland to your right as you wind among the islands, mud flats, and oyster bars to reach Palm Bay and the Mud Bay–Goodland Route in 1 mile. If you're heading for Fish Hawk Creek, keep southeast, skirting a finger island to enter a maze of mangrove and oyster bars. (Map #0 at the back of the book will help you plot your route here.) As a bonus, the shallows and jagged oysters bars in this area discourage motorboaters. Open into Buttonwood Bay, still keeping southeast to bisect the gates of Gator Bay.

At 10.5 miles, deep Fish Hawk Creek leaves extremely shallow Gator Bay, where snags rise from the water. The stream curves southwest, alternately widening and narrowing before opening into the Gulf near a peninsula of Turkey Key (not to be confused with Turkey Key inside Everglades National Park) at 12 miles. The Gulf fully opens before you and the beaches of Gullivan Key are visible to the south. Reach Gullivan Key at 13.5 miles. The primary camping area is situated along Gullivan Key's west-facing beaches. From here, it is 6.5 miles southeast to Tiger Key and 10 miles west around Gullivan Bay to Cape Romano via the White Horse Key Route.

Morgan River Route

Begin: Cape Romano	End: Snook Hole Channel
Distance: 3 miles	Time: 1.5 hours
Potential tidal influence: 4 challenge: 3	Potential wind influence: 3 Navigational

Highlights: Inside route through Cape Romano

Hazards: Motorboats and jet skis; shallows

Campsites: Cape Romano Island

Connections: White Horse Key Route

The short Morgan River Route allows paddlers to loop around Cape Romano Island, avoiding a backtrack while experiencing narrow waters different from those of wide-open Gullivan Bay and the Gulf of Mexico. On the other hand, being so close to Marco Island has its drawbacks. On nice weekends, motorboats and jet skis tour this same route. Also, because of changes wrought by Hurricane Wilma, the land and waterscape no longer coincide with the nautical charts. As shown on the nautical charts, for instance, the mouth of Morgan Pass extends from the tip of Cape Romano. In reality, the Morgan River is now accessed by a new mouth west of Carr Island. More accurate, the aerial charts will be helpful here.

The route starts at the south tip of Cape Romano. Leave the wide beach surrounding the abandoned white-domed house and head northwest with the open Gulf to your left. Pass more beaches and storm-damaged coastline before making the watery, shoal-wracked opening that leads into Morgan Bay. Sandy camps border the entrance, but these, like the shoals, are unlikely to deter a canoe or kayak the way they would a motorboat. The route curves north along the Morgan Keys, following a normally staked channel that winds among the myriad mud flats in this shallow bay.

Leave Morgan Bay to make the Morgan River at 1.5 miles. The river soon splits; take the left and narrower channel overarched with mangrove. Stay right after emerging from the channel before reentering the Morgan River at 2.1 miles. From here, take the now-wide Morgan River north, meeting Blind Pass and the north tip of Cape Romano Island at 3 miles. To your right, southeast, it is a short distance to a high, clamshell beach landing and campsite. To the north stands Helen Key, across Snook Hole Channel. It is 3 miles to Coon Key via the White Horse Key Route and a little over 2 miles farther to Goodland via the Mud Bay–Goodland Route.

Mud Bay–Goodland Route

Begin: Collier-Seminole State Park   End: Coon Key

Distance: 9 miles   Time: 5.5 hours

Potential tidal influence: 5   Potential wind influence: 3

Navigational challenge: 3

Highlights: Historic shell mounds; waterside community; varied waters

Hazards: Motorboats; extremely shallow bays and mud flats

Campsites: Grocery Place, Coon Key

Connections: Fish Hawk Creek Route, White Horse Key Route

The Mud Bay–Goodland Route not only leads you from Collier-Seminole State Park into the Gulf, but it is also part of the Collier-Seminole Canoe Trail, which forms a 14.4-mile loop, the other half of which—the Fish Hawk Creek Route—is described above. In fact, to start the Goodland–Mud Bay Route, you must first travel a portion of the Fish Hawk Creek Route. This route passes the village of Goodland, which also provides a jumping-off point that paddlers use to access the Gulf or to take "inside routes," traveling south toward Everglades City. Leave the Blackwater River at Collier-Seminole State Park, tracing a small creek to pass extremely shallow Mud Bay. Then, pass a pair of shell mounds along Royal Palm Hammock Creek to enter shallow Palm Bay. From here, the route skitters through an island maze to enter Goodland Bay, passing the houses and marinas of Goodland before taking Coon Key Pass into Gullivan Bay and the Gulf.

Start at channel marker #47 on the Blackwater River, 1.9 miles from the boat ramp at Collier-Seminole State Park. Head southwesterly from the larger channel of the Blackwater and paddle beneath a mangrove-canopied passage to join a tidal creek leading to Mud Bay at one-half mile. Once in Mud Bay, you may find out what happens if you don't catch a rising or high falling tide. It's called "mud dogging"—getting stuck and having to drag your boat through the slop. A slender, shallow, ever-changing tidal channel flows through Mud Bay, and hopefully you will find it. It is often the only water *in* the bay: strong post-front north winds can prevent the tidal push from getting to Mud Bay, leaving it waterless. Waters being favorable, head generally south through the bay, then curve back to the north, entering Royal Palm Hammock Creek at 1.7 miles. The stream narrows and curves south, as West Palm Run continues west.

Stay with Royal Palm Hammock Creek. On your left at 2.2 miles, pass Old Grove, a bit of high ground marked by palms. The stream snakes sharply back and forth, building up mud bars on the insides of bends. Reach the north access of Grocery Place on river right at 2.9 miles. Grocery Place is a designated backcountry campsite for which a permit from Collier-Seminole State Park is required. The primary, sign-posted access is around the south end of the boot-shaped mound at 3.3 miles. An old cistern on the main shell mound indicates a post-Calusa settlement. Back in the woods, a second cistern can be found. Grocery Place offers level tent sites, but it can be buggy. Just ahead of the Grocery Place access, a stream continues in a northwesterly direction, while Royal Palm Hammock Creek opens south into Palm Bay.

Palm Bay can be troublesome, but it isn't as shallow as Mud Bay. If you're paddling the Collier-Seminole Canoe Trail loop, keep due south until you reach the southeastern corner of Palm Bay. Here, curve easterly, keeping the mainland to your left, to finally reach the Blackwater River and its channel markers. For the Mud Bay–Goodland Route, I recommend that you keep south in Palm Bay, then curve northwest along the edge of the islands that form the lower end of this shallow area. Try to catch a rising or high falling tide to push you on now-moving tidal waters through the island mangrove maze that links Palm Bay to Goodland Bay.

Once you clear this island maze at 5.5 miles, watch for mud flats. The buildings of Goodland are visible across Goodland Bay. Instead of bee-lining for them, head toward the Florida Highway 92 Bridge, then curve south, passing channel marker #10 and joining marked Coon Key Pass. Here, the Big Marco River heads toward the north side of Marco Island.

Goodland offers alternate jumping-off points from some of the marinas there. It is also the quickest way to the Gulf, at a little over 2 miles. I recommend Calusa Island Marina (www.calusaisland-marina.com). Leave Goodland by the busy, marked and numbered Coon Key Pass. As the pass widens, the pocket beaches of Tripod Key show, along with channel marker #2. The north sand spit of Coon Key is visible ahead, and the open waters of Gullivan Bay extend to the horizon. Reach Coon Key and the end of this route at 9 miles. From here, it is 5.5 miles westerly to the tip of Cape Romano and 11 miles southeasterly to Tiger Key via the White Horse Key Route.

White Horse Key Route

Begin: Tiger Key   End: Cape Romano

Distance: 16.5 miles   Time: 8 hours

Potential tidal influence: 3   Potential wind influence: 5

Navigational challenge: 2

Highlights: Beach islands; camping opportunities; wide-open water

Hazards: Wide-open water; big winds; many motorboats on north end

Campsites: Tiger Key, Camp Lulu Key, Round Key, Panther Key, Hog Key, White Horse Key, Gullivan Key, Coon Key, Helen Key, Cape Romano Island

Connections: West Pass Route, Indian Key Pass Route, East River Route, Fish Hawk Creek Route, Mud Bay–Goodland Route, Morgan River Route

---

White Horse Key Route skirts the Gulf islands extending from the north border of Everglades National Park all the way to Cape Romano, as far north as the wild Everglades coast extends. It travels through multiple state and federal management areas: Ten Thousand Islands National Wildlife Refuge, Fakahatchee Strand State Preserve, and Rookery Bay Preserve. The Gulf islands here are very much like those within Everglades National Park but have fewer rules and regulations. For the paddler, this means more heavily camped islands but also freedom from the strict itinerary national park rules necessitate. This area also receives more motorboat traffic than the park, especially around Cape Romano.

Heading northwest, leave Tiger Key and cross deep West Pass, aiming for Camp Lulu Key. Reach this over-camped island at 1.5 miles. Camp Lulu Key is famed for being the home of Mike Ward, the last hermit of the Everglades, who died in the early 2000s. His locked cabin on stilts still overlooks one of the main camping areas. Round Key appears to stand alone in the distance. Keep westerly, staying close to shore if you're not going to Round Key. Beware the extensive shallows. From Round Key it is 5 miles to Fakahatchee Island and 12.5 miles to U.S. 41 via the East River Route.

The beaches of Panther Key loom larger as you cross open Fakahatchee Pass. Note the marked channel leading from the Gulf to the Faka Union Canal and the Port of the Islands Marina. On a clear day, the high-rise hotels of Marco Island are visible to the west. Reach Gomez Point, the south tip of Panther Key, at 4 miles. This popular camping island, with sites on both its east and west sides, has a long history of habitation. In the late 1800s, homesteader John Gomez resided here with his wife in a palmetto shack. The couple tried, among other things, to raise goats, but panthers kept snagging them—hence the island's name. A well on the island attracted passing boaters and was later home to another semi-recluse named Roy Osmer. Everglades National Park allowed Osmer to live on Comer Key until Hurricane Donna did in Comer Key and Osmer's house in the 1960. He later left the park, then came to Panther Key.

Keeping northwest, more deep water lies between Panther Key and Hog Key, which has a small but heavily used camping area. Most paddlers simply aim for White Horse Key and its beachfront. If the winds are high, stay on the inside of White Horse Key and Gullivan Key. Be mindful of the shallows on the Gulf-facing side of the islands, divided by the deep waters of Dismal Key Pass. Both islands are fine camping destinations.

Leave Gullivan Key at 6.5 miles and begin the great curve around Gullivan Bay, paddling deep waters before reaching the broken beaches of Turtle Key. West of Turtle Key are some interesting waters—alternating deep passes divided by shallow, fingerlike underwater ridges, one of which is called Long Rock. At low tide, you will either have to paddle around or carry your craft over Long Rock.

At 10 miles, skirt Brush Island, with its gumbo-limbo trees standing tall on a sheer bluff. Cross open waters while aiming for Coon Key—its pocket beaches clearly visible. Large Tripod Key covers the horizon to the north. This is one stretch of water without a nearby inside "cheat route," so make sure the weather is favorable while

Morning on Gullivan key. Photo by Constance Mier.

passing through. Also be aware of the increased motorboat traffic coming out of Goodland via Coon Key Pass. Reach Coon Key at 11 miles. The sandy north spit makes for a good stopping spot. The best campsites are on its east side. Relic pilings extend from the now-wooded southeast tip of the undersized island into the water. Open your eyes and ears as you keep west, crossing busy Coon Key Pass, a marked channel out of Goodland. A small set of wooded islands, bookended by Neal Key and Ramsey Key, precede another deep marked channel coming out of Coxambas Bay. Shore birds often light among the scattered shoals of this area, especially near channel marker #6 in Gullivan Bay.

You are now turning southwest, and the beaches of Helen Key shine across the water. This large, southeast-facing mangrove island offers limited camping. Cross the marked and busy Snook Hole Channel ahead, as you curve southward for the northern tip of Cape Romano Island at 14 miles. Here, the Morgan River Route leads west then south along the inside of Cape Romano Island to emerge on the

A stretch of beach on Cape Romano. Photo by author.

Gulf and the actual tip of Cape Romano at 3 miles. The White Horse Key Route, by contrast, curves around the outside of Cape Romano Island, passing a small sloping clamshell beach and camping area backed by gumbo-limbo and buttonwood. A mangrove shoreline resumes, before palm and sea grape beachfront takes its place a mile further along. Pass parcels of private land.

At 15.5 miles, as the island curves southwest, a high beachfront mound, crowned with gumbo-limbo, marks the beginning of a long beach—backed by sea oats, palm, and sea grape—stretching around Cape Romano. This is not only a popular camping area, but also where motorboats tie up while their passengers explore the shoreline. Other parcels of privately owned land stand here—a series of narrow waterfront lots unlikely to be developed. Pilings and other shoreline detritus reveal relatively recent but incomplete development attempts. A now-lost well in the vicinity once drew in mariners—from the Caslusa to the Spaniards—long before the Florida of today. While curving around the island's tip you may see the exposed shoals of Cape Romano in the Gulf, although a deep passage runs along the southeastern side of the island.

Reach the tip of Cape Romano and the end of this route at 16.5 miles. As you curve around the actual island tip, an odd, dilapidated, white-domed house is now, along with the shells, a beachcomber attraction. Not long ago, the Morgan River exited in this vicinity, but Hurricane Wilma in 2004 moved the opening north about half a mile. From here, it is a little over 3 miles back to the north end of Cape Romano Island via the Morgan River Route.

The Campsites

The Campsites

Everglades campers heading into the backcountry are required to stay at designated campsites. This concentrates the human impact into fewer and certain locations to minimize damage to natural resources. And out here, there aren't a whole lot of places to overnight, other than designated campsites, that are above water, especially on the "inside."

The park offers three types of campsites. Each has its positive and negative characteristics. First are chickees, located where no dry land exists. These are elevated wooden platforms with open sides and sloped metal roofs. A vault toilet is connected to the platform by a gangway. Double chickees have two platforms but very limited space.

The second type of campsite is a ground campsite. These are primarily old shell mounds built up over time by the Calusa and more recently used by white and Seminole settlers. They are often covered in tropical hammock vegetation and as laden with bugs as with history.

Finally, there are the beach campsites, located along the Gulf of Mexico on crushed-shell sands. Access to the beaches is strongly affected by winds and tides. On shore, winds can blow your tent down, and low tides can mean a long carry to get your boat to paddleable water. Bugs can be either very troublesome or nonexistent depending on the winds. But the walking room of a beach camp can be a relief after being stuck in a boat all day.

Chickees have limited room as shown by the tent-crowded platform at Hells Bay chickee. Photo by Constance Mier.

The park service opens and closes campsites for various reasons, so inform yourself about the latest changes. Shark Point campsite, for instance, was closed for lack of use. Kingston Key chickee was destroyed by a hurricane. Jewel Key was a last minute addition and is now open. I have added new campsites to this edition of my book. These camps, located north of the park, include Fakahatchee Strand State Preserve, Ten Thousand Islands National Wildlife Refuge, Rookery Bay National Estuarine Reserve, Collier-Seminole State Park, plus a scattering of private lands. Because all of these areas are maintained by different land management agencies, campsite availability and regulations will vary. To be on the safe side, I recommend you check each area's Web site for the latest information on camping guidelines, reservations, and permits. No matter what the management plan of each site, your plan should be to follow the Leave No Trace rule, which is also a good idea within the boundaries of Everglades National Park.

The following list of campsites starts with an easy-to-scan information box, giving the Everglades camper a quick site overview.

First, the type of campsite and type of landing for your boat are listed. After that, there's a scenery rating, ranging from 1 (poor) to 5 (excellent). Campsite use on a scale of very high to low is next given to help you determine whether you are likely to have company or even be able to get on a site. Next listed are maximum number of people and parties allowed at the campsite. When the maximum number of either people or parties is met, the campsite is full. For example, Lard Can campsite has a 10-person capacity and a 4-party limit. If one group of 10 people reserves a night at Lard Can campsite, then the campsite is full for that night. If four parties of one camper each reserve the same night at Lard Can, the campsite is still considered full, even though only four people will be there. The listing for maximum number of nights tells you the most nights in a row a party can stay at that site. You will also find listed whether the campsite allows fires and has a toilet.

"GPS coordinates" (WGS84 datum) identifies the campsite's latitude and longitude, while "On which route" names the exact route the campsite is located on. If the campsite lies at the terminus of two routes, then both routes are listed. Nearby connecting routes are next identified. Finally, under "Nearby campsites," you will find listed other camping possibilities in the same general area, in case the site you are trying to get is full and you want to be in the same vicinity.

Reserving Campsites

Campsites must be reserved when you get your backcountry permit (see "Planning Your Trip" in the introduction for details). Permits are issued in person up to 24 hours in advance of your trip, so have several campsites in mind in case the ones you want are full. A permit will be issued only for available campsites. At present, the permit fee is $10, plus $2 per person per night. (For two people going on a five-night trip, for instance, the fee would be $30.) Once your permit is issued and you have an itinerary, you must stick to it. However, do not imperil yourself or your party by trying, no matter what, to stay on permit. Rangers will understand legitimate extenuating circumstances (big storms, injuries), that force you to go off permit. On the other hand, if you just don't feel like paddling any farther, don't try to catch on at a campsite for which you don't have reservations, especially a chickee. There simply isn't spare camping room available. To reserve or check the availability of campsites north of the park, consult individual Web sites. Information about Florida state parks can be found at floridastateparks.org.

Florida Bay

Alligator Creek

Type of campsite: Ground	Landing: Ground
Scenery: 4	Use: Very low
Max. # of campers: 8	Max. # of parties: 3 Max. # of nights: 2
Fires: No	Toilet: No

GPS coordinates: N25° 10.569', W80° 47.601'

On which Route: West Lake Canoe Trail, Snake Bight Route

Nearby connecting routes: West Lake Canoe Trail, Snake Bight Route

Nearby campsites: None

If you like camping in solitude in a little-visited area of the Everglades backcountry, stay at Alligator Creek. Your camping buddies will be the wildlife, active day and night. This is a ground campsite, located at the mouth of Alligator Creek where it enters Garfield Bight, a part of Florida Bay. The actual landing, which may be muddy at low tide, is on Alligator Creek, less than 100 feet from the bight. You may be lucky enough to see an alligator sunning itself at the landing. The camping area, situated on a flat marl prairie, is largely overgrown with dill weed, purslane, and other ground cover, though a portion of the campsite is worn to bare earth.

The mangroves along the shore of Alligator Creek and a few other trees provide partial shade. Foot trails extend into the marl prairie where you can get obstructed views of Garfield Bight. Although the West Lake Canoe Trail is intended for hand-propelled craft only, motorboaters can access the little-used campsite from Florida Bay. (Few do as a practical matter because Garfield Bight is so shallow.)

Little Rabbit Key

Type of campsite: Ground	Landing: Dock
Scenery: 4	Use: Low
Max. # of campers: 12	Max. # of parties: 4 Max. # of nights: 2
Fires: No	Toilet: Yes

GPS coordinates: N24° 58.885', W80° 49.570'

On which route: Dildo Bank Route, Man of War Route

Nearby connecting routes: Dildo Bank Route, Man of War Route

Nearby campsites: None

Little Rabbit Key lies at the heart of Florida Bay. It is the first stop of the two-night, three-day Florida Bay loop and is an all-day paddle from Flamingo. This small island is ringed by trees, with a grassy, brushy center covered by a creeping plant known as sea purslane. Red mangrove, with its prop roots, faces out on the ocean, while the more massive black mangrove grows inland. Little Rabbit Key has no beach.

A small dock with cleats protrudes from an opening in the mangroves on the northwest side of the island. A clearing and the center of the island lie behind the dock. Camping areas are located directly behind the dock and off to one side in the shade of some big black mangroves. The preferred tent sites are here, though you won't get much breeze.

A picnic table and two vault toilets make Little Rabbit Key somewhat civilized. Little footpaths circle the perimeter of the key. Your only clear ocean views are from the dock and landing area. From there you can see Big Rabbit Key and waters to the west; plus you can take in a fabulous sunset. After dark, go out to the dock and shine your flashlight into the water—look at the shrimp, crabs, minnows, and other marine creatures that make up a strand in the web of life in Florida Bay.

North Nest Key

Type of campsite: Beach	Landing: Beach and dock
Scenery: 5	Use: High
Max. # of campers: 25	Max. # of parties: 7 Max. # of nights: 7
Fires: Yes	Toilet: Yes

GPS coordinates: N25° 9.138', W80° 30.655'

On which route: North Nest Key Loop

Nearby connecting routes: None

Nearby campsites: None

This beach campsite lies all alone in northeast Florida Bay near Key Largo—maybe because it's in a class all by itself. A large island, North Nest Key is punctuated with small beaches amid the mangroves hugging its shoreline. The western side of the island has a swim beach, marked with "No Wake" buoys, and shallow waters ideal for wading. Just around the corner is the actual camping area. A 40- by 3-foot dock allows for easy landing of your craft, but the gentle beach here is paddler friendly, too. The colorful waters and green keys of Florida Bay offer a superlative view from the camping area. Understandably popular, North Nest Key is as heavily visited by motorboats as by paddlers.

Mangrove and buttonwood provide shade for several small-tent areas beneath their limbs. Footpaths lead farther into the island and a couple of more open tent sites, next to a shallow pond. Other tent sites are located right next to the bay. None of the camping areas is particularly large, but campers can disperse and get a little privacy if they so desire.

Cape Sable, Whitewater Bay, and the South

Clubhouse Beach

Type of campsite: Beach	Landing: Beach
Scenery: 4	Use: Low
Max. # of campers: 24	Max. # of parties: 4 Max. # of nights: 3
Fires: Yes	Toilet: No

GPS coordinates: N25° 7.745', W81° 2.444'

On which route: East Cape Route

Nearby connecting routes: Snake Bight Route, Buttonwood Canal Route, First National Bank Route, Dildo Key Route, Middle Cape Route

Nearby campsites: East Clubhouse Beach, East Cape

Clubhouse Beach campsite is just a few miles distant from East Clubhouse Beach campsite and, with few exceptions, closely resembles its neighbor. The prairie here is larger, and the beach is more interspersed with shoreline mangrove, but it offers an equally good view of northern Florida Bay.

Clubhouse Beach was named by the Model Land Company, which tried to develop the Cape Sable area during the Florida real estate boom of the early 1920s. The company built a large clubhouse on stilts, which extended out from the beach. Here, company salespeople entertained potential clients, who were boated in from Miami and environs. As far as I can tell, nothing remains of the clubhouse today. Hurricanes can be very rough on old wooden structures.

Level sandy spots big enough for a tent are hard to find here, although you can find a few flat, vegetation-free areas back up from the beach. In case of windy or cold weather, try out one of the tent sites shielded by mangrove forest on the west end of the beach.

Beachcombers can go east for a decent walk, provided they don't mind going inland here and there and walking over the prairie.

East Cape

Type of campsite: Beach	Landing: Beach
Scenery: 5	Use: Medium
Max. # of campers: 60	Max. # of parties: 15 Max. # of nights: 7
Fires: Yes	Toilet: No

GPS coordinates: N25° 6.967', W81° 5.049'

On which route: East Cape Route, Middle Cape Route, First National Bank Route

Nearby connecting routes: East Cape Route, Middle Cape Route, First National Bank Route

Nearby campsites: Clubhouse Beach, Middle Cape

The large East Cape campsite occupies the most southerly tip of land in the mainland United States. The actual campsite starts at the most westerly creek that links Florida Bay with Lake Ingraham, which lies behind East Cape and Middle Cape. Just beside the creek is a flat tent site that looks south over Florida Bay. The south-facing portion of the Cape was battered by the 2005 hurricanes as its skeletal trees testify. The rest of the campsite swings west around the point of the cape. Old dock pilings, remnants of an old boat concession tour which landed here, mark the popular camping spot. Tent sites extend for hundreds of yards along the beach.

The strip of beach, widened by the storms, is backed by a few coconut palms, cactus, grass, sea purslane, and Jamaica dogwood and other trees. Back in the 1830s the cape looked very different. It was the site of Fort Poinsett, when the U.S. Army and the Seminoles were at war. Army personnel thought the Seminoles were getting arms from Spanish fishermen who operated in the area and that Cape

Sable was a meeting place for arms deals. The log fort was later abandoned and obliterated by storms. Only the story remains.

East Clubhouse Beach

Type of campsite: Beach   Landing: Beach

Scenery: 4   Use: Low

Max. # of campers: 24   Max. # of parties: 4   Max. # of nights: 3

Fires: Yes   Toilet: No

GPS coordinates: N25° 7.584', W80° 59.656'

On which route: East Cape Route

Nearby connecting routes: Snake Bight Route, Buttonwood Canal Route, First National Bank Route, Dildo Key Bank Route, Middle Cape Route

Nearby campsites: Clubhouse Beach, East Cape

Looking southeast from East Clubhouse Beach. Photo by author.

This beach campsite is the closest campsite to Flamingo. First-time Everglades paddlers are often disappointed when they reach this ambitiously named campsite, expecting a bona fide beach. Instead, the very narrow strip of sand is interspersed with pockets of mangrove that grow right up to and along the 300-yard shoreline. Behind what little beach there is lies an open prairie of sea purslane, an edible plant, which extends far back to a dense woodland that sweeps around the prairie all the way to the shore west of the beach. Turtle grasses often pile up between the water and the beach.

The east side of the beach is the largest and most popular camping area and one of the few spots big enough to pitch a tent or two. As you head westward, vegetation grows nearly to the shoreline.

Hells Bay

Type of campsite: Chickee	Landing: Dock
Scenery: 3	Use: High
Max. # of campers: 12	Max. # of parties: 2 Max. # of nights: 1
Fires: No	Toilet: Yes

GPS coordinates: N25° 15.197', W80° 52.714'

On which route: Hells Bay Canoe Trail, Lane River Route, East River Route

Nearby connecting routes: Hells Bay Canoe Trail, Lane River Route, East River Route

Nearby campsites: Pearl Bay chickee, Lane Bay chickee

Because the Hells Bay chickee stands at the confluence of three primary paddle routes east of Whitewater Bay, it is popular with campers. The most popular of the three approaches to the chickee is the marked Hells Bay Canoe Trail, which comes from Main Park Road. This campsite is also a regular stop for paddlers coming up the East River from lower Whitewater Bay. The surrounding water is shallow and clear, with a coffee-colored tint. In the past, food-habituated alligators hung around this chickee, so avoid swimming here and use caution getting water from around the chickee. Never feed an alligator or other wild animal. They lose their wildness that way and become a danger to humans.

The Hells Bay double chickee lies at the south end of Hells Bay in a small cove of low-growing mangrove. It is well away from the shoreline, which makes for adequate breezes and fewer insects. The structure faces east, which means a great sunrise followed by an early blazing sun. But your best views are to the north and the bulk of Hells Bay, so named because it is hell to get into and hell to get out of.

Joe River

Type of campsite: Chickee	Landing: Dock
Scenery: 2	Use: High
Max. # of campers: 12	Max. # of parties: 2 Max. # of nights: 1
Fires: No	Toilet: Yes

GPS coordinates: N25° 16.789', W81° 3.940'

On which route: Cormorant Pass Route, Joe River Route

Nearby connecting routes: Big Sable Route, Cormorant Pass Route

Nearby campsites: South Joe River chickee, Oyster Bay chickee

Joe River is a very sturdy newer double chickee that doesn't sway as you walk around it, as some of the older ones do. It is set in a tiny cove off the east side of a bend in Joe River, just south of Oyster Bay. The view both up and down the river is somewhat limited. Behind the southwest-facing chickee, open to strong afternoon sun, stands a tall forest of mangrove on three sides, broken by two small creeks flowing into and out of the tiny cove. This creates daily tidal flow directly under the chickee.

Two 13-foot-square platforms with 6-foot-wide gangplanks come together at a common vault toilet. Cook tables on each chickee are useful. Be careful to hold on to small items here, as the spaces between the planks on the chickees are wide. The whole camping area is set 20 feet away from the mangroves, which may help some as far as insects are concerned. But don't expect too much of a breeze here. This campsite has the high use you would expect on a popular paddling route.

Lane Bay

Type of campsite: Chickee	Landing: Dock	
Scenery: 4	Use: Medium	
Max. # of campers: 6	Max. # of parties: 1	Max. # of nights: 1
Fires: No	Toilet: Yes	
GPS coordinates: N25° 17.001', W80° 53.525'		
On which route: Lane River Route		
Nearby connecting routes: Hells Bay Canoe Trail, Roberts River Route		
Nearby campsites: Hells Bay chickee, Roberts River chickee		

The Lane Bay single-camping-party chickee backs up against a hardwood hammock at the north end of Lane Bay. The standard camping platform is connected to a vault toilet by a 4-foot-wide gangplank that was replaced in the mid-2000s. A south-facing platform, even with a roof, gets its share of the sun, but the view of Lane Bay is worth it. This perch offers campers a commanding view of wooded shores with a larger variety of vegetation than the average mangrove waterfront. The hardwood hammock directly behind the chickee gives you close-up views of the setting—ferns, wax myrtle, coco plums—though this forest may contribute to insect problems at times. In the bay directly in front of the chickee is the beginning of the Lane River.

Lard Can

Type of campsite: Ground	Landing: Ground
Scenery: 3	Use: Low
Max. # of campers: 10	Max. # of parties: 4 Max. # of nights: 2
Fires: No	Toilet: Yes

GPS coordinates: N25° 14.953', W80° 50.822'

On which route: Hells Bay Canoe Trail

Nearby campsites: Pearl Bay, Hells Bay

Lard Can is an old spot of heavily wooded solid ground that humans have inhabited since the Calusa discovered it hundreds of years ago. In pre-park days, gladesmen often set up base camps here for hunting and fishing and stored their supplies in big tin lard cans, the driest storage available. That's how the campsite got its name.

A ring of mangrove borders the water, except for a small landing split by a buttonwood tree, where two boats can pull up onto mud and roots. There is a small clearing here surrounded by ferns, palm trees, and coco plums. Campsites extend to the right of the main landing, but the encircling vegetation limits insect-clearing breezes.

This low-use campsite makes for a good first night's stop, especially if you're getting a late start or the chickees are full. It's good for solitude as well; I've never encountered another party camping here. If you've come to fish, you can angle for bass and freshwater species in the ponds on the way in without having to worry about making a frenzied paddle to camp before dark. (Lard Can is only 3 miles away from Main Park Road.)

Set in dense woods, Lard Can will be very buggy following rains. It can be muddy as well. Before you camp here, check the gauge (PVC pipe marked in inches) on the left of the Hells Bay Canoe Trail dock. If the gauge reads 2 feet or the dock is submerged, Lard Can will be pretty sloppy, too.

Middle Cape

Type of campsite: Beach	Landing: Beach
Scenery: 5	Use: Medium
Max. # of campers: 60	Max. # of parties: 15 Max. # of nights: 7
Fires: Yes	Toilet: No

GPS coordinates: N25° 9.442', W81° 8.475'

On which route: Middle Cape Route

Nearby connecting routes: East Cape Route, Big Sable Route, Little Sable Creek–Lake Ingraham Route

Nearby campsites: East Cape, Northwest Cape

A long stretch of beach, including Middle Cape itself, occupies this campsite. On the south end of the cape is an open, palm-dotted field paralleling the beach. A few old pilings, exposed at low tide, mark the start of the popular camping section of the beach. Shade here is nonexistent. Closer to the cape are some gumbo-limbo and Jamaica dogwood trees, along with some agave whose barren flower stalks tower in the air.

The cape itself offers relatively high ground at its sharp tip and tremendous views both north and south and, of course, into the Gulf of Mexico. North of the cape are some excellent tent sites. Then the beach narrows beside a small grassy field, which gives way to mangroves that grow to the Gulf's edge. The 2005 hurricanes opened up a sandy campsite, with scattered mangrove, on the north side of the Mid Cape Canal.

Middle Cape was once known as Palm Point. According to legend, several tall palms grew at the cape and passing mariners used them as a guide to their location. In the early 1800s the palms were cut down, but the spot was still known as Palm Point until the Coast and Geodetic Survey renamed it.

North River

Type of campsite: Chickee	Landing: Dock
Scenery: 2	Use: Medium
Max. # of campers: 6	Max. # of parties: 1 Max. # of nights: 1
Fires: No	Toilet: Yes

GPS coordinates: N25° 19.905', W80° 56.233'

On which route: The Cutoff Route

Nearby connecting routes: North River Route, The Labyrinth Route, Roberts River Route, Cormorant Pass Route

Nearby campsites: Watson River chickee, Roberts River chickee

The North River chickee is not actually on the North River, but on the river north of the North River. This river has no name. The covered camping platform named for the nearby North River lies on the east side of a small mangrove island (less than 100 feet in diameter) that sits in the middle of this unnamed river, which is only a couple hundred feet wide itself here.

This is an older chickee of standard size connected to a vault toilet by a 3-foot-wide gangplank. There is also a built-in ladder leading to the shallow clear waters that deepen quickly, making for good swimming. The view is somewhat limited by mangrove branches that extend around three sides of the structure. The chickee front overlooks the main river channel and a creek. This small island presents few bug problems.

Be prepared for bright early-morning light here. Arise early to enjoy the sunrise and get moving before the rays really heat up the chickee. At night, the lights of Miami will shimmer across the water, but with minimal powerboat traffic and a lot of bird life your sense of solitude in nature will remain overpowering. By day, you can investigate the upper reaches of the North River above The Cutoff.

Northwest Cape

Type of campsite: Beach   Landing: Beach

Scenery: 5   Use: Medium

Max. # of campers: 36   Max. # of parties: 9   Max. # of nights: 7

Fires: Yes   Toilet: No

GPS coordinates: N25° 13.281', W81° 10.262'

On which route: Middle Cape Route, Big Sable Route, Little Sable Creek–Lake Ingraham Route

Nearby connecting routes: Middle Cape Route, Big Sable Route, Ponce De Leon Bay Route

Nearby campsites: Middle Cape, Graveyard Creek

Vines creep along Northwest Cape. Photo by author.

The Northwest is my favorite of the cape campsites. It gets the least use of these campsites because it is the hardest to access. You get a real sense of going back in time to old Florida here. This spot is as beautiful as any in the country.

The beach follows the gentle contour lines of Northwest Cape, and the sand is wide enough to camp anywhere in the cape's immediate vicinity. Behind the beach is a pretty grass plain that goes back a good half mile and is punctuated with palm trees and several hardwood hammocks. In spots, Jamaica dogwood grows right along the beach line. Patches of agave grow among the grass.

Northwest Cape curves gently north. Up the way, palms grow closer to the beach. An interesting hammock of gumbo-limbo and dildo cactus grows close to the sea. The beach extends for a little way farther north until it hits a stand of storm-damaged mangrove skeletons at the ocean's edge. There is fine camping all along here.

Oyster Bay

Type of campsite: Chickee | Landing: Dock

Scenery: 2 | Use: High

Max. # of campers: 12 | Max. # of parties: 2 | Max. # of nights: 1

Fires: No | Toilet: Yes

GPS coordinates: N25° 19.412', W81° 3.969'

On which route: Big Sable Route, Cormorant Pass Route, Shark Cutoff Route

Nearby connecting routes: Big Sable Route, Cormorant Pass Route, Whitewater Bay Route, Joe River Route

Nearby campsites: Shark River chickee, Joe River chickee

Oyster Bay is one of the larger double chickees that sees use from both paddlers and motorboaters. It is on the route for those who circle Cape Sable and those who loop Whitewater Bay. Being so close to the Wilderness Waterway keeps it hopping, too.

The camping platform lies just west of Cormorant Pass in northern Oyster Bay. Two 14- by 12-foot platforms are connected by 7-foot-wide gangplanks that meet at a common vault toilet. A central ladder descends into the water. All this makes for extra room for walking around. Also, you can set up your tent earlier in the day and still have room to do things on your larger-than-average chickee. The right-hand chickee has been upgraded and a cooking table added.

Situated among a group of mostly small islands, the chickee faces east and will get some early-morning sun. But the west side backs up to a mangrove island a mere 15 feet distant. This chickee does not offer outstanding views, but it is sheltered from the elements by the surrounding islands. On the other hand, wind can be a good thing when the bugs are out—Oyster Bay campsite is notorious for no-see-ums, which bothered me during all of my stays there.

Pearl Bay

Type of campsite: Chickee	Landing: Dock
Scenery: 3	Use: High
Max. # of campers: 12	Max. # of parties: 2 Max. # of nights: 1
Fires: No	Toilet: Yes

GPS coordinates: N25° 15.560', W80° 51.404'

On which route: Hells Bay Canoe Trail

Nearby connecting routes: East River Route, Lane River Route

Nearby campsites: Lard Can, Hells Bay chickee

Pearl Bay campsite is the Cadillac of chickees—the largest and the best built. It serves an additional important function by being the park's only handicapped-accessible backcountry campsite.

This accessibility starts with a covered canoe slip. Astride this slip are two canoe-length steps with metal handrails that lead to an extra-wide 15-foot-square chickee. The wooden guardrails that border the platform have conspicuous openings for accessing the water around the chickee. A 6-foot-wide gangway leads to a large handicapped-accessible toilet. Another gangway leads to an adjoining, equally large chickee that also has wooden guardrails and a correspondingly large roof. All this translates to extra room to move around in for campers who feel cramped in their boats.

The Pearl Bay chickee lies at the north end of Pearl Bay and looks south over the largest part of the inlet. A good 30 feet separates the chickee from the shoreline behind it, which reduces insect problems. During the day, canoers paddling the Hells Bay Canoe Trail may pass by, but by evening it will be just you and the permanent residents of the Everglades.

Roberts River

Type of campsite: Chickee   Landing: Dock

Scenery: 4   Use: Medium

Max. # of campers: 12   Max. # of parties: 2   Max. # of nights: 1

Fires: No   Toilet: Yes

GPS coordinates: N25° 18.973', W80° 54.496'

On which route: Roberts River Route, The Cutoff Route

Nearby connecting routes: Roberts River Route, The Cutoff Route, Lane River Route

Nearby campsites: Lane Bay chickee, North River chickee

Roberts River chickee is a two-camper group affair tucked in a little cove at the head of an elongated stretch of the Roberts River. It is a newer chickee, with wider (6-foot) walkways than the older chickees. The walkways connect the covered camping platforms with a common vault toilet.

Just a stone's throw away is an old wooded hammock with ample dry land—a historic camping ground for all kinds of folks who traversed this section of the Everglades in times past. The hammock,

A cold day at Roberts River chickee. Photo by author.

now grown up with huge ferns, tall hardwood trees, and a few palms, may have inspired the decision to locate this west-facing chickee where it is.

Having the bulk of the bay in front of the chickee means warm sunsets, and the woods so close behind delay the morning sun from becoming too hot too early. The chickee's overall protection from the elements makes for a nice camp in inclement weather. It could be a little on the buggy side, but that hasn't been the case on any of my stays here.

Roberts River chickee makes a good base camp for exploring the headwaters of the Roberts River, which splits off into several streamlets above The Cutoff, less than a mile distant. It is also good for peace and quiet, as it's off the beaten path of the motorboating crowd.

South Joe River

Type of campsite: Chickee	Landing: Dock
Scenery: 3	Use: High
Max. # of campers: 12	Max. # of parties: 2 Max. # of nights: 1
Fires: No	Toilet: Yes

GPS coordinates: N25° 13.248', W81° 1.121'

On which route: Joe River Route

Nearby connecting routes: Cormorant Pass Route, Whitewater Bay Route, Buttonwood Canal Route, East River Route

Nearby campsites: Joe River chickee

The South Joe camping platform is a popular first night's destination for paddlers who depart from Flamingo. (I stayed here my very first night in the Everglades backcountry.) Located off the main waterway in a side bay of the Joe River, it has the advantage of quiet. This bay is drained by two creeks, so you can enter it from two directions, depending on which part of the Joe River you are coming from.

This east-facing chickee has a superior view of the entire bay. The two camping platforms are 12 feet square with 5- by 15-foot gangplanks merging to a common vault toilet. The whole chickee is a good 40 feet removed from the one mangrove shore. This spells better breezes and fewer insects. Expect company here on weekends, mainly paddlers. In pre-park days, gladesmen used to hunt and camp on patches of land west of the South Joe River.

Watson River

Type of campsite: Chickee	Landing: Dock
Scenery: 3	Use: High
Max. # of campers: 6	Max. # of parties: 1 Max. # of nights: 1
Fires: No	Toilet: Yes

GPS coordinates: N25° 19.958', W80° 58.833'

On which route: The Cutoff Route, Cormorant Pass Route, The Labyrinth Route

Nearby connecting routes: The Cutoff Route, Cormorant Pass Route, The Labyrinth Route, Whitewater Bay Route, Shark Cutoff Route

Nearby campsites: North River chickee, Shark River chickee, Oyster Bay chickee

---

Watson River chickee is set in a mangrove stand on the north side of a Whitewater Bay key, somewhat protected by a couple of other small keys nearby. From here you can access the big bay, small streamlets, and the little-paddled Watson River. The single-party covered chickee here is an older model with weathered boards and a short narrow walkway leading to a vault toilet. The camping platform faces north across open water to a manatee warning sign (which you can use to locate the chickee). Because it's surrounded by mangrove on three sides, north is its only view, scanning the beginning of the Watson River. Chilly north winds, a periodic occurrence in the Everglades during the paddling season, may bear down on the camper here.

The shady Watson River spot is welcome on a hot day, though the nearby mangrove could lead to bug problems. During the day you may hear powerboats, but at night, there won't be another person for miles—just the mangrove, the water, and the stars.

The Central Rivers Area

Broad River

Type of campsite: Ground	Landing: Dock
Scenery: 3	Use: Low
Max. # of campers: 10	Max. # of parties: 3 Max. # of nights: 2
Fires: No	Toilet: Yes
GPS coordinates: N25° 28.754', W81° 8.534'	

On which route: Broad River Route

Nearby connecting routes: Highland Beach Route, The Nightmare Route, Rodgers River Route, Wood River Route

Nearby campsites: Highland Beach

Broad River campsite is set on a piece of dry ground 2 miles up the south bank of the Broad River from the Gulf of Mexico. It lies west of the site location shown on nautical charts and is a 10-minute paddle from the north end of The Nightmare. Many paddlers camp here, waiting for the right tides to paddle The Nightmare. This mostly open ground site gets shade from Jamaica dogwood, palm, and too much of the invasive Brazilian pepper. Assorted vines such as morn-

Broad River campsite at midday. Photo by author.

ing glory complement the more substantial vegetation. A few small mangroves front the Broad River.

A dock and small ground landing provide boaters access to the campsite, where there is also a vault toilet. Campers spend much of their time on the dock, though, attempting to escape the mosquitoes and no-see-ums sometimes found in the vicinity. Tent sites are scattered on the land, including secluded sites well away from the water—if you are willing to venture into the thickets. You can find any variation of sun and shade you desire here. Picnic tables make cooking and eating easier.

Camp Lonesome

Type of campsite: Ground	Landing: Dock
Scenery: 4	Use: Low
Max. # of campers: 10	Max. # of parties: 3 Max. # of nights: 3
Fires: No	Toilet: Yes

GPS coordinates: N25° 29.287′, W80° 59.984′

On which route: Broad River Route, Wood River Route

Nearby connecting routes: Broad River Route, Wood River Route, Rodgers River Bay Route

Nearby campsites: Rodgers River chickee

Camp Lonesome is an old shell mound that has been lived and camped on for hundreds of years. The original Everglades settlers, the Calusa, augmented these bits of land by piling up discarded shells, which over time combined with the slowly accumulating soil to form the mounds on which they lived. Seminoles occupied this locale as late as the 1940s as a homesite and trading post.

Today, a T-shaped dock leads into a mound of land grown up with palms, fig, gumbo-limbo, and the ever-present pest, Brazilian pepper. Ferns, brush, and vines enclose the campsite on all sides, so the

Broad River is visible only from the dock. A USGS survey marker stands at the site.

A couple of picnic tables make Camp Lonesome more camper friendly than some of the other ground sites. Expect to share this very small campsite with weekend motorboaters coming here to fish. Despite the company and tight quarters, this spot exudes an aura of the wild Everglades, especially during the week.

Canepatch

Type of campsite: Ground   Landing: Dock

Scenery: 4   Use: Medium

Max. # of campers: 12   Max. # of parties: 4   Max. # of nights: 3

Fires: No   Toilet: Yes

GPS coordinates: N25° 25.3086', W80° 56.6078'

On which route: North Harney River Route, Harney River Route, Little Banana Patch Route

Nearby connecting routes: North Harney River Route, Harney River Route, Shark Cutoff Route, Little Banana Patch Route

Nearby campsites: None

The Canepatch ground site is a historic mound used for centuries by the Calusa, then by Seminole and white settlers. It was known for a long time as Avocado Mound, for the avocado trees planted there by the Seminoles. Its final agricultural incarnation was as a cane, lemon, and banana farm. Today, you can find remnants of all three plants growing on the mound.

To reach the campsite, come to the T-shaped dock on your arrival. Next, cross the long gangway from the water onto the mound and come to a clearing amid the numerous banana trees dominating the campsite. A few palms, guava trees, and cane add to the heavy peripheral vegetation. Though the center of the clearing is unshaded, save for a lone guava tree, shaded tent sites can be found along the wood's edge. The mound itself is sizable, but because the area is very overgrown only a small area is left for camping. Intrepid explorers who don't mind being bug bit and scratched up can investigate the site, maybe searching out the two USGS survey markers in the camping area. Remember, if you stumble on an artifact, leave it for others to discover and enjoy as you did.

Expect motorboat campers on weekend nights in the peak season. Try to come during the week and stay a couple of nights to paddle the Little Banana Patch Route, an 8.5-mile circuit through the creeks northeast of the camp.

Graveyard Creek

Type of campsite: Ground	Landing: Beach and ground
Scenery: 5	Use: Medium
Max. # of campers: 12	Max. # of parties: 4 Max. # of nights: 3
Fires: No	Toilet: Yes

GPS coordinates: N25° 22.959', W81° 8.546'

On which route: Highland Beach Route, Graveyard Creek Route, Ponce De Leon Bay Route

Nearby connecting routes: Highland Beach Route, Graveyard Creek Route, Ponce De Leon Bay Route, Harney River Route

Nearby campsites: Harney River chickee, Shark River chickee

Lying on the northern edge of a small inlet where Graveyard Creek meets the Gulf of Mexico, the Graveyard Creek campsite is officially designated a ground campsite even though it has characteristics of both a ground and a beach campsite. The actual camping area sits on a spit of high ground that runs along the Gulf of Mexico and then doglegs back east along Graveyard Creek.

Much of the land here was washed away by the 2005 hurricanes. Because the sand and shells were pushed back into the mangrove thickets, campers nowadays pitch their tents among the standing mangroves, both living and dead. The best access for this campsite is up mangrove-studded Graveyard Creek. The creek is deepest here and will allow boaters to exit and enter the campsite no matter what the water level, as falling tides can leave some access points high and dry. Two vault toilets are located beside Graveyard Creek. The campsite also provides the amenity of picnic tables.

Harney River

Type of campsite: Chickee	Landing: Dock
Scenery: 3	Use: High
Max. # of campers: 12	Max. # of parties: 2 Max. # of nights: 1
Fires: No	Toilet: Yes

GPS coordinates: N25° 25.958', W81° 5.455'

On which route: Harney River Route, The Nightmare Route

Nearby connecting routes: Harney River Route, The Nightmare Route, North Harney River Route, Highland Beach Route

Nearby campsites: None

The old Harney River single chickee has been dismantled and replaced by a new double chickee across the river. This new camping platform, 4 miles east of the Gulf, is strategically placed at the south end of an overgrown and tidally influenced area of the Wilderness Waterway at marker #12, where the waterway veers north from the Harney River. From this chickee you can paddle on a rising or high tide through heavily vegetated Broad Creek and the occasionally shallow Nightmare on The Nightmare Route. Because of its strategic location, the campsite is a bottleneck for those traveling the length of the Wilderness Waterway and can be difficult to reserve. If you can't get on here, consider the Graveyard Creek campsite as an alternative.

The two 12-foot-square platforms with covered roofs have an

The Harney River double chickee has wide tidal variations. Photo by author.

offset gangway connected to a shared vault toilet. A small ladder descends from the gangway into the water. Variations of 4 feet between the tidal high and low are not uncommon at this easterly facing chickee, making loading and unloading of your craft, especially sea kayaks, difficult at times.

Highland Beach

Type of campsite: Beach	Landing: Beach
Scenery: 5	Use: Medium
Max. # of campers: 24	Max. # of parties: 4 Max. # of nights: 3
Fires: Yes	Toilet: No

GPS coordinates: N25° 28.509', W81° 10.785'

On which route: Highland Beach Route, Broad River Route

Nearby connecting routes: Broad River Route, Wood River Route, Highland Beach Route, The Nightmare Route, Lostmans River Route

Nearby campsites: Broad River

Highland Beach is one of my favorite campsites—a classic natural beach that takes effort for paddlers to access. And for the Everglades, it's high ground. Farmed by the Rewis family in pre-park days, this high land has since reverted to what seems an undisturbed coastline. The long shell ridge was formed by the Gulf of Mexico's wave action, while hurricanes—despite leaving patches of barren mangrove skeleton—have, over time, enhanced the beach. Thick underbrush has been cleared from the sand and long stretches of mangrove have been uprooted, leaving the beach longer and more open and exposing trees, such as palm, formerly hidden in the tangle. Big Creek, shown on nautical charts, is gone.

Palms add a tropical touch to Highland Beach. Photo by author.

The beach starts at the northern edge of the bay formed by the Rodgers and Broad rivers. It continues north and becomes higher the farther north you go. A grass prairie backs the sand and is dotted with cabbage palm, Spanish bayonet, and an occasional Jamaica dogwood, strangler fig, and cactus. Mangrove guards the back side of the prairie. Palms grow thickest at the beach's edge where the sand is highest. The beach is nearly continuous from the north to Highland Point. Bay bean, bay cedar, and sea purslane cling to the sand closest to the Gulf, and shells abound along the strand.

Beware of the shallow approach to the beach on a low tide. Conversely, you may be left high and dry at this campsite until the tide has risen sufficiently to allow your departure. Due to this shallow water and to its distance from either Everglades departure point, this campsite is not heavily used. Expect to see a few motorboats zipping around the vicinity, though.

Rodgers River

Type of campsite: Chickee	Landing: Dock
Scenery: 3	Use: Medium
Max. # of campers: 12	Max. # of parties: 2 Max. # of nights: 1
Fires: No	Toilet: Yes

GPS coordinates: N25° 32.148', W81° 3.861'

On which route: Willy Willy Route, Cabbage Island Shortcut, Rodgers River Route, Toms Creek Route

Nearby connecting routes: Willy Willy Route, Cabbage Island Shortcut, Rodgers River Route, Toms Creek Route

Nearby campsites: Willy Willy

Rodgers River double chickee is located a mile west of the Wilderness Waterway in the south portion of Rodgers River Bay. Because it's situated in the dead center of the Everglades paddling area, canoeists and sea kayakers must put forth considerable effort to get to it.

The view from here is worth the effort. All of Rodgers River Bay lies before you to the south, the direction in which the chickee faces. Behind you is a shallow inlet. The mangrove shoreline is more than 40 feet away, making bug problems minimal. On the other hand, you had better weight down your gear; if the wind blows hard, there is little to block it. I once spent a cold rainy evening huddling behind my tent while cooking and eating dinner.

The platforms are 11 by 13 feet with gangways leading to a common vault toilet. The shelter overhead will provide some shade, but a south-facing chickee bears the brunt of the sun. If you share the site at all, you will more than likely share it with fellow paddlers.

Shark River

Type of campsite: Chickee	Landing: Dock
Scenery: 3	Use: High
Max. # of campers: 6	Max. # of parties: 1 Max. # of nights: 1
Fires: No	Toilet: Yes

GPS coordinates: N25° 22.128', W81° 2.704'

On which route: Shark Cutoff Route, The Labyrinth Route, Graveyard Creek Route

Nearby connecting routes: Shark Cutoff Route, The Labyrinth Route, Graveyard Creek Route, Big Sable Route, Cormorant Pass Route

Nearby campsites: Graveyard Creek, Oyster Bay chickee, Watson River chickee

---

Shark River is a vestige of the original chickee system first put together by the park service in the 1970s. It is a single 10- by 12-foot camping platform backed against a deep forest of red mangrove on a side creek of the Little Shark River. A 4-foot-wide gangway leads to a vault toilet and a small ladder descending into the water. This platform has the least overall square footage of all the chickees.

A north-facing position makes Shark River chickee a shady place. Close proximity to the mangroves can mean fewer breezes and more bugs, but only in comparison to other chickees. Overall, it is a quiet, pleasant spot, though as a single chickee on the Wilderness Waterway it can be in high demand.

The side creek of the Shark River chickee is also the beginning of The Labyrinth Route. The Graveyard Creek Route leads west from here to Graveyard Creek campsite. The Wilderness Waterway continues northeast on the Shark Rivers and southwest through the Shark Cutoff to Whitewater Bay.

Willy Willy

Type of campsite: Ground	Landing: Dock	
Scenery: 4	Use: Low	
Max. # of campers: 10	Max. # of parties: 3	Max. # of nights: 3
Fires: No	Toilet: Yes	
GPS coordinates: N25° 34.836', W81° 3.327'		
On which route: Willy Willy Route, Rodgers River Bay Route		
Nearby connecting routes: Willy Willy Route, Rodgers River Bay Route, Lostmans River Route, Rodgers River Route, Cabbage Island Shortcut, Toms Creek Route		
Nearby campsites: Rodgers River chickee		

Willy Willy is an old shell mound turned campsite deep in the eastern part of the Everglades paddling area, near Big Cypress National Preserve. Freshwater creeks surround this shady hammock of gumbo-limbo, palm, ferns, and dense undergrowth. An L-shaped dock connects the shell mound to the water. Pull your boat alongside the dock and enter the camp. Two picnic tables and a vault toilet add to campers' convenience.

By Everglades standards, the site is sloped. The mound drains well but can still get muddy. Willy Willy does have level tent sites but, crowded by vegetation, the campsite's space is limited. (Stay friends with your camping neighbors.) On weekends you are likely to encounter motorboaters who have brought the kitchen sink with them. Try to stay here for a couple of nights during the week to explore the adjacent freshwater creeks using aerial maps downloaded onto your GPS.

Ten Thousand Islands

Darwins Place

Type of campsite: Ground	Landing: Ground
Scenery: 4	Use: Medium
Max. # of campers: 8	Max. # of parties: 2 Max. # of nights: 3
Fires: No	Toilet: Yes

GPS coordinates: N25° 41.6394', W81° 12.1412'

On which route: Darwins Place Route, Gopher Key–Charley Creek Route

Nearby connecting routes: Chatham River Route, Last Huston Bay Route, Gopher Key–Charley Creek Route

Nearby campsites: Sweetwater chickee, Plate Creek chickee

Darwins Place is a ground camp with a lot of good and a little bit of bad. It is located atop an old Calusa mound by a small creek connecting Chevelier and Cannon bays. This mound was the home of the last man to homestead in Everglades National Park: Arthur Leslie Darwin, a hermit, whose concrete block house foundation still adorns the site today. He moved here in 1945 and grew bananas to sell, living out his days on Opossum Key, the common name of the shell mound here.

Possum Key was much more open in Darwin's day and has grown in considerably. Explorers can find an old lemon tree and a lone coconut palm if they make their way back through the heavy overgrowth of Brazilian pepper (a persistent pest despite park service attempts to get rid of it) and through the fig, gumbo limbo, Simpson stopper, and cabbage palms.

Solitude seekers will be disappointed by the campsite's heavy use and the weekend boat parade on the adjacent Wilderness Waterway. Expect fellow campers to occupy one of the tightly clustered tent sites here on weekends. If you decide to stay here, consider a layover or short day to explore Gopher Key, via the Gopher Key–Charlie Creek Route.

Hog Key

Type of campsite: Beach	Landing: Beach	
Scenery: 5	Use: Medium	
Max. # of campers: 8	Max. # of parties: 2	Max. # of nights: 2
Fires: Yes	Toilet: No	
GPS coordinates: N25° 34.284', W81° 13.986'		
On which route: Turkey Key Route		
Nearby connecting routes: Lostmans River Route, Highland Beach Route		
Nearby campsites: Turkey Key, New Turkey Key		

Hog Key is really not an island but a peninsula jutting out into the Gulf of Mexico. From shallows in the water, the beach slopes more than 6 feet to a storm-widened plain of prickly pear cactus, sea oats, and grass. Behind this stretches an extensive forest of tall sea grape, tamarind, buttonwood, and cabbage palm. Look for the giant tamarind tree spreading its branches over the campsite. It survived the 2005 hurricanes but doesn't look too good these days. From Hog Key, your view is of Wood Key and the Plover Keys.

Sunset from Hog Key makes for a fine ending to an Everglades day. Photo by author.

Besides the main camping area, Hog Key offers several other campsites. These include a small beach on the southeast side of the island, good for when northerly winds blow; several sites to the north that were opened up by the hurricanes; and a small spit by an inlet in Wood Key Cove that catches a due east wind, good for buggy times. It may be hard to find a perfectly level tent site here, but you will certainly be above the high tide line. Speaking of tides, try to time your arrival with a rising tide, as the shallow approach can make this a hard camp to get to at the same time that it makes it the domain of sea kayakers and canoers.

This area was settled by Richard Hamilton in the early 1900s. He ran hogs here, but the swines' diet of oysters and crabs left their meat inedible. Hamilton changed the hogs' diet to table scraps, which improved their flavor. Wild hogs still roam the key today—I've seen one while camped here.

Lopez River

Type of campsite: Ground	Landing: Ground
Scenery: 3	Use: High
Max. # of campers: 12	Max. # of parties: 3 Max. # of nights: 2
Fires: No	Toilet: Yes

GPS coordinates: N25° 47.271', W81° 18.374'

On which route: Lopez River Route

Nearby connecting routes: Last Huston Bay Route, Hurddles Creek Route, Rabbit Key Pass Route

Nearby campsites: Sunday Bay chickee

The author looks for an inscription at Lopez River campsite. Photo by Jean S.

Lopez River campsite is an old shell mound first occupied by the Calusa and later by Gregorio Lopez, who came to the area from Spain in the 1890s. The boat landing is actually part of the shell mound that extends into the river. There are several small landing spots here, but the main one is right in front of an old cistern built by Lopez. The year "1892" appears on the part of the cistern right by the river. Mangrove fronts the rest of the campsite. Modern amenities include several picnic tables and a vault toilet.

The ground here is high and dry. Shady tent sites are located beneath a large buttonwood and a few gumbo-limbos upriver of the cistern, wherein trees now grow. Another more isolated tent site is located below the cistern near a partially fallen tamarind tree. Dense thickets that include the shrub blackbead enclose the main camping area away from the river, but the shell mound extends in both directions along the Lopez.

Lostmans Five

Type of campsite: Ground	Landing: Dock
Scenery: 3	Use: Low
Max. # of campers: 15	Max. # of parties: 3 Max. # of nights: 3
Fires: No	Toilet: Yes
GPS coordinates: N25° 38.036', W81° 8.552'	
On which route: Darwins Place Route, Willy Willy Route	
Nearby connecting routes: Darwins Place Route, Willy Willy Route, Lostmans River Route	
Nearby campsites: Plate Creek chickee	

The Lostmans Five ground site is very low and noted for being muddy at times. For this reason, a platform resembling a chickee has now been built atop the campsite to keep conditions drier. The setting is attractive. Most of the ground sites in the interior are blocked from a water view by heavy vegetation. But Lostmans Five is right on the water, and about half the campsite overlooks Lostmans Five Bay at the mouth of Lostmans Creek. A T-shaped dock extends into the water for easy landing. There is a vault toilet on the dock. Picnic tables make the campsite more user friendly.

Buttonwood, ferns, and small bushes such as saffron plum surround the mostly open part of the campsite that doesn't abut the bay. A few palm trees break up the open area. Even though the site is open, shaded tent sites are available on the camp's perimeter.

Concrete blocks and old pilings indicate a previous presence, perhaps from the Poinciana land operation, headquartered on nearby Onion Key. In the 1920s, potential land buyers were driven to Pinecrest, off the Tamiami Trail, and then walked to a canoe landing at Lostmans Five, where they boated about a mile to Onion Key. This spot is very likely the old canoe landing. The 1926 hurricane ended the Poinciana development. Lostmans Five was later a site for a cabin on stilts.

Though generally a low-use area, Lostmans Five is sometimes occupied on weekends by angling motorboaters. You might prefer to visit during the week when you're more likely to have the site to yourself. Take some time to paddle toward the freshwater Glades up Lostmans Five Creek. The name Lostmans Five, by the way, came about because it is the fifth major bay coming north from the mouth of Lostmans River. Count them: First Bay, Second Bay, Onion Key Bay, Two Island Bay, then Lostmans Five Bay.

Mormon Key

Type of campsite: Beach	Landing: Beach	
Scenery: 4	Use: High	
Max. # of campers: 12	Max. # of parties: 2	Max. # of nights: 3
Fires: Yes	Toilet: No	
GPS coordinates: N25° 40.435′, W81° 17.368′		

On which route: Pavilion Key Route, Huston River Route, Chatham River Route, Turkey Key Route

Nearby connecting routes: Pavilion Key Route, Huston River Route, Chatham River Route, Turkey Key Route, Gopher Creek–Charley Creek Route

Nearby campsites: Pavilion Key, New Turkey Key, Watsons Place

---

Mormon Key lies at the mouth of the Chatham River in a long-occupied area known as Chatham Bend. The Calusa stayed here; you can see their broken conch and clamshells. Later the island was occupied by whiter settlers, one of whom lived here with his first and second wives simultaneously, which gave it the name Mormon Key. At low tide, concrete remnants of a dock can be seen at the west point of the island.

The primary northwest-facing beach here is high but small. A field of grass, cactus, and brush parallels the beach. This clearing gives way to backdrop stands of buttonwood, sea grape, and mangrove. Other hammock species can be found in the interior of the island. The main beach allows views across Chatham Bend to the mouth of the Chatham River, Gun Rock Point, Pavilion Key, and other points north.

A sandy campsite on the shallow southwestern edge was opened up by the 2005 hurricanes. Jamaica dogwood and sea grape trees provide shade. Small beaches between clumps of mangrove provide cold weather campsites on the south side of the island.

New Turkey Key

Type of campsite: Beach	Landing: Beach	
Scenery: 4	Use: High	
Max. # of campers: 10	Max. # of parties: 2	Max. # of nights: 2
Fires: Yes	Toilet: Yes	

GPS coordinates: N25° 38.800', W81° 16.874'

On which route: Turkey Key Route

Nearby connecting routes: Pavilion Key Route, Huston River Route, Chatham River Route, Gopher Key–Charley Creek Route

Nearby campsites: Mormon Key, Turkey Key

New Turkey Key campsite lies at the center of a very slender, small island at the extreme south end of the Ten Thousand Islands. The north tip of New Turkey faces the mainland and is sandy but subject to flooding when high tides and winds mix. I found this out the hard way—do not camp here. The center portion of the island is buffered with black mangrove and a little sea grape. Access can be from both the Gulf and the mainland side of the island. I recommend the mainland side, as a deep channel runs beside the island here. The primary tent sites are situated on the island's north end by a sand spit and under some mangrove near the slenderest part of the island. Another isolated tent site can be found on the south end of the key—a grassy flat punctuated with Spanish bayonet.

This small key has a two-party limit. On weekdays you will usually have it to yourself. Expect motorboat campers on weekends—they like the deep channel which allows them to pull their boats close to shore without leaving them stranded in the shallows. If you're planning to make a fire, be prepared: New Turkey Key is normally picked clean of firewood.

Pavilion Key

Type of campsite: Beach	Landing: Beach
Scenery: 5	Use: High
Max. # of campers: 20	Max. # of parties: 4 Max. # of nights: 3
Fires: Yes	Toilet: Yes

GPS coordinates: N25° 42.323', W81° 21.186'

On which route: Pavilion Key Route

Nearby connecting routes: Chatham River Route, Huston River Route, Rabbit Key Pass Route

Nearby campsites: Rabbit Key, Mormon Key

Pavilion Key is the largest island campsite in the park. The primary camping area is on the northern tip of the island, where a long sandy spit extends out from the forested part of the island. Vegetation on this peninsula includes sea oats, grass, mangrove, and buttonwoods, but there isn't much shade here. On the plus side are the ocean views and breezes from both sides of the spit. But if the wind is gusty your tent could be blown away.

Farther from the spit is a beach area forested on its south side by sea grape, mangrove, and a tangle of vines. This growth acts as a buffer that slows some winds, especially from the south. Tent sites extend along this stretch of beach, where you can also beachcomb a fair distance. The farther northwest you go on the island, the more storm damage you will see. Other campsites are located on the sandy

Looking over open water from Pavilion Key. Photo by Constance Mier.

southeast tip of the island near what remains of Dog Key and on a Gulf-facing beach that looks southwest.

If you are looking for solitude, don't come here. This is a large-capacity campsite, as is evidenced by its having two vault toilets. Pavilion is popular with paddlers and some motorboaters, because it's far out in the Gulf and has such a large beach. This popularity is not lost on the island's raccoons, who lurk under cover of the darkness to steal food and water. Store your goods appropriately.

Picnic Key

Type of campsite: Beach	Landing: Beach
Scenery: 4	Use: High
Max. # of campers: 16	Max. # of parties: 3 Max. # of nights: 3
Fires: Yes	Toilet: Yes

GPS coordinates: N25° 49.381', W81° 28.995'

On which route: Indian Key Pass Route, West Pass Route, Pavilion Key Route

Nearby connecting routes: Indian Key Pass Route, West Pass Route, Pavilion Key Route, White Horse Key Route

Nearby campsites: Tiger Key, Camp Lulu Key

Picnic Key campsite is located in the heart of the Ten Thousand Islands, 7.5 miles from the Gulf Coast Ranger Station, just north of Indian Key Pass. Most of the U-shaped island is mangrove, but a southwest-facing beach makes it a camping pleasure. A park service sign marks the beach; the only other park presence is a vault toilet. This beach runs more than 100 yards in length and is backed by sea oats, palms, and a multitude of sea grape trees. Some mangrove is mixed among these trees, along with Jamaica dogwood. In pre-park days, residents of Chokoloskee came to Picnic Key to harvest fall's sea grapes, spreading their blankets under the trees and shaking the fruits from them, turning the event into a picnic. Later, the sea grapes were turned into a tasty jam.

Your view from this busy camp is of the Gulf of Mexico and nearby Tiger Key to the west and the Stop Keys to the south. Welcome morning shade is provided by the woods east of the beach. A word of caution: Be careful wading or swimming near the beach; it is somewhat rocky.

Plate Creek

Type of campsite: Chickee	Landing: Dock
Scenery: 4	Use: Medium
Max. # of campers: 6	Max. # of parties: 1 Max. # of nights: 1
Fires: No	Toilet: Yes

GPS coordinates: N25° 38.4594', W81° 8.9379'

On which route: Darwins Place Route

Nearby connecting routes: Willy Willy Route, Lostmans River Route

Nearby campsites: Lostmans Five

Plate Creek is the most unusual chickee in the park. A single unit, but with more room than most double chickees, it was built on the pilings of an old land development office. The large pilings of the shaded portion of the platform were taken from an old water tower that fed the various floating buildings here. Park chickee builders got imaginative using these and other leftover pilings. First, they built a 50- by 4-foot dock with a vault toilet at one end. A short gangway leads to the main platform. This platform, 20 by 14 feet, is only partly covered, but is more than adequate for a paddler's tent. Spread your gear out on the rest of the platform and walk the dock to stretch your legs.

Plate Creek chickee is located on the east side of an island in the center of Plate Creek Bay, which is graced with lots of palms. Because the chickee backs up against it, this island stops a cold north-west wind but allows possible insect and critter problems. Store your food with care.

Rabbit Key

Type of campsite: Beach	Landing: Beach
Scenery: 4	Use: High
Max. # of campers: 8	Max. # of parties: 2 Max. # of nights: 2
Fires: Yes	Toilet: Yes

GPS coordinates: N25° 45.048', W81° 22.659'

On which route: Rabbit Key Pass Route, Pavilion Key Route, Sandfly Island Route

Nearby connecting routes: Rabbit Key Pass Route, Pavilion Key Route, Sandfly Island Route

Nearby campsites: Pavilion Key, Lopez River

Rabbit Key campsite is located at the southern end of the Ten Thousand Islands adjacent to the Gulf of Mexico, but the primary camping area faces north and east, toward the mainland. Across a lagoon from the camp, you can see Lumber Key, Crate Key, and another unnamed island. Expect to share Rabbit Key with other campers on weekends and most weekdays. It is a popular place—with its scenic blend of sand and trees and its proximity to Chokoloskee and Everglades City.

The primary camping area has only limited space. It is on a small beach backed with grass and mangrove beside a tiny rill that drains a pond in the center of the island. There is another tent site south of the island's vault toilet, under some trees by a swath of grass, sea purslane, and prickly pear cactus. The west side of the island has a couple of shaded tent sites that can be used when the weather is cool and windy. (Otherwise, these spots are too buggy.) A few north-facing sites can be found among the shoreline trees as well.

Sunday Bay

Type of campsite: Chickee	Landing: Dock
Scenery: 3	Use: High
Max. # of campers: 12	Max. # of parties: 2 Max. # of nights: 1
Fires: No	Toilet: Yes

GPS coordinates: N25° 48.17', W81° 16.36'

On which route: Hurddles Creek Route, Huston Bay Route

Nearby connecting routes: Lopez River Route, Huston River Route, Last Huston Bay Route

Nearby campsites: Lopez River, Sweetwater

Sunday Bay chickee is an excellent first night's destination from Chokoloskee. It is not too far to paddle and is one of the larger double chickees, with a special treat for one of the two groups that can stay here. This south-facing platform is located half a mile from the Wilderness Waterway on the north edge of a small bay that splinters off larger Sunday Bay. The close proximity of Chokoloskee and the Wilderness Waterway make it a popular camping destination, so expect to have company, especially on weekends.

The two 11- by 13-foot shaded platforms are connected to a central vault toilet by 4-foot-wide gangways. One of the platforms has the added bonus of a bench seat built along its north edge, where campers can sit and overlook the bay. The first campers to arrive at the chickee always take this platform first. The whole structure stands a good 30 feet distant from the mangrove, making for fewer bugs.

Sweetwater

Type of campsite: Chickee	Landing: Dock
Scenery: 4	Use: High
Max. # of campers: 12	Max. # of parties: 2 Max. # of nights: 1
Fires: No	Toilet: Yes

GPS coordinates: N25° 44.40', W81° 12.43'

On which route: Chatham River Route

Nearby connecting routes: Last Huston Bay Route, Darwins Place Route

Nearby campsites: Watsons Place, Darwins Place, Sunday Bay

Sweetwater chickee is off the beaten path. It is 2 miles up Sweetwater Creek, off the Wilderness Waterway, near the Chatham River. *You cannot access Sweetwater chickee via Last Huston Bay, only from Sweetwater Creek.* The mouth of Sweetwater Creek is narrow and hard to find, but once you get here, this camping platform will reward your determination. Few motorboaters use this area, because the creek ends towards the freshwater Glades and is not on a commonly traveled waterway, making it a quiet setting.

The 12- by 13-foot camping platforms are connected to a common vault toilet by 5-foot-wide gangways. Situated in a lagoon of the creek, the chickee faces south. A palm-topped island sits nearby, but not too close, just like the rest of the shore. The 50 feet of water between the camping platform and the mangrove minimizes insect problems. Tidal variations are minor this far from the Gulf, which makes unloading and loading your craft easier.

Tiger Key

Type of campsite: Beach	Landing: Beach	
Scenery: 5	Use: High	
Max. # of campers: 12	Max. # of parties: 3	Max. # of nights: 3
Fires: Yes	Toilet: No	

GPS coordinates: N25° 49.675', W81° 29.489'

On which route: West Pass Route, White Horse Key Route

Nearby connecting routes: Indian Key Pass Route, Pavilion Key Route

Nearby campsites: Picnic Key, Camp Lulu Key

Tiger Key is the most northerly of all the campsites in Everglades National Park. It is a west-facing beach camp on the outer edge of the Ten Thousand Islands. No matter which way you access this key, you must paddle out to the Gulf side of the island to a shallow cove, where the campsite is located near the island's center. Try to avoid low tide when approaching this camp, or you may have to portage your boat and gear a fair distance to the key.

A sign marks the long beach where most campers stay. Grass dotted with prickly pear cactus grows above the sand. Behind this grassy area is dense brush, occasional sea grape, buttonwood, and a lot of mangrove. Occasional mangrove interrupts the beach. Here your view is the expansive Gulf, Camp Lulu Key, and the Ten Thousand Islands Wildlife Refuge. Other tent sites are available on the sandy spit at the northwest tip of the island, overlooking West Pass.

Turkey Key

Type of campsite: Beach	Landing: Beach	
Scenery: 4	Use: Medium	
Max. # of campers: 12	Max. # of parties: 3	Max. # of nights: 3
Fires: Yes	Toilet: No	

GPS coordinates: N25° 38.536', W81° 16.370'

On which route: Turkey Key Route, Gopher Key–Charley Creek Route

Nearby connecting routes: Chatham River Route, Pavilion Key Route, Huston River Route

Nearby campsites: New Turkey Key, Mormon Key

Turkey Key is a beach campsite on a mangrove island a little south of the Chatham River. Running north to south, this island is just a short distance off the mainland. The primary camping areas are found on a west-facing beach marked with a park service sign. Other smaller camping sites are located further south and on the south tip of the island.

Everglades beaches are comprised of whole and crushed shells. Photo by author.

Vegetation is mostly mangrove, with scattered stands of sea grape. Grass and sea oats stabilize the beach areas, broken here and there by mangrove that extends all the way to the water. Be careful of the shallow approach to the key; if the tide is out, you will end up carrying your gear to the beach. This is what is known as an "Everglades portage." The shallow approach makes Turkey Key mostly a paddlers' campsite. While you're on the beach, note the amazing quantity of clam and conch shells. The preponderance of shells suggests a commercial operation in times past. Turkey Key was once the site of fishing shacks and a rendezvous point for fishermen and their suppliers. At the same time, the 2005 hurricanes threw an abundance of new shells onto the beach. These storms also denuded much of the mangrove on the west side of the key, opening it up a bit.

Watsons Place

Type of campsite: Ground   Landing: Dock

Scenery: 3   Use: High

Max. # of campers: 20   Max. # of parties: 5   Max. # of nights: 2

Fires: No   Toilet: Yes

GPS coordinates: N25° 42.547', W81° 14.738'

On which route: Chatham River Route

Nearby connecting routes: Last Huston Bay Route, Darwins Place Route, Huston River Route

Nearby campsites: Sweetwater chickee, Mormon Key

Watsons Place campsite stands on the north bank of the Chatham River, about 3 miles inland from the Gulf. It was once a thriving cane and vegetable farm of 35 acres, built atop an old shell mound. The farm, known as Chatham Bend, was operated by the notorious Ed Watson, who allegedly murdered several people on the site. Today, the cleared area is less than an acre, but you can see the remains of a syrup kettle, a cistern, and rusty farm implements. Determined explorers who venture through the thickets to see more evidence of Watson's operation, including the old house foundation, should know that the bodies of several of his victims were never found. . . .

Others folks resided here after Watson, but the park service let the place grow over. A T-shaped dock with a short walkway connects the land to a long landing where boats can tie up. There is also a vault toilet on the dock. A shell landing lies on the far side of a buttonwood and a Jamaica dogwood tree fronting the river. These trees provide one of the few shady spots at this campsite, with the exception of a tamarind tree by the tall part of the mound where Watson's house once stood. Dense brush borders the other sides of the campsite, which has picnic tables.

With the campsite's capacity of 5 parties or 20 campers, expect company here, especially on weekends. And if you are here by yourself, don't be surprised if the spirits of Watson's victims keep you company, whispering in the wind.

North of the Park

Camp Lulu Key

Type of campsite: Beach	Landing: Beach
Scenery: 4	Use: Very high
Max. # of campers: No limit	Max. # of parties: No limit Max. # of nights: No limit
Fires: Yes	Toilet: No

GPS coordinates: N25° 50.004', W81° 30.555'

On which route: White Horse Key Route

Nearby connecting routes: West Pass Route, White Horse Key Route, Pavilion Key Route, East River Route

Nearby campsites: Picnic Key, Tiger Key, Round Key, Panther Key

Camp Lulu Key is probably the most heavily used campsite in the entire Everglades paddling region. Why? Because it is nearest beach-camping locale to Everglades City for which a camping permit isn't required. When other campsites in the Everglades National Park reach permitted capacity, Camp Lulu Key is the number one alternative. The small island offers several camping spots, the first of which is the southeast-facing beach that looks toward Tiger Key. Curving west, a narrow strip of sand—formerly home to the last Everglades hermit, Mike Ward—is very popular. You can still see his locked stilt-house here. Tents can also be set up on the sandy point that extends into a lagoon on the back side of the island. Be prepared for close quarters and lots of company at all of these spots. No matter where your site, you will probably see evidence of previous campers: exposed trash, including the distasteful and unhygienic disposal of personal items. Avoid this place unless you have no other alternative.

Cape Romano Island

Type of campsite: Beach	Landing: Beach
Scenery: 5	Use: High
Max. # of campers: No limit	Max. # of parties: No limit
Max. # of nights: No limit	
Fires: Yes	Toilet: No

GPS coordinates: N25° 50.478', W81° 40.942'

On which route: White Horse Key Route, Morgan River Route

Nearby connecting routes: White Horse Key Route, Morgan River Route

Nearby campsites: Helen Key, Coon Key

Cape Romano is a large, spread-out camping area that extends around the outer edge of Cape Romano Island. Facing Helen Key, a mound and a small clamshell beach on the island's north end is the least-used camping area. The south end of Cape Romano has the most beachfront, but it is also the busiest area, with numerous motorboats and day users. The southwest part of the island, known as Morgan Beach, is also heavily used but offers plenty of sandy sites to pitch your tent. The hotels of Marco Island are visible from this beach, though. The sandy mouth of Morgan Bay, exposed in 2004 by Hurricane Wilma, is also popular.

If you are looking for solitude, Cape Romano Island is not the place. It does, however, offer wide-open views and deep waters around its edges. As you curve around the island, you will encounter undeveloped parcels of privately owned land. Please respect the property rights of the landowners by not camping on these spots.

Coon Key

Type of campsite: Beach	Landing: Beach
Scenery: 4	Use: Medium
Max. # of campers: No limit	Max. # of parties: No limit
Max. # of nights: No limit	
Fires: Yes	Toilet: No

GPS coordinates: N25° 53.542', W81° 38.217'

On which route: White Horse Key Route, Mud Bay–Goodland Route

Nearby connecting routes: White Horse Key Route, Mud Bay–Goodland Route

Nearby campsites: Helen Key, Cape Romano Island

Coon Key is a small, appealing island campsite in the northern part of Gullivan Bay near Goodland. Being located at the head of Coon Key Pass has its good and bad points. On the good side, Coon Key offers paddlers the shortest route between a put-in and a Gulf Island. (The put-in is at Goodland, only slightly more than 2 miles away.) On the bad side, Coon Key Pass is one of the most heavily used motorboat accesses in the entire Everglades paddling region, so you will never be far from motorboat noise on nice weekends. If you decide to stay here anyway, camps can be made along the eastern front on undersized pocket beaches backed by sea grape and buttonwood. A narrow spit extending from the north tip of the island offers another campsite possibility.

Fakahatchee Island

Type of campsite: Ground	Landing: Shell
Scenery: 5	Use: Medium
Max. # of campers: No limit	Max. # of parties: No limit
Max. # of nights: No limit	
Fires: Yes	Toilet: No

GPS coordinates: N25° 52.120', W81° 29.185'

On which route: East River Route

Nearby connecting routes: White Horse Key Route, West Pass Route

Nearby campsites: Round Key, Panther Key

The northeast side of Fakahatchee Island offers two camping areas. The first—a small spot on a high shell mound, with gumbo-limbo and plentiful cacti—looks north over Fakahatchee Bay. The tent site is set back from the mound's high point. Trails extend around the mound to a nearby cistern and the walls and foundation of an old homesite. The second campsite is situated one-tenth of a mile east around the island and overlooks tiny isles. This spot has a narrow access between buttonwood and mangrove, which also screen the water view a bit. Larger than the first, this camping area also has trails, including a path to an old cemetery. You can usually get one

A paddler taste tests the water from a cistern on Fakahatchee Island. Photo by author.

of the two available sites, but have the bug dope ready for as soon as you land your craft.

Grocery Place

Type of campsite: Ground	Landing: Shell
Scenery: 3	Use: Low
Max. # of campers: 10	Max. # of parties: No limit
Max. # of nights: No limit	
Fires: Yes	Toilet: No

GPS coordinates: N25° 57.098', W81° 36.838'

On which route: Mud Bay–Goodland Route

Nearby connecting routes: Fish Hawk Creek Route

Nearby campsites: None

Grocery Place campsite is situated on a high shell mound located along Royal Palm Hammock Creek at a sharp bend in the waterway. Coming from the Collier-Seminole State Park boat ramp, you will see the north side access first, at 5 miles. Palms mark the site. The landing here is somewhat muddy. Paddle around the shell mound to the sign-posted south access with its shell landing. A level, shaded camping area sits adjacent to an old cistern here. A second cistern is located on a spur trail. Though the underbrush gets thick away from the camp, narrow user trails keep parts of the mound open. Pray for breezes, as the bugs can be very troublesome in hot, still weather.

Gullivan Key

Type of campsite: Beach	Landing: Beach
Scenery: 5	Use: High
Max. # of campers: No limit	Max. # of parties: No limit
Max. # of nights: No limit	
Fires: Yes	Toilet: No

GPS coordinates: N25° 51.952', W81° 34.836'

On which route: White Horse Key Route, Fish Hawk Creek Route

Nearby connecting routes: White Horse Key Route, Fish Hawk Creek Route

Nearby campsites: White Horse Key, Panther Key

Gullivan Key is a Gulf-front destination offering camping areas on all sides. A long spit extends from the north tip of the island, but most of it is submerged by the tides. As you curve around a cove here, mangrove takes over. The east side has small beach clearings good for tent sites, while another camping spot is located on the extreme southern tip of the island. The west and southwest sides of the key offer the most beachfront and are backed by buttonwood, sea grape, and mangrove. Visible from here across Gullivan Bay, the high-rise hotels of Marco Island shimmer at night, providing a busy contrast to your quiet island respite.

Helen Key

Type of campsite: Beach	Landing: Beach
Scenery: 4	Use: Low
Max. # of campers: No limit	Max. # of parties: No limit
Max. # of nights: No limit	
Fires: Yes	Toilet: No

GPS coordinates: N25° 53.012', W81° 40.071'

On which route: White Horse Key Route

Nearby connecting routes: Morgan River Route

Nearby campsites: Coon Key, Cape Romano Island

Facing Gullivan Bay, Helen Key is situated near the very popular Cape Romano Island and, as a result, gets much less use. A long stretch of southeast-facing beach is broken by red mangrove stands.

In many areas, the sandy shore rises immediately to black mangrove, a few palms, and sea purslane, leaving little room for tents. The southwest end of the long beach has the most palms and the most open sand frontage. From here, you can look across the Snook Hole Channel and the greater Cape Romano area. You will have little company on this underused and underappreciated beach, but expect motorboats whizzing by when the sun shines.

Hog Key

Type of campsite: Beach	Landing: Beach
Scenery: 3	Use: High
Max. # of campers: No limit	Max. # of parties: No limit
Max. # of nights: No limit	
Fires: Yes	Toilet: No
GPS coordinates: N25° 51.797', W81° 33.448'	
On which route: White Horse Key Route	
Nearby connecting routes: East River Route	
Nearby campsites: Panther Key, White Horse Key, Gullivan Key	

Not be confused with Hog Key in Everglades National Park, this Hog Key is a smaller island tucked between the popular camping islands of Panther Key and White Horse Key. The only significant camping area on Hog Key is next to an inlet on its northwest side that has merged with an unnamed adjacent island. Water runs between these islands, but not even a canoe can bisect them because of the thick bordering mangrove. A level sandy area can be accessed from the north or south. Buttonwood and mangrove grow nearby but don't offer much shade. This campsite is heavily used, so expect to see other people.

Panther Key

Type of campsite: Beach   Landing: Beach

Scenery: 5   Use: Very high

Max. # of campers: No limit   Max. # of parties: No limit
Max. # of nights: No limit

Fires: Yes   Toilet: No

GPS coordinates: N25° 51.065', W81° 32.762'

On which route: White Horse Key Route

Nearby connecting routes: East River Route

Nearby campsites: Round Key, White Horse Key, Gullivan Key

Running north to south, Panther Key is a large island with a large number of campsites and a large number of campers. Even so, it seems to keep its attractive nature. Paddlers tend to frequent the southeast-facing areas, especially the palm-studded cove near Gomez Point. As you curve around to the island's west side, a mix of sea grape, buttonwood, palm, and mangrove rise above a long beach bordered by sea oats. The deep channel running just offshore here brings motorboat campers to the most northwest side of the island. Panther Key, like most of the keys north of the park, is much greener and shows much less damage from the 2005 hurricanes than islands inside Everglades National Park.

Round Key

Type of campsite: Beach   Landing: Beach

Scenery: 4   Use: High

Max. # of campers: No limit   Max. # of parties: No limit
Max. # of nights: No limit

Fires: Yes   Toilet: No

GPS coordinates: N25° 50.365', W81° 31.701'

On which route: East River Route, White Horse Key Route

Nearby connecting routes: West Pass Route

Nearby campsites: Camp Lulu Key, Picnic Key, Tiger Key, Panther Key

Round Key is a tiny, rocky island out in the Gulf. Surrounded by extensive shallows, fragile Round Key's small camps face primarily southeast and northwest. Sea grape and mangrove shade parts of the island, which you can circle on foot—traveling the rocky shore and under the trees—in about 10 minutes. Avoid this island in high winds, and expect the probability of having to tote your boat and gear at low tide. You might enjoy investigating the remains of a forgotten foundation on the island's southeast point.

White Horse Key

Type of campsite: Beach	Landing: Beach
Scenery: 5	Use: High
Max. # of campers: No limit	Max. # of parties: No limit
Max. # of nights: No limit	
Fires: Yes	Toilet: No

GPS coordinates: N25° 51.719', W81° 34.218'

On which route: White Horse Key Route

Nearby connecting routes: East River Route

Nearby campsites: Round Key, Panther Key, Gullivan Key

Gulf-facing White Horse Key has three distinct—and busy—camping areas. On the east side, a small sheltered sandy spot overlooks a narrow channel just a stone's throw away from an unnamed island. A deep channel for avoiding tidal shallows is the advantage here. Curving around the island an alluring beach faces southwest and offers the longest stretch of open sand. Sea grape and mangrove provide some shade here. On the northwest tip, an open, shadeless beach area, bordered by sea oats, overlooks Dismal Key Pass.

Looking out from the mangrove forest at White Horse Key. Photo by author.

Appendix

Route Chart

This chart combines the numerical information given at the beginning of each route description. "Wind" is potential wind influence. "Tide" is potential tide influence. "Nav" is navigational challenge. All variables are rated on a scale of 1 to 5, with 1 being low and 5 being high.

Route	Start	End	Miles	Wind	Tide	Nav
Florida Bay						
Dildo Key Bank Route	Flamingo	Little Rabbit Key	14	5	5	3
East Cape Route	Flamingo	East Cape	10	5	5	2
First National Bank Route	Little Rabbit Key	East Cape	20.5	5	5	3
North Nest Key Loop	Key Largo	Key Largo	16	5	4	3
Snake Bight Route	Alligator Creek	Flamingo	12	5	4	2
Cape Sable, Whitewater Bay, and the South						
Big Sable Route	Northwest Cape	Oyster Bay chickee	13	5	5	2
Buttonwood Canal Route	Flamingo	CG marker #10	5	2	2	1
Cormorant Pass Route	Joe River chickee	Watson River chickee	12	4	3	3
The Cutoff Route	Roberts River chickee	Watson River chickee	7	3	3	3
East River Route	CG marker #10	Hells Bay chickee	5.5	4	2	3
Hells Bay Canoe Trail	Main Park Road	Hells Bay chickee	6.5	2	1	1
Joe River Route	CG marker #10	Joe River chickee	12	3	3	2
The Labyrinth Route	Shark River chickee	Watson River chickee	7.5	1	2	5
Lane River Route	Hells Bay chickee	Confluence of Lane & Roberts rivers	5	3	2	3
Little Sable Creek–Lake Ingraham Rte.	Northwest Cape	East Cape	14	5	4	4
Middle Cape Route	East Cape	Northwest Cape	10.5	5	5	2
Mud Lake There and Back	Main Park Road	Main Park Road	8	3	2	2
Nine Mile Pond Loop	Main Park Road	Main Park Road	5.7	3	1	1
Noble Hammock Loop	Main Park Road	Main Park Road	2.3	2	1	1
North River Route	CG marker #30	The Cutoff at North River	4.5	3	2	2

continued

Route	Start	End	Miles	Wind	Tide	Nav
Roberts River Route	CG marker #18	Roberts River chickee	5.5	4	2	2
West Lake Canoe Trail	Main Park Road	Alligator Creek at Florida Bay	9.5	2	2	3
Whitewater Bay Route	CG marker #10	CG marker #40	12	5	2	1
The Central Rivers Area						
Broad River Route	Gulf	Camp Lonesome	12	3	4	2
Cabbage Island Shortcut	Rodgers River chickee	Broad River	3.5	2	2	3
Graveyard Creek Route	Shark River chickee	Graveyard Creek	7	3	4	3
Harney River Route	Canepatch	Gulf	13.5	3	4	2
Highland Beach Route	Mouth of Lostmans River	Graveyard Creek	13	5	4	2
Little Banana Patch Route	Canepatch	Canepatch	8.5	2	2	3
Lostmans River Route	WW marker #52	Mouth of Lostmans River	6	3	4	2
The Nightmare Route	Broad River campsite	Harney River chickee	8.5	2	2	4
North Harney River Route	WW marker #11	Canepatch	10.5	3	4	4
Ponce De Leon Bay Route	Shark River Island	Graveyard Creek	4	5	4	2
Rodgers River Route	Gulf	Rodgers River chickee	11.5	3	3	3
Rodgers River Bay Route	Willy Willy	WW #26 at Broad River Bay	7	3	2	3
Shark Cutoff Route	WW marker #9 at Tarpon Bay	Oyster Bay chickee	9	2	4	2
Toms Creek Route	Rodgers River chickee	Lostmans River	7	3	3	3
Wood River Route	Camp Lonesome	WW marker #24 at The Nightmare	11	2	2	2
Ten Thousand Islands						
Causeway Route	Chokoloskee	Gulf Coast Ranger Station	3	3	4	2
Chatham River Route	Mormon Key	Sweetwater chickee	8	3	4	3

Route	From	To				
Darwins Place Route	WW marker #99 at Chatham River	Lostmans Five	9.5	4	2	2
Gopher Key–Charley Creek Route	Darwins Place	Turkey Key	8	2	2	4
Halfway Creek Canoe Trail	Tamiami Trail	Gulf Coast Ranger Station	7.5	2	3	2
Halfway Creek Loop	Sea Grape Drive	Sea Grape Drive	8.8	2	3	2
Hurddles Creek Route	Chokoloskee	Sunday Bay chickee	7.5	2	3	3
Huston River Route	WW marker #119 at Sunday Bay	Mormon Key	9	3	4	2
Indian Key Pass Route	Gulf Coast Ranger Station	Picnic Key	7.5	3	5	2
Last Huston Bay Route	Sunday Bay chickee	WW marker #99 at Chatham River	7	4	2	2
Lopez River Route	Chokoloskee	WW marker #125 at Crooked Creek	7	4	3	2
Pavilion Key Route	Picnic Key	Mormon Key	15.5	5	5	3
Rabbit Key Pass Route	Rabbit Key	Chokoloskee	5.5	4	4	2
Sandfly Island Route	Gulf Coast Ranger Station	Rabbit Key	8	4	4	2
Turkey Key Route	Mormon Key	Mouth of Lostmans River	11	5	5	2
Turner River Canoe Trail	Tamiami Trail	Chokoloskee	9	2	2	4
West Pass Route	Gulf Coast Ranger Station	Picnic Key	9.5	4	4	4
Willy Willy Route	Lostmans Five	Willy Willy campsite	10	3	3	3

North of the Park

Route	From	To				
East River Route	Tamiami Trail	Round Key	12.5	4	3	4
Fish Hawk Creek Route	Collier-Seminole SP	Gullivan Key	13.5	4	4	4
Morgan River Route	Cape Romano	Snook Hole Channel	3	3	4	3
Mud Bay–Goodland Route	Collier-Seminole SP	Coon Key	9	3	5	3
White Horse Key Route	Tiger Key	Cape Romano	16.5	5	3	2

Campsite Chart

This chart combines information for the backcountry campsites in the paddling region of the Everglades National Park. The length-of-stay limits indicated apply to peak-use season, November through April. Campsite capacities apply year round. Campsite capacities are subject to change; check at a ranger station before departing. Campsites must be vacated by noon. (NL means no limit.)

Campsite	Type of site	# of people	# of parties	# of nights	Toilet	Table	Dock	Use
Florida Bay								
Alligator Creek	Ground	8	3	2				L
Little Rabbit Key	Ground	12	4	2	*	*	*	L
North Nest Key	Beach	25	7	7	*		*	M
Cape Sable, Whitewater Bay, and the South								
Clubhouse Beach	Beach	24	4	3				L
East Cape	Beach	60	15	7				M
East Clubhouse Beach	Beach	24	4	3				L
Hells Bay	Chickee	12	2	1	*		*	H
Joe River	Chickee	12	2	1	*		*	H
Lane Bay	Chickee	6	1	1	*		*	M
Lard Can	Ground	10	4	2	*			L
Middle Cape	Beach	60	15	7				M
North River	Chickee	6	1	1	*		*	M
Northwest Cape	Beach	36	9	7				M
Oyster Bay	Chickee	12	2	1	*		*	H
Pearl Bay	Chickee	12	2	1	*		*	H
Roberts River	Chickee	12	2	1	*		*	M
South Joe River	Chickee	12	2	1	*		*	H
Watson River	Chickee	6	1	1	*		*	H

continued

The Central Rivers Area

Campsite	Type of site	# of people	# of parties	# of nights	Toilet	Table	Dock	Use
Broad River	Ground	10	3	2	*	*	*	L
Camp Lonesome	Ground	10	3	3	*	*	*	L
Canepatch	Ground	12	4	3	*	*	*	M
Graveyard Creek	Ground	12	4	3	*		*	M
Harney River	Chickee	12	2	1	*		*	H
Highland Beach	Beach	24	4	3				M
Rodgers River	Chickee	12	2	1	*		*	M
Shark River	Chickee	6	1	1	*		*	H
Willy Willy	Ground	10	3	3	*	*	*	L

Ten Thousand Islands

Campsite	Type of site	# of people	# of parties	# of nights	Toilet	Table	Dock	Use
Darwins Place	Ground	8	2	3	*	*		M
Hog Key	Beach	8	2	2				L
Lopez River	Ground	12	3	2	*	*		H
Lostmans Five	Ground	15	3	3	*	*	*	L
Mormon Key	Beach	12	2	3				M
New Turkey Key	Beach	10	2	2	*			H
Pavilion Key	Beach	20	4	3	*			H
Picnic Key	Beach	16	3	3	*			H
Plate Creek	Chickee	6	1	1	*		*	M

Rabbit Key	Beach	8	2	2	*			H
Sunday Bay	Chickee	12	2	1	*		*	H
Sweetwater	Chickee	12	2	1	*		*	H
Tiger Key	Beach	12	3	3				H
Turkey Key	Beach	12	3	3				M
Watsons Place	Ground	20	5	2	*	*	*	H

North of the Park

Camp Lulu Key	Beach	NL	NL	NL				H
Cape Romano Island	Beach	NL	NL	NL				H
Coon Key	Beach	NL	NL	NL				M
Fakahatchee Island	Ground	NL	NL	NL				M
Grocery Place	Ground	10	NL	NL				L
Gullivan Key	Beach	NL	NL	NL				H
Helen Key	Beach	NL	NL	NL				L
Hog Key	Beach	NL	NL	NL				M
Panther Key	Beach	NL	NL	NL				H
Round Key	Beach	NL	NL	NL				M
White Horse Key	Beach	NL	NL	NL				H

Paddler's Checklist

☐ Coast Guard–approved life vest
☐ Paddles, with spare for each person in boat
☐ Bailer
☐ Bow and stern lines
☐ Waterproof bags for gear
☐ Flares
☐ Light for operating at night
☐ Waterproof nautical chart
☐ Compass, with spare
☐ GPS, with downloaded nautical charts
☐ Tide chart
☐ Binoculars
☐ Backcountry permit
☐ Fishing license and regulations
☐ Weather forecast
☐ NOAA weather radio
☐ Freestanding tent with no-see-um netting
☐ Sleeping bag, comfort rated to 40 degrees
☐ Sleeping pad
☐ Water—1 gallon per person per day

- ☐ Food, with extra day's supply
- ☐ Raccoon-proof storage container for food and water
- ☐ Portable stove or grill
- ☐ Fuel for stove
- ☐ Waterproof matches and lighter
- ☐ Cooking gear and utensils
- ☐ Biodegradable soap
- ☐ Rain gear
- ☐ Cold- and warm-weather clothing
- ☐ Long-sleeved shirt and long pants for sun protection
- ☐ Wide-brimmed hat
- ☐ First-aid kit
- ☐ Knife, with spare stowed away
- ☐ Wristwatch for calculating tides
- ☐ Sunglasses
- ☐ Sunscreen and chapstick
- ☐ Insect repellent
- ☐ Personal items—toothbrush, etc.
- ☐ Trowel
- ☐ Biodegradable toilet paper

Boat Rentals and Outfitters

Everglades City

Ivey House/Everglades Rentals and Eco Adventures
P.O. Box 5038
Everglades City, Fla. 34139
(877) 567-0679 (toll free); (239) 695-3299
www.IveyHouse.com; www.EvergladesAdventures.com
These fine folks rent canoes, kayaks, and gear; lead eco tours; and provide shuttles to launch sites throughout the Glades. They also offer showers and overnight lodging at Ivey House, located adjacent to Everglades Adventures in Everglades City.

Glades Haven Marina
875 South Copeland Avenue
Everglades City, Fla. 34139
(888) 956-6251 (toll free); (239) 695-2746
www.gladeshaven.com
Located in Everglades City, this business rents canoes and kayaks and provides shuttles. They have a boat launch and also rent cabins and houses.

Florida City

Everglades International Hostel
20 SW 2nd Avenue, Florida City, Fla. 33034
(800) 372-3874 (toll free); (305) 248-1122
www.evergladeshostel.com
Located only 15 minutes from the east entrance to Everglades National Park, this outfit provides inexpensive lodging, canoe and kayak rentals, guided tours, and shuttle services.

Flamingo

Flamingo Lodge Marina & Outpost Resort
1 Flamingo Lodge Highway
Flamingo, Fla. 33034
(239) 695-3101
www.flamingolodge.com
High on convenience and price, this group offers canoes and kayaks for rent from the main jumping-off spot for the southern Everglades. Showers are available as well.

Key Largo

Florida Bay Outfitters
104050 Overseas Highway
Key Largo, Fla. 33037
(305) 451-3018
www.kayakfloridakeys.com
Florida Bay Outfitters is your Keys connection for canoe and kayak rentals. They also sell boats and all kinds of paddling gear and offer guided tours ranging from half a day to a week.

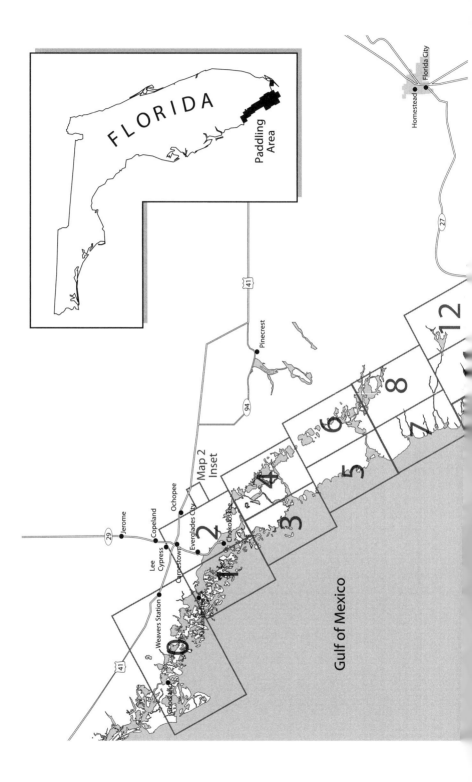

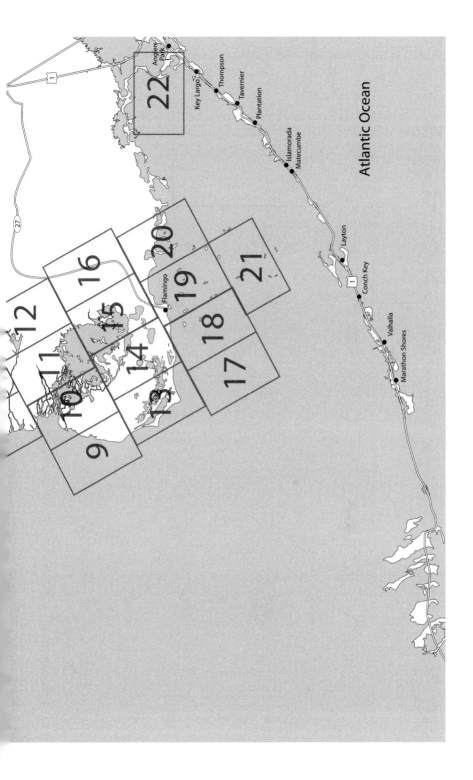

Atlantic Ocean

Anglers Pak
Key Largo
Thompson
Tavernier
Plantation
Islamorada
Matecumbe
Layton
Conch Key
Valhalla
Marathon Shores
Flamingo

9 10 11 12
13 14 15 16
17 18 19 20
21 22

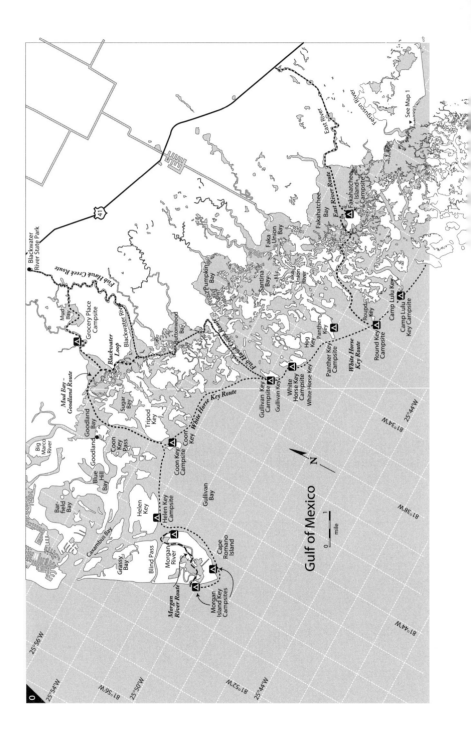

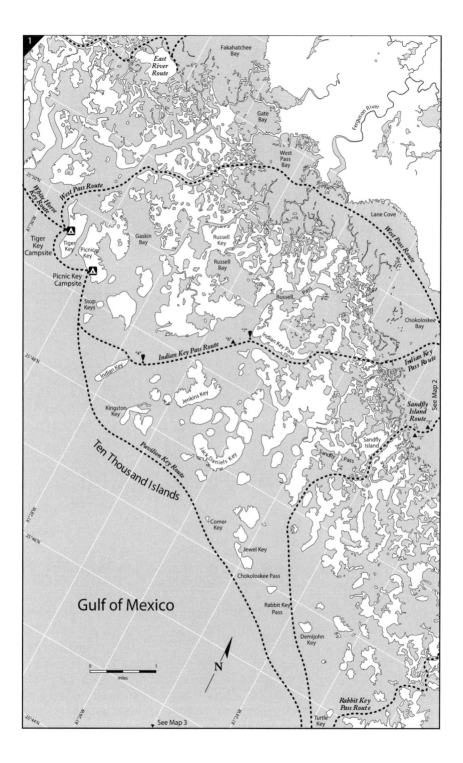

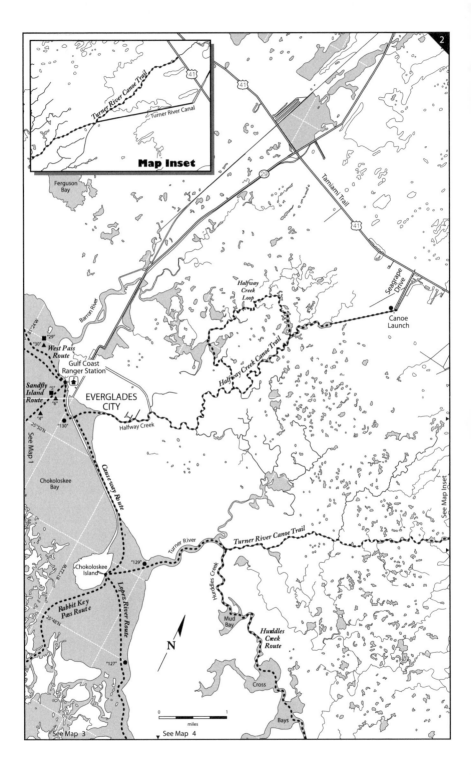

Map Inset

Turner River Canoe Trail

Turner River Canal

41

41

Tamiami Trail

29

Ferguson Bay

Barron River

Halfway Creek Loop

Seagrape Drive

Canoe Launch

81°24'W

"29"

"30"

West Pass Route

Gulf Coast Ranger Station

Sandfly Island Route

"5"

"6"

"A"

EVERGLADES CITY

25°50'N

"130"

Halfway Creek

Halfway Creek Canoe Trail

See Map 1

Chokoloskee Bay

Causeway Route

Turner River

Turner River Canoe Trail

Chokoloskee Island

"129"

Hurddles Creek

81°22'W

Lopez River Route

Rabbit Key Pass Route

25°48'N

Mud Bay

Hurddles Creek Route

"127"

N

Cross

0   1
miles

See Map 3

See Map 4

Bays

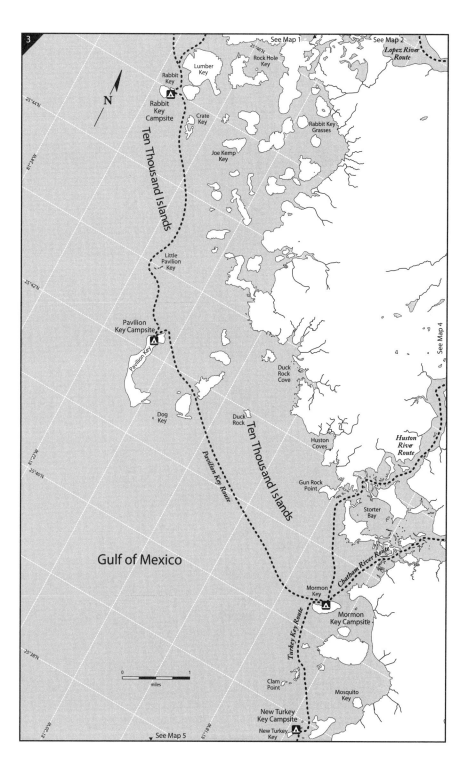

See Map 1

See Map 2

3

Lopez River Route

25°44'N

25°42'N

25°40'N

25°38'N

N

Ten Thousand Islands

Rabbit Key

Lumber Key

Rock Hole Key

25°46'N

Rabbit Key Campsite

Crate Key

Rabbit Key Grasses

Joe Kemp Key

Little Pavilion Key

Pavilion Key Campsite

Pavilion Key

Dog Key

Duck Rock

Ten Thousand Islands

Duck Rock Cove

See Map 4

Huston Coves

Huston River Route

Pavilion Key Route

Gun Rock Point

Storter Bay

Gulf of Mexico

Chatham River Route

Mormon Key

Turkey Key Route

Mormon Key Campsite

Clam Point

Mosquito Key

0   1
miles

New Turkey Key Campsite

New Turkey Key

See Map 5

81°24'W

81°22'W

81°20'W

81°18'W

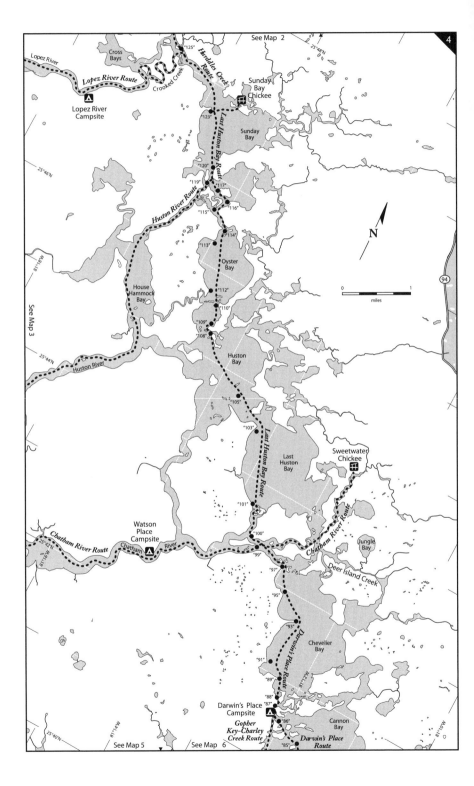

See Map 2

Lopez River

Cross Bays

Lopez River Route

Crooked Creek

Humilles Creek Route

Sunday Bay Chickee

Lopez River Campsite

"125"

"123"

Sunday Bay

Last Huston Bay Route

"120"

"119"

Huston River Route

"117"

"116"

"115"

"114"

"113"

Oyster Bay

House Hammock Bay

"112"

"110"

"109"

"108"

Huston Bay

Huston River

"105"

"103"

Last Huston Bay Route

Last Huston Bay

Sweetwater Chickee

"101"

Watson Place Campsite

"100"

Chatham River Route

Chatham River

"99"

Chatham River Route

Jungle Bay

Deer Island Creek

"97"

"95"

"93"

Chevelier Bay

Darwin's Place Route

"91"

"89"

"88"

"87"

Darwin's Place Campsite

Gopher Key–Charley Creek Route

"86"

Cannon Bay

"85"

Darwin's Route

N

0   1
miles

94

See Map 3

See Map 5

See Map 6

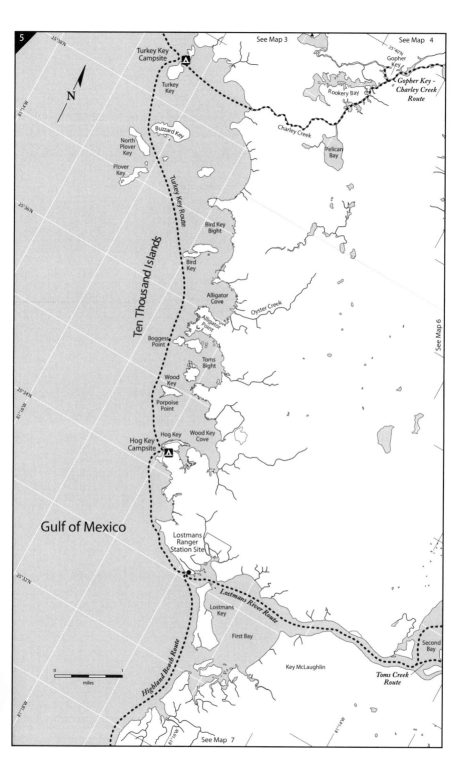

25°38'N

See Map 3

See Map 4

25°40'N

Gopher
Key

Turkey Key
Campsite

*Gopher Key –
Charley Creek
Route*

N

Turkey
Key

Rookery Bay

Buzzard Key

Charley Creek

North
Plover
Key

81°14'W

Pelican
Bay

Plover
Key

25°36'N

Bird Key
Bight

Ten Thousand Islands

Turkey Key Route

Bird
Key

Alligator
Cove

Oyster Creek

Alligator
Point

See Map 6

Boggess
Point

Toms
Bight

Wood
Key

25°34'N

81°16'W

Porpoise
Point

Hog Key   Wood Key
Cove

Hog Key
Campsite

Gulf of Mexico

Lostmans
Ranger
Station Site

25°32'N

Lostmans River Route

Lostmans
Key

First Bay

Second
Bay

Key McLaughlin

*Toms Creek
Route*

0   1

miles

Highland Beach Route

81°18'W

81°14'W

See Map 7

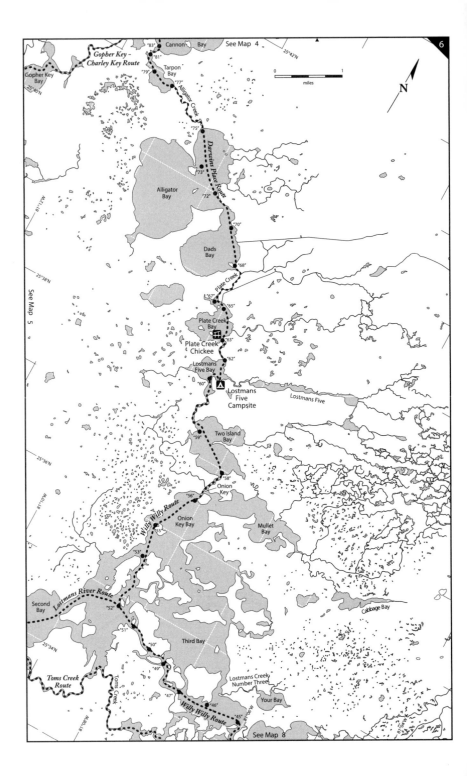

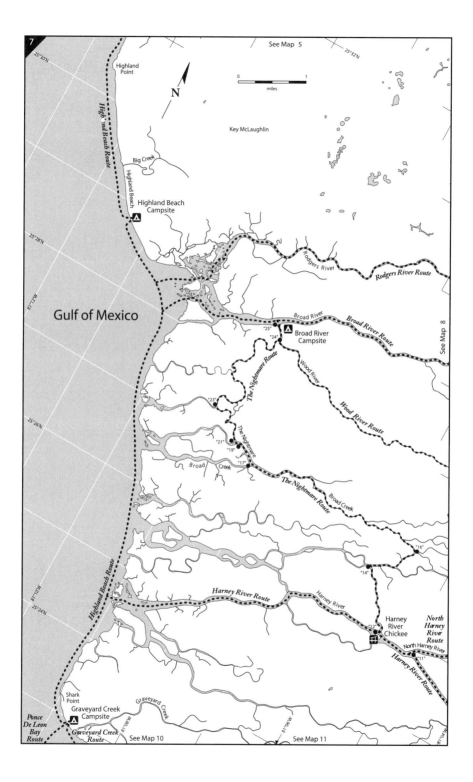

7

25°30'N

See Map 5

25°32'N

Highland
Point

N

0   1
miles

Key McLaughlin

*High*land *Beach Route*

Big Creek

Highland Beach

Highland Beach
Campsite

25°28'N

Rodgers River

Rodgers River Route

Gulf of Mexico

Broad River

Broad River Route

"25"

"24"

Broad River
Campsite

See Map 8

The Nightmare Route

Wood River

Wood River Route

25°26'N

"23"

"21"
"19"
"17"

The Nightmare

Broad   Creek

The Nightmare Route

Broad Creek

"16"

"14"

Highland Beach Route

Harney River Route

Harney River

25°24'N

Harney
River
Chickee

*North
Harney
River
Route*

"12"

North Harney River

Harney River Route

"11"

Shark
Point

Graveyard Creek
Campsite

Graveyard   Creek

*Ponce
De Leon
Bay
Route*

*Graveyard Creek
Route*

See Map 10

See Map 11

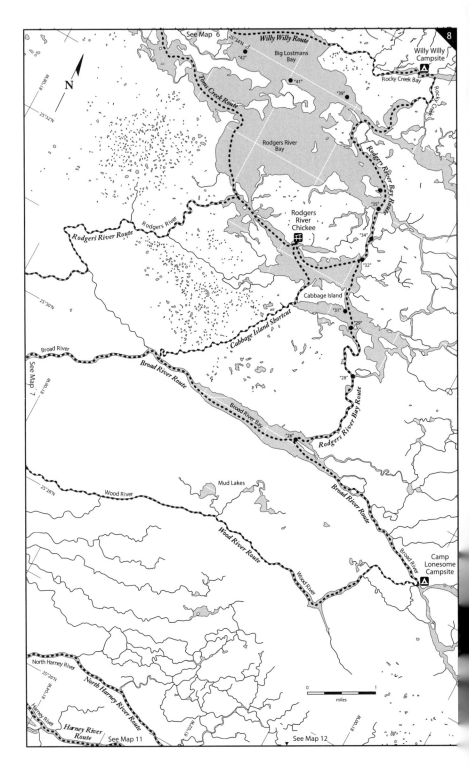

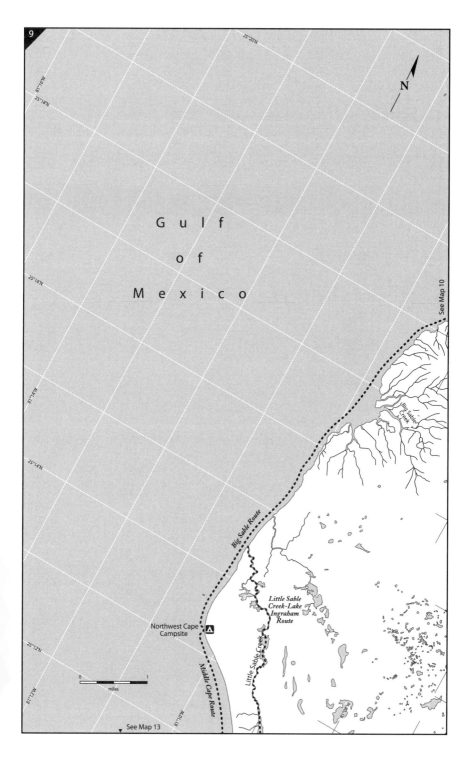

9

25°20'N

N

25°18'N

G u l f

o f

M e x i c o

25°16'N

See Map 10

Big Sable
Creek

25°14'N

Big Sable Route

Little Sable
Creek–Lake
Ingraham
Route

Northwest Cape
Campsite

Little Sable Creek

0   1

miles

Middle Cape Route

See Map 13

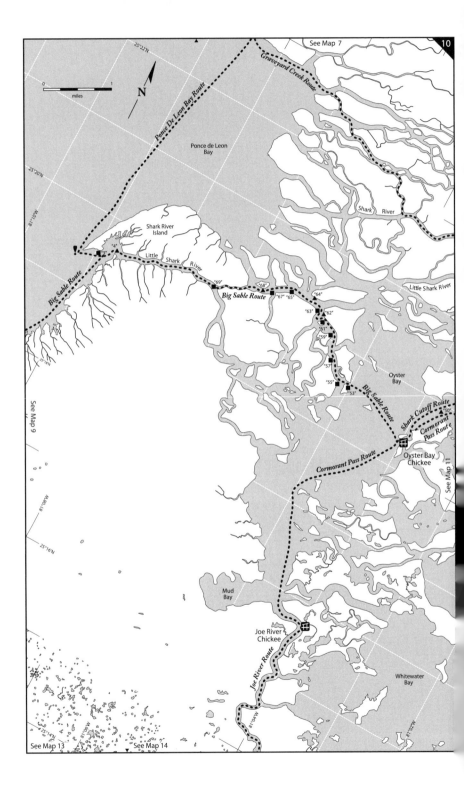

25°22'N

0   miles   1

N

Ponce De Leon Bay Route

Graveyard Creek Route

Ponce de Leon
Bay

25°20'N

81°10'W

Shark   River

Shark River
Island

Big Sable Route

Little   Shark   River

Little Shark River

"69"

Big Sable Route

"68" "64"
"67" "65"

"63" "62"

"61"
"59"

"57"

Oyster
Bay

"55"

"53"

Big Sable Route

Shark Cutoff Route

"50"

Cormorant
Pass Route

Oyster Bay
Chickee

25°18'N

See Map 9

See Map 11

Cormorant Pass Route

81°08'W

25°16'N

Mud
Bay

Joe River
Chickee

Joe River Route

Whitewater
Bay

81°06'W

81°04'W

81°02'W

25°14'N

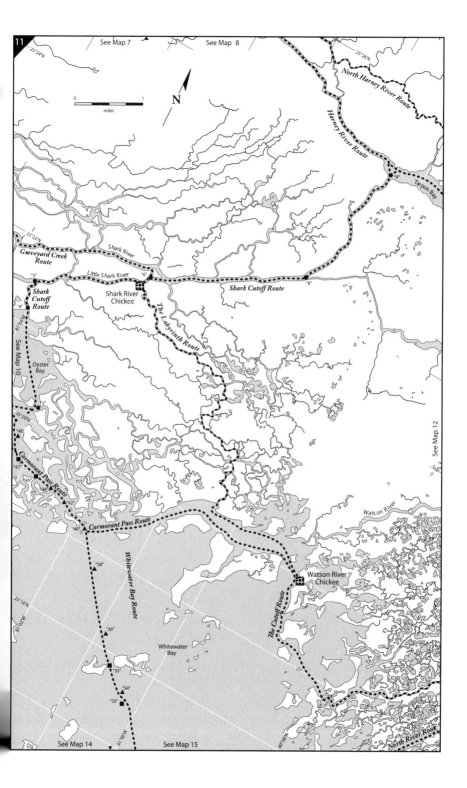

See Map 7

See Map 8

25°24'N

N

0   1
miles

North Harney River Route

25°26'N

Harney River Route

"9"

Tarpon Bay

25°22'N

Graveyard Creek Route

Shark River

Little Shark River

"6"

Shark Cutoff Route

"8"

"5"

Shark Cutoff Route

Shark River Chickee

"4"

See Map 10

The Labyrinth Route

Oyster Bay

"2"

25°20'N

"48"

Cormorant Pass Route

"47"

"45"

"44"

"42"

Watson River

Cormorant Pass Route

"40"

Cormorant Pass Route

See Map 12

Watson River Chickee

"38"

Whitewater Bay Route

25°18'N

"36"

The Cutoff Route

Whitewater Bay

"35"

"34"

"33"

See Map 14

See Map 15

North River Route

80°56'W

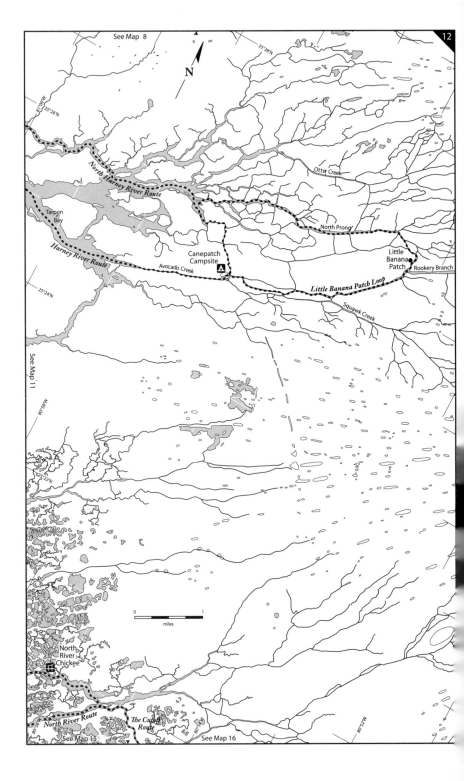

N

25°26'N

80°00'W

North Harney River Route

Otter Creek

Tarpon Bay

North Prong

Little Banana Patch

Rookery Branch

Harney River Route

Canepatch Campsite

Avocado Creek

Little Banana Patch Loop

25°24'N

Squawk Creek

See Map 11

80°58'W

25°22'N

0   1
miles

North River Chickee

North River Route

The Cutoff Route

80°57'W

See Map 15   See Map 16

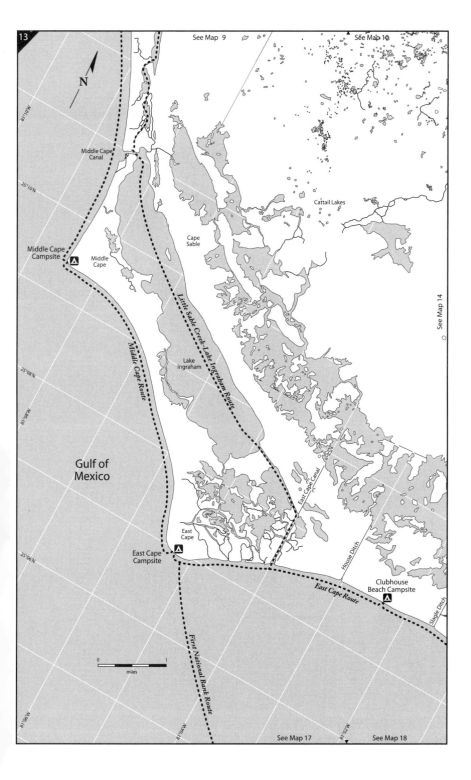

See Map 9
See Map 10

N

Middle Cape
Canal

Cattail Lakes

Cape
Sable

Middle Cape
Campsite

Middle
Cape

See Map 14

Little Sable Creek–Lake Ingraham Route

Lake
Ingraham

Middle Cape Route

Gulf of
Mexico

East Cape Canal

East
Cape

East Cape
Campsite

House Ditch

Clubhouse
Beach Campsite

East Cape Route

Slagle Ditch

First National Bank Route

0   1
miles

See Map 17
See Map 18

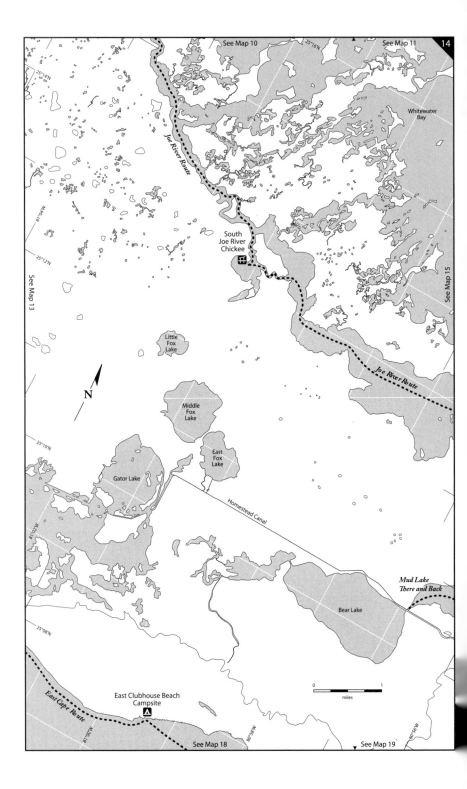

See Map 10
See Map 11
See Map 13
See Map 15
See Map 18
See Map 19

Whitewater Bay

Joe River Route

South Joe River Chickee

Joe River Route

Little Fox Lake

Middle Fox Lake

East Fox Lake

N

Gator Lake

Homestead Canal

Mud Lake
There and Back

Bear Lake

East Cape Route

East Clubhouse Beach Campsite

0   1
miles

25°14'N
25°12'N
25°10'N
25°08'N
25°16'N
81°00'W
80°58'W
80°56'W

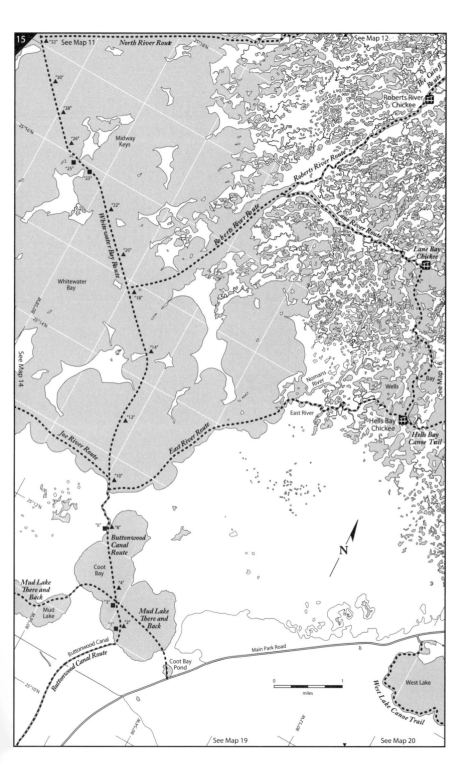

15

See Map 11

North River Route

See Map 12

▲ "32"
▲ "30"
▲ "28"
▲ "26"
■ "25"
▲ "23"
▲ "22"

The Cutoff Route

Roberts River
Chickee 🏠

Roberts River Route

25°16'N

Midway
Keys

▲ "20"

Roberts River Route

Lane River Route

Lane Bay
Chickee 🏠

○ "18"

Whitewater
Bay

Whitewater Bay Route

25°14'N

▲ "14"

Nomans
River

Wells

80°22'W

25°12'N

▲ "12"

Joe River Route

East River Route

East River

See Map 16

Bay

Hells Bay
Chickee 🏠

Hells Bay
Canoe Trail

▲ "10"

■ "6"
▲ "8"

*Buttonwood
Canal
Route*

Coot
Bay

▲ "4"

*Mud Lake
There and
Back*

■ "3"

Mud
Lake

■ "1"
■ "2"

*Mud Lake
There and
Back*

Buttonwood Canal

Buttonwood Canal Route

Coot Bay
Pond

Main Park Road

25°10'N

80°24'W

80°22'W

See Map 14

0   1
miles

West Lake

West Lake Canoe Trail

See Map 19   N   See Map 20

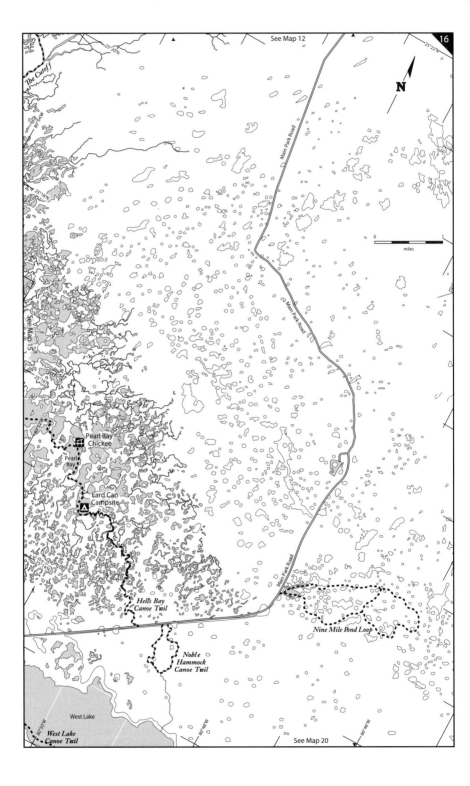

See Map 12

N

0
miles

The Cutoff

25°20'N

25°18'N

Main Park Road

See Map 15

25°16'N

Pearl Bay
Chickee

Pearl
Bay

Lard Can
Campsite

Main Park Road

Hell's Bay
Canoe Trail

Nine Mile Pond Loop

Noble
Hammock
Canoe Trail

80°50'W

West Lake

West Lake
Canoe Trail

80°48'W

80°46'W

See Map 20

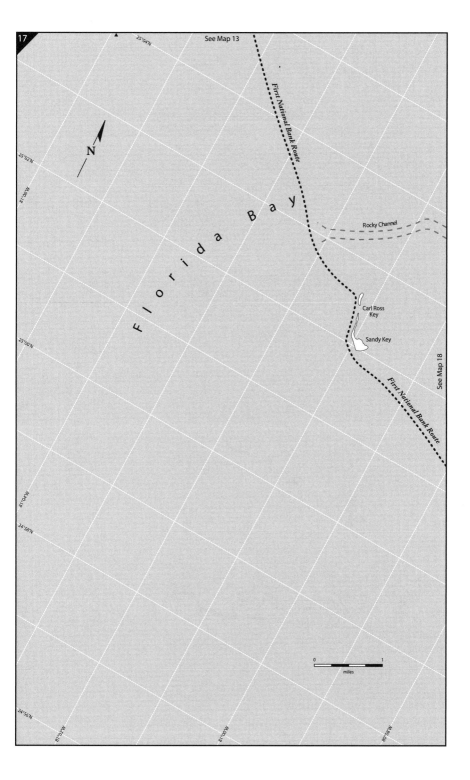

See Map 13

N

First National Bank Route

F l o r i d a B a y

Rocky Channel

Carl Ross Key

Sandy Key

First National Bank Route

See Map 18

25°04'N
25°02'N
25°00'N
24°58'N
24°56'N

81°06'W
81°04'W
81°02'W
81°00'W
80°58'W

0   1
miles

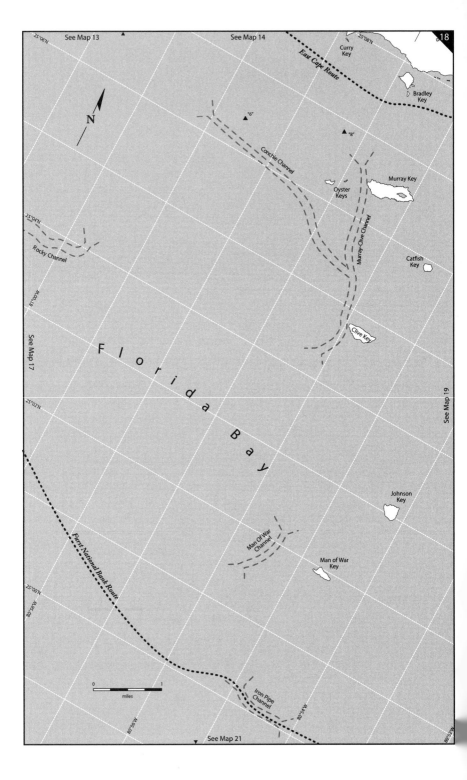

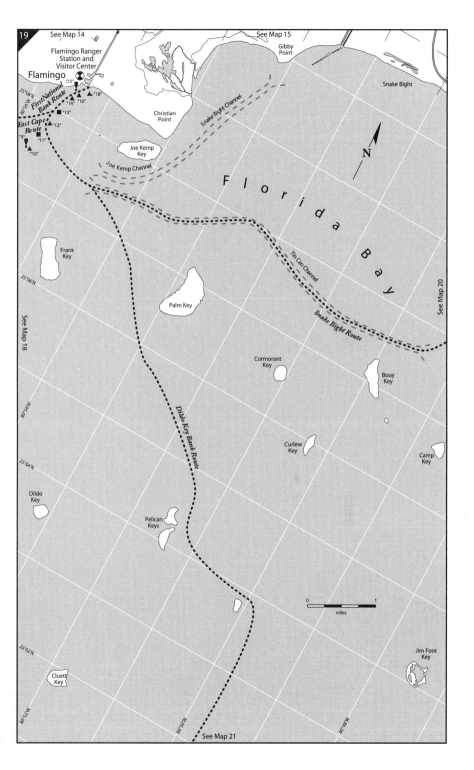

See Map 14

See Map 15

Flamingo Ranger
Station and
Visitor Center

Flamingo

Gibby
Point

Snake Bight

First National
Bank Route

25°08'N

East Cape
Route

"15"

"18"

"14"   "16"

"13"

"12"

"9"

"11"

"10"

Christian
Point

Snake Bight Channel

Joe Kemp
Key

Joe Kemp Channel

N

F l o r i d a   B a y

Frank
Key

25°06'N

Palm Key

Tin Can Channel

See Map 20

Snake Bight Route

See Map 18

Cormorant
Key

Bouy
Key

25°08'N

25°04'N

Dildo Key Bank Route

Curlew
Key

Camp
Key

Dildo
Key

Pelican
Keys

0   1
miles

25°02'N

Jim Foot
Key

Cluett
Key

80°30'W

80°28'W

See Map 21

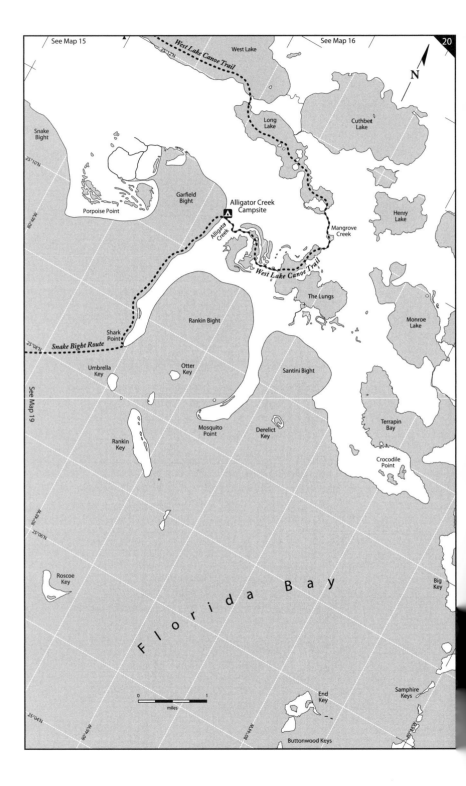

N

West Lake Canoe Trail

West Lake

25°12'N

Cuthbert
Lake

Long
Lake

Snake
Bight

25°10'N

Henry
Lake

80°30'W

Garfield
Bight

Alligator Creek
Campsite

Porpoise Point

Alligator
Creek

Mangrove
Creek

West Lake Canoe Trail

The Lungs

Monroe
Lake

Rankin Bight

Shark
Point

25°08'N

Snake Bight Route

Umbrella
Key

Otter
Key

Santini Bight

Rankin
Key

Mosquito
Point

Derelict
Key

Terrapin
Bay

Crocodile
Point

80°48'W

25°06'N

Roscoe
Key

F l o r i d a   B a y

Big
Key

0   1
miles

End
Key

Samphire
Keys

25°04'N

80°46'W

80°44'W

Buttonwood Keys

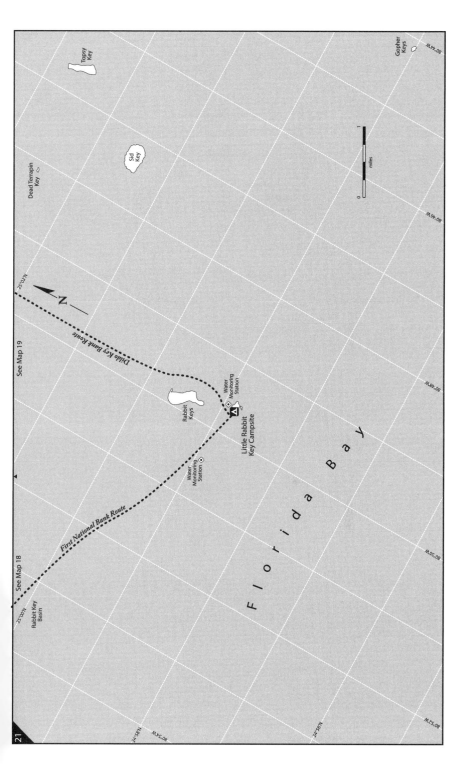

21

Topsy Key

Gopher Keys

80-44'W

Dead Terrapin Key

Sid Key

miles

80-46'W

25-02'N

See Map 19

N

Dildo Key Bank Route

80-48'W

Rabbit Keys

Water Monitoring Station

Water Monitoring Station

Little Rabbit Key Campsite

F l o r i d a   B a y

First National Bank Route

See Map 18

80-50'W

25-00'N

Rabbit Key Basin

80-54'W

80-52'W

24-58'N

24-56'N

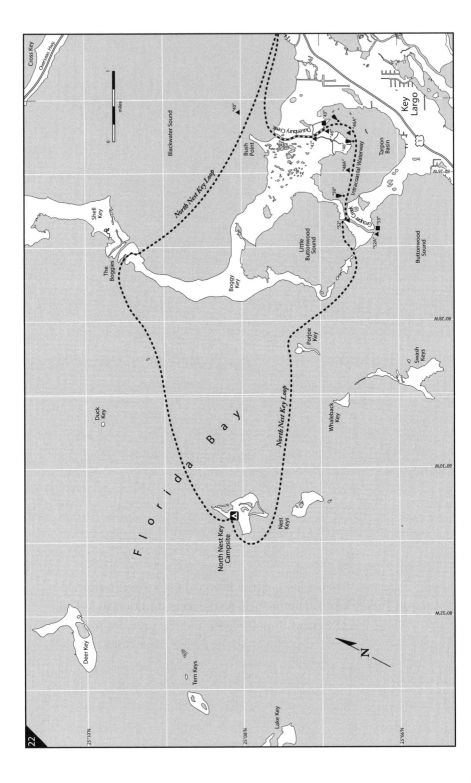

Acknowledgments

I would like to thank the following folks for their invaluable help in writing this book. Easily first are my friends from Minnesota, John and Barb Haapala, who let me base camp at The Empire. Thanks also to Louie and Alice Toth. From the Flamingo campground kiosk, the very friendly Chris Cagle, Chris Ryan, Jase Harris, Holly Bartlett, and Tim Downey. Thanks also to Michiganders John and Donna Buckley for keeping an eye on the backcountry. From the Flamingo Ranger Station, the folks who answered my persistent questions: Kris Stoehr, Steve Robinson, William "Buzz" Potts, Sarah Beckwith, John Waters, Lori Rome, Nancy Holman, Roy Wood, and Allyson Polocz. I also would like to thank the folks from the park headquarters: Reed Detring, Deborah Nordeen, Rick Cook, and Cal Singletary of the Florida National Parks and Monuments Association for his guidance. From the Gulf Coast Ranger Station, I thank Mike Mayer, Judy Hayes, Tom Iandimarino, Eugene Wesloh, Greg Podany, Kathy Clossin, Candace Tinkler, Carl Hilts, Noreen Brown, Dola Berg, Patrick Buerkle, John Russell, Sid Capo, and Gary and Gail Eaton.

Thanks to Vivian Oliva—a true Everglades aficionado—for typing on Turkey Key and for her help on the second edition, as well; to T. J. Keefe, Alex Peterson, Tom Rodgers, and the guy from Manhattan at Lopez River campsite who entertained me with his tales of life in the city; to the folks at the Ivey House; and to Linda and her daughter Meredith from Rabbit Key. Thanks to Big Agnes for a quality bug-proof tent, the Seedhouse 3, and to Wenonah for their boat, the *Spirit II*.

Thanks to everyone at University Press of Florida for their help. Thanks to Debbie Lauria, Tom Lauria, Anthony Lauria, and Kristina Lauria for boarding me in Coral Gables between paddling trips. Thanks to William "World Wide" Armstrong for coming down to lend his photographic expertise and fish-cooking artistry. Thanks to Constance Mier and Mark Carroll for the photos. Also, thanks to Steve "Devo" Grayson, Ellen Connolly, John Cox, Tina Dean, Jeff Cochran, Roxanne Bamond, Aaron Marable, Holly and Kerry Nicholson, Frank Carroll, and Jean S. for paddling with me and making the Glades adventures more memorable.

Johnny Molloy is the author of more than thirty books, including hiking, camping, and paddling guidebooks, comprehensive guidebooks about specific areas, and outdoor adventure books. For the latest on Johnny, please visit www.johnnymolloy.com.